AF469307

Hussars, Horses and History

Hussars, Horses and History

John Strawson

Pen & Sword
MILITARY

First published in Great Britain in 2007 by
Pen & Sword Military
an imprint of
Pen & Sword Books Ltd
47 Church Street
Barnsley
South Yorkshire
S70 2AS

ISBN 978 1 84415 5828

A CIP catalogue record for this book is
available from the British Library

Typeset in 11/13pt Sabon by
Lamorna Publishing Services

Printed and bound in England by Biddles Ltd

For a complete list of Pen & Sword titles please contact
PEN & SWORD BOOKS LIMITED
47 Church Street, Barnsley, South Yorkshire, S70 2AS, England
E-mail: enquiries@pen-and-sword.co.uk
Website: www.pen-and-sword.co.uk

Contents

List of Illustrations between pages 118-119

Acknowledgements

First I would like to thank Brigadier Henry Wilson, Publishing Director of Pen & Sword Books Limited for his readiness to look at the first draft of these memoirs and for his subsequent suggestions and encouragement for some amendments to it.

I am most grateful to the following for permission to reproduce the painting *Ladies Bathing* by JEC Mathews as the dust cover of this book: Lieutenant Colonel MJR Rothwell TD; The Royal Wessex Yeomanry; Lieutenant Colonel PRH Clifford TD MFH; The Royal Gloucestershire Hussars Charitable Trust; the Trustees of the Cavalry and Guards Club, where the picture now hangs. John Mathews (1842-1927) was a captain in The Royal Gloucestershire Hussars and commanded the RGH contingent at Queen Victoria's Diamond Jubilee celebrations. I also wish to thank Colonel Tom Hall CVO OBE for his initiative and assistance in obtaining this permission.

In describing my adventures with the Staff College Draghounds, the Pipe Band competition and life in Cairo, I have drawn upon some stories I wrote for *Blackwood's Magazine* in the 1960s and 1970s. Similarly my account of taking 1½ couple of foxhounds from Buckinghamshire to Trieste is based on an article I wrote for *The Times* in the 1960s.

The author and publishers wish to thank the following for their kind permission to reproduce photographs to illustrate the text (details are given on another page): The Photograph Archive of the Imperial War Museum – the author would particularly like to express his gratitude to Laura Clouting and Yvonne Oliver for their prompt, courteous and effective assistance; The Queen's

Royal Irish Hussars short history (of which I am a co-author); Professor Amedeo Montemaggi, author of *La Linea Gotica 1944* and many other learned publications about the war in Italy 1943-1945 and in particular the battles for the Gothic Line 1944-1945; the Regimental Archives of The Queen's Royal Irish Hussars and the Regimental Journal *Crossbelts*.

I wish to express my profound gratitude to my son-in-law, Tim Barker, for his meticulous work in reproducing many of the illustrations for this book in the form and dimension in which they appear. My thanks go to Bruce Hunter and Alice Wilson for their tactful assistance with the contractual arrangements.

I would like to thank the photocopying staff of Coates & Parker, Warminster for their cheerful and courteous help in making copies of my typescript.

Finally I wish to thank my wife for her customary help with the proof-reading, index checking and general support in the production of this book.

Chapter 1

The Churchill Touch

'The 4th Hussars is a very good Cavalry Regiment, & Colonel Brabazon an excellent Commanding Officer so I think your selection is in that respect a very good one.'

[Extract from a letter dated 6 February 1895 from the Duke of Cambridge – Army Commander-in-Chief – to Lady Randolph Churchill]

'Twelve days after the Duke's letter Churchill reported to the 4th Hussars at Aldershot, and on February 20 he received his Commission.'

Winston S. Churchill by Randolph S. Churchill

In 1941 my Regiment, the 4th Hussars, suffered a grievous blow to its morale, which was then substantially restored by an unlooked-for fillip. In each case the same man was at the centre of affairs. It was Winston Churchill who, together with General Wavell, C.-in-C. Middle East, had insisted on succouring Greece and, in that ill-fated campaign, the 4th Hussars, put in a hopeless tactical position, were overwhelmed by the *Wehrmacht*'s Panzer and Stuka power, losing many officers and men into the captivity of POW camps. This was the grievous blow. The Regiment reformed in Egypt, however, with those who had evaded capture and was reinforced by officers and men from other regiments. Shortly afterwards Winston Churchill was appointed colonel of his old Regiment. Here was the fillip. During the four years of war still ahead, Churchill visited the 4th Hussars four times, and what follows is an account of two of these visits.

In November 1943 the Regiment was at Beni Yusef camp, not

far from Mena and the Giza pyramids. We had just finished re-equipping with Sherman and Honey tanks, and were daily expecting a call to action. Just before noon one morning, as we troop leaders – the military day being over – were on the point of leaping into an open 15cwt truck and driving to Gezirah Sporting Club for luncheon and some sporting fixture, the call appeared to come. Our Squadron Sergeant Major, pregnant with news, doubled to the vehicle. We had frequently observed him making others double – including even ourselves on those mercifully rare occasions when the squadron leader's ire bubbled over into an order for a subalterns' drill parade – but never before seen him execute so undignified a movement himself:

> Excuse me, Sir. The squadron leader's compliments and will you all attend a conference in his office at 2 o'clock. I think we must be on the move, Sir.

There was an ill-concealed glint of anticipation in the Sergeant Major's eye.

At 2 o'clock the 'O' group duly assembled in the Squadron Leader's little hutted office. Present were the Squadron Leader himself, the second-in-command, five troop leaders, the Squadron Sergeant Major, Squadron Quartermaster Sergeant and the Transport Sergeant. The last named had two favourite words which interlarded almost every sentence he uttered. The first he shared with many other men in uniform and needs no elucidation or iteration here, but was the cause of such complaint by a sensitive member of the Transport Troop that the Squadron Leader was obliged to remind this driver that he was not running a kindergarten. The other word, also not exclusively his, but less common, manifested itself in the Sergeant's constantly expressed intention of 'gripping' somebody or something. If an ordered vehicle arrived late, he could be relied upon to 'grip' the driver; if at guard mounting a trooper's boots fell short of perfection, he too and his boots would be 'gripped'; if again, any of his men allowed their hair to exceed what he regarded – and his standards were severe – as the very minimum to adorn the crown of the head, then they would be marched off to the regimental barber and 'gripped' there. When he used the word he would bare and grind his teeth as if to suit the action to it; as if in fact these same molars would be actively employed in the dreaded process.

The Squadron Leader's news was milder than the Sergeant Major had led us to suppose. A party of VIPs, unnamed but unquestionably important, would be arriving at Mena House Hotel during the next few days in order to confer together and we, that is the Regiment as a whole, had been given the great honour of guaranteeing their security from the desert flank. The three Sabre Squadrons and the Reconnaissance Troop were to deploy appropriately and to ensure that no vehicles or men infiltrated towards the hotel from the desert. Closer guards were to be provided by the military police and an infantry battalion.

We were to be in position by last light on this very day and would remain on guard for about a week, subject to the conference's progress. All the necessary orders were then given in detail. Only at the last moment of our meeting did the Squadron Leader reveal who one of the VIPs was to be – the Colonel of the Regiment and, as it happened, Prime Minister, First Lord of the Treasury, Minister of Defence – Winston Churchill himself. 'If anyone tries to get at Winston,' I heard the Transport Sergeant growl as we filed from the Squadron Leader's office, 'I'll grip 'im'.

The guard duty was tedious. Each troop was given a sector to watch by day, well out in the desert, and a much tighter perimeter to patrol on foot at night. How bored we got, scanning the same stretch of desert, patrolling the same stretch of wire. Two hours on, four hours off, for six long days and nights. No sign of Winston, no sign of anything. Yet our spirits were kept up by the anticipation that our Colonel might take this opportunity to visit his Regiment. At first it seemed not. The VIP meeting broke up. Churchill went to Teheran. We returned to our routine of training, going for a hack on the Veterinary Corps' horses at Abassia and playing bridge at Gezirah.

Then suddenly on 1 December, immediately after morning parade, there was another conference for troop leaders. Winston Churchill was to inspect the Regiment in two days' time. Parades are usually the prerogative of the Adjutant and the Regimental Sergeant Major. But on this occasion, with so little time for so important an affair, preparations took on the atmosphere of a serious military operation. Reconnaissance for a suitable site was followed by formal orders for rehearsal on a different stretch of desert, so that the actual one would not be disturbed. The actual site was a beautifully smooth area not far from the Giza pyramids. What a backcloth! The RSM, who had never been really happy since the horses went, was in ecstasy; never had he had so majestic a parade ground to play with. Whitewashed stones were then deployed to mark the positions where tanks and crew would be. A marquee rose up so that the Colonel could take 'refreshment' if he wished. Pride of the RSM's heart, a saluting dais, was positioned. The form of parade was simple. The Colonel would arrive, stand on the dais, receive a general salute, inspect the Regiment, address us if he so wished and depart. We should have known, knowing him, that it would not be quite like that.

The day dawned. The parade was to be early to avoid the heat of the sun, and at 8 o'clock the Regiment was lined up by Squadrons with Regimental HQ on the right of the line. It was a magnificent sight. About eighty tanks in two lines, officers and men at 'Crews front', transport lined up behind the tanks, also with commanders and crews. Every officer and man wore a new battledress, some sporting a Military Cross or Military Medal; most unadorned in spite of much desert fighting, and thereby hung a tale, shortly to be told. The Regimental flag flew bravely by the saluting base. All was ready.

A posse of staff cars escorted by military police swung in from the Cairo-Alexandria road and drove across the hard sand towards us. A familiar figure alighted and was shown to his position on the dais. With him were a bevy of generals, ADCs and his daughter, Sarah, most elegant in her WAAF uniform.

'4th Hussars – AttenSHUN!' rang out the Commanding Officer's order. 'General SALUTE.' Formalities over, the inspection then proceeded. We all saw him close to, some of us for the first time. Winston, the Prime Minister, leader of the nation, champion of freedom, and *our* Colonel, wearing *our* uniform and *our* cap badge. Every man's heart glowed within him. Winston stopped here and there to speak to the soldiers, and then asked Bobby Kidd, our Commanding Officer, a question which turned out to be a facer:

'Why is the Regiment not wearing the Africa Star?'

Consternation! When, during an inspection of this sort, a really difficult question is posed, it is customary for the senior officer present simply to turn to his subordinate and demand an answer from him. This procedure is then repeated until the most junior man present is taxed with it, perhaps the one least likely to know, yet upon him may depend the reputation of his masters. In this case, the process was reversed initially. Bobby Kidd turned to the General Officer Commanding British Troops in Egypt and asked him. Then the normal custom was resumed until a mere major, deputy assistant adjutant and quartermaster general, was required to give an explanation. His reply was short and to the point. 'They haven't been issued yet.' This information was relayed back to the great man, who looked far from pleased.

Winston then returned to the front of the Regiment; he climbed onto a jeep and with an all-embracing gesture invited us to gather round. We massed round his jeep. Then the words came tumbling out – how proud he was to see us in such splendid array, geared for battle, so clearly ready to go to Italy and take up the struggle again, how we would win more fame for the Regiment, how he would assuredly visit us again there, and how he relied on us to reinforce the Eighth Army's renown as one of the most valiant in British arms. Then came a surprise. He told us that he had instructed the GOC Egypt that the ribbon of the Africa Star would be on the tunics of all of us entitled to it by tomorrow morning. Even then he had not finished, but blandly announced that he had asked the Commanding Officer whether the Regiment would now march past and that his request had been granted. Three hurried 'O' groups followed; the CO and his squadron leaders; squadron leaders and their troop leaders; troop leaders and their tank commanders.

The orders were given, all crews were once more in front of their tanks, the order 'Mount', a signal to start up and a radio order to begin. So, unexpected and unrehearsed, we marched past the Colonel. As each tank passed him on the saluting dais, up went each tank commander's hand in salute. Gravely and formally Winston returned each salute, until towards the end of the line one of C Squadron's tanks went by. All C Squadron's tanks had been named after English villages, and on the side of this one painted in foot high capital letters was – CHURCHILL, the name of a Somerset village. No formal salute from the Colonel this time, but the V sign.

Next the Colonel *did* take refreshment in the marquee, met the officers and warrant officers, and then took his leave. Back at camp the Adjutant found a dramatic signal from GHQ Cairo, which declared that a team of seamstresses would report to Beni Yusef camp that evening to sew the Africa Star medal ribbon on tunics of all ranks entitled to wear it. It was clear that a more or less universal 'gripping' of the staff had taken place. On the whole we all took kindly to having medal ribbons sewn on to our uniforms by a team of not ill-looking and largely French-speaking seamstresses. Some future rendezvous were arranged. C Squadron Sergeant Major was very active in inspecting all barrack huts and thus all seamstresses there present, although the Transport Sergeant was heard to announce that he would personally 'grip' any member of his troop who laid a finger on 'one of them bints with needles'.

Who else but the Colonel could have done it? What a star turn he was! How unforgettable had his visit been! And next time we saw him, we would be about to battle our way through the Gothic Line and so be eligible to have another medal ribbon sewn on our tunics. Mr Churchill's visit to us in Italy was far less formal and yet somehow more fitting. We were bivouacked near Ancona and about to move north. It was in August 1944. We were paraded with our tanks on a huge grass airfield and shortly after Mr Churchill's aircraft had landed and he, together with General Alexander, had been greeted by our Commanding Officer, a bizarre occurrence interrupted, although only momentarily, the planned programme. Despite efforts to guide him to the saluting base by another route, the great man, dressed as before as Colonel 4th Hussars, stepped out purposefully in a direct line from the aircraft to the position where the Regiment was paraded, only to be confronted soon afterwards by an anti-tank ditch, part of the airfield's defences. None daunted, he plunged down into it to the obvious dismay of General Alexander, as always elegantly attired in bush-shirt and shorts. Nevertheless Alexander, our Commanding Officer and various aides-de-camp followed. It was just as well for when the Prime Minister attempted to climb out of the anti-tank ditch he found it beyond his powers and only combined heaving at his not inconsiderable posterior by the Commander-in-Chief and other lesser military mortals succeeded in extricating him.

The inspection and parade then proceeded and was brought to a close by Mr Churchill indicating – as he had in Cairo – that all ranks should close round him while he stood on a jeep to address us. Then came one more of those fine extempore declarations about the state of the game, and his expression of pride that his old Regiment would shortly be giving the Hun another knock. Finally he had tea with us in a tent when all the officers were presented to him. Once more our morale was at an all time high – the Churchill Touch. You couldn't beat it. We were to see more of our Colonel after the war at Regimental dinners and a further visit to the 4th Hussars at Hohne. And we had a sombre duty to perform some twenty years after the war had ended, and Sir Winston Churchill had succumbed to the last enemy. But an account of the part we played in his funeral must await a later chapter.

Chapter 2

Joining the Regiment

'Never forget: the Regiment is the foundation of everything.'
Wavell

In the Cavalry's mounted days it was traditional that when it came to looking after things, the horses came first, the men second, and yourself last. When it comes to penning a memoir, however, there will be times when you are obliged to put yourself first in order, as it were, to get off the ground. But, there will, in these pages, be plenty of room for nights at the opera, days in the hunting field, encounters with the hospitality of Dyak longhouses, high table talk at Oxford colleges, arguing the toss with the *Wehrmacht* in the Apennines, riding high with the Corazzieri in their magnificent indoor school at the centre of Rome, relishing Shakespeare's plays at Stratford, contributing to General Shan Hackett's bestselling books about future wars, wrestling matches with females of the species – in short a mixed bag. Above all, of course, come the people – family, friends, comrades in arms, generals under whose command I served, the soldiers under my own command, publishers, sportsmen, kennel huntsmen, grooms, fellow villagers, generous hearted Kentuckians in the Blue Grass country, Arab generals and councillors and negotiations with them.

Not far behind the people come the four-legged friends – foxhounds, gun dogs, mares and geldings of all characteristics, bold, wilful, playful, obstinate, loveable, noble and, for those fortunate enough to have owned, ridden, hunted or played polo on, schooled, cherished, revered – an absolutely indispensable ingredient of leading a full life.

To the cavalryman, as indeed to the infantryman too, it is his Regiment which matters most, and I suppose the greatest piece of good fortune to befall me – apart from my marriage – was to become a 4th Hussar. How well I remember the day I joined. It was towards the end of 1942, and the Regiment had been withdrawn from the Western Desert after distinguishing itself at El Alamein and was resting, re-equipping and training in Cyprus. Together with two other officers and a dozen soldiers I arrived at a hutted camp to the east of Nicosia. The nearest village was Kokini Trimithia. I was posted to C Squadron, commanded at that time by Major Porgy Archer MC, who had acquired his nickname by virtue of a well-rounded figure and a florid complexion. He had done well in the Alamein battle – hence the Military Cross. I did not meet him at once on arrival, but was greeted by two fellow lieutenants. Arthur Hoare was the son of General Sir Reginald Hoare, who had served in the 4th Hussars with Winston Churchill and, like him, was a member of the Regimental polo team which won a famous victory in the India tournament of 1899. Arthur was kind enough to supply me with a few regimental accoutrements which I lacked. The other member of C Squadron was Guy Wheeler, known as the Puffin Bird – the British Army has always loved nicknames – by virtue of his somewhat prominent spectacles. Guy became a great friend and we served together in the Regiment for some sixteen years. Later on he commanded The Royal Scots Greys. Second in command of the squadron was James Fryer, a delightful, Falstaffian figure; a lawyer, a wit and an expert with the sun compass, indispensable for navigation in the Western Desert. He was a kindly, avuncular fellow and would offer friendly advice to us troop leaders when we strayed from conduct regarded by Porgy as fitting and proper – our failure to salute the Squadron Leader as he made his way towards his own specially constructed thunder-box was one such misdemeanour which he felt obliged to correct.

Porgy himself, a pre-war regular 4th Hussar, was not in appearance the beau ideal of a British cavalryman. His figure was against him here, but he had proved himself as Joint Master of a military pack of foxhounds, was always well turned out, had an agreeable sense of humour, sometimes, alas, at the discomfort of others, loved to mimic his fellow officers and generally demanded a high standard of personal conduct and military competence. He was devoted to his wife and his correspondence to and from her was frequent and continuous. If he had a major fault it was a tendency to bully, on detecting weakness in a subordinate. There was little chance of his indulging this fault with his troop leaders, however, for they were not prone to be bullied. There were some notable characters among other members of C Squadron. The Quarter Master Sergeant, Geordie Hoyle, had once been caught by the military police in a forbidden street in Cairo with only his boots on. His explanation that he must have mistaken his way in the blackout was not well received by the Colonel, who dealt out some suitable justice of fines and threats. The lesson was not wasted on him. A few weeks later, when in command of three Honey tanks, he reported a group of Mark IV panzers approaching his position and asked for guidance. Curtly told to engage them, his acknowledgement of the order, while not observing the radio procedure then in vogue, was a model of courtesy and military discipline. 'Very good, sir.' He was as good as his word, beat the enemy off, and was subsequently awarded the DCM.

Two other C Squadron characters deserve mention before I come to my own 3rd Troop and the men under my command. Trooper Thorneley was our Officers' Mess waiter – each squadron had its own Mess as we were widely dispersed – and was known by his fellow soldiers as The Duke, because of his dignified bearing and refined accent. It was said that he had murdered at least one Egyptian in a bar brawl occasioned by what he had regarded as a bill which owed more to multiplication than addition. But from his demeanour in Mess, you would not have suspected that he was a man of violence. Gliding silently to and fro, bearing whiskys and soda or a platter of bully beef fritters – these latter treated with the same deference as deserved by the daintiest of dishes to satisfy the taste of a most rigorous gourmet – he wore the kind of expression which Jeeves would assume when deprecating one of Bertie Wooster's more extravagant lapses in taste. He contrived somehow to appear more distinguished than those he was serving. Loyal, efficient, deferential and elegant, he added tone to our simple Mess. He was, in short, a treasure. Not to be outdone in condescension was the Squadron Clerk, Corporal Cowper. Because of our limited accommodation, he sat in the corner of Porgy's office and thus, unless excluded for some confidentiality regarded as unsuitable for his ears, was privy to the squadron's ins and outs. Each day he would, in his neat copperplate hand, write out the squadron orders for the next day – incredible as it may seem, we had no typewriter – and ensure that we troop leaders had taken due note of them. Every now and again something would go wrong, precipitating Porgy's wrath and his demand for retribution. When as a last resort Cowper's judgement on the matter in hand was sought, his standard reply, which usually brought the investigation to a close, was: 'I know nothing about it at all, Sir, nothing!'

When I took over 3rd Troop, Sergeant Harrison had been acting as Troop Leader. He had been awarded the DCM for his courageous and effective conduct in the desert. A fine looking man, upright, honourable and able, I counted myself fortunate indeed to have such a reliable subordinate. But it was not to last, for a few weeks later, he was posted to an OCTU and subsequently commissioned into the 10th Hussars. In his place came Sergeant Pope; jovial, a competent tank commander, good with the men, but his nerve was not as steady as I would have liked. Not so my Troop Corporal Hill – tough, determined, a disciplinarian, and like Sir Richard Strachan 'longing to be at 'em'. Yet I lost him too. He had developed some obscure malady. There, however, my ill-luck ended. The others in my troop were a fine lot. Corporal Little refuted his name. Grave, brave, steady in action, a brilliant wireless operator, he was possessed too of a dry humour. On one occasion during a disagreeable engagement with a Panzer Grenadier Division of the *Wehrmacht*, when he heard another of my fellow Troop Leaders, who had joined the 4th Hussars late in 1943, loudly trying to keep his spirits up with an aria from *Le Nozze di Figaro* and had reached the line 'What a glorious thing is war', Corporal Little blandly enquired: 'Do you really think so, Sir?' He went on to become a sergeant and was wounded, happily not seriously, in one of the final battles in Italy.

I was particularly fortunate in my own tank crew. Trooper Tyson was a dark skinned, dark haired Cornish man, my driver and a wizard with gearboxes, engine and clutches. Imperturbable in action, a good cook – it was vital that one member of your crew should both enjoy and be skilful at turning our rations into something you actually liked eating – and fiercely proud of his maintenance skills which ensured that our tank was always on the road, he had but one fault. He was not the smartest member of my troop, but in view of his predilection for oils, grease and other lubricants, I was able to forgive him his sartorial inadequacies. Next was Trooper Grigg, a quiet, honest, steady man from Gloucester, who had formerly been a butcher and now was the best gunner in the squadron. With such men as these you knew there would be no hesitations when it came to fighting. Last of my crewmen, the wireless operator and gun loader, was Trooper Batey, a Scotsman who, I learned, had made a habit of questioning the equity of ration distribution between the three – later four – tanks in the troop. The solution was clear. Batey became the arbiter of sharing out the rations. Among the less attractive items for our consumption were such things as soya sausages, a margarine more suitable for greasing tank tracks than for victualling tank crews, beans more like bullets and very hard biscuits. But we were able to supplement the edible portion of the rations – bully beef being the great standby – with eggs, fruit and an occasional chicken purchased with cigarettes from the *contadini* of Puglia, Abruzzi, Marche and the Romagna. I should add that the cigarette issue was one of the so-called V variety. As a non-smoker, the handing over of my ration to my crew was only half appreciated as I was informed that although better than none at all, they were awful.

Other notables in my troop were Nobby Clark, scruffy, ill-disciplined and not amenable to orders, he was nonetheless a rock of cool courage in action, defiant of danger; Lance Corporal Day, thin, quiet, an excellent driver and later tank commander; Trooper Morris, mischievous, bouncy and cheerful, even when wounded by shrapnel from one of the most disagreeable weapons the *Wehrmacht* had – Moaning Minnie – a large calibre mortar whose missiles made a fiendish kind of noise as they approached you, halfway between a shriek and a sigh. I remember Morris making a point of thanking me for getting him quickly to our first aid post, where our medical officer, Captain Leigh, patched him up and dispatched him to a field hospital further back.

I have almost forgotten to mention Corporal Haversham, a West Country stalwart, whose laconic comments and slow, broad smile defused many an awkward moment. He was one of those men worth his weight in diamonds when it came to tricky situations and his sense of humour was infectious. On one occasion when I had taken the whole troop for a day's swimming at Kyrenia – where, unlike today, the Dome Hotel was the sole hostelry and the broad sandy beaches were uncluttered – he indulged this trait at my expense. Haversham was in command of a small rowing boat with a few troopers, while I was lazily swimming in the agreeably tepid greenish-blue water. Suddenly a cry from Haversham broke the calm. 'Look out, Zir! There's an octopus close behind you.' I looked behind me and sure enough there was just such a creature, rather small, but nonetheless waving some menacing tentacles about. I also caught sight of the sheer delight on the faces of Haversham and his crew at the prospect of their troop leader's discomfort. I decided, like Falstaff that the better part of valour was discretion and with a fair imitation of Johnny Weissmuller, made for the shore. Haversham had already proved himself a reliable tank commander in the desert battles, and after our next encounter with Kesselring's panzer and parachute divisions in Italy, where again his steadiness and competence proved a great support to me, he was promoted to sergeant and posted to another squadron.

I will not prolong my account of regimental characters, but there are still a few who should be mentioned in this dispatch. The 4th Hussars were at this time commanded by Bobby Kidd, formerly a Royal Dragoon – most of the senior 4th Hussar officers had been made prisoners of war in the ill-fated Greek campaign and it had been necessary to look elsewhere for the seniority and experience required. Bobby Kidd had been a great race rider in his day, although one might not have thought so from his mild manner and light touch on the reins of command. As he enjoyed playing tennis and bridge I was quite often called for to make up the numbers. Tennis at Gezirah Sporting Club was made easier for us by the presence of ball boys, who would retrieve the scattered balls and bounce them towards whoever was serving at the time. Bobby Kidd was short and, whether by intention or not, the ball boys would bounce the ball towards him so hard that it frequently went over his head, despite a desperate grasp. Then the Colonel would show the fire that still burned in him. 'You bloody kora wallah' he would hiss and later on when we had finished the game it demanded all my powers of persuasion to ensure that the poor kora wallahs received an adequate tip. When it came to battle, although I did not appreciate it at the time – so engrossed was I in what my own troop was required to do – it seemed to me that the Colonel did not adhere to some of the basic rules of combat, that is ensuring that his subordinates were fully briefed as to the situation and that their squadrons would enjoy the full support of our artillery and infantry comrades in arms. Confronted with some puzzling or disconcerting circumstance, Bobby Kidd was apt to stretch out his right arm, with fingers crooked, and give voice to a hesitant: 'Oh, my God!' It was a gesture and pronouncement that my Squadron Leader, Porgy, loved to enact.

The Regimental Sergeant Major, Chesty Read, was one of the strongest horsemen in the British cavalry. Slight in height, muscular in body, powerful in voice, intimidating in manner – when he wished – with piercing blue eyes, an infinite capacity for Stella beer, and an absolute conviction that the horse had not been born and never would be that he, Chesty, could not school to perfection. He was all that any regiment could wish for and we in the 4th Hussars were proud of him. An acknowledgement from him that our own performance, when mounted, had not been a disgrace to the cavalry in general and the Regiment in particular was something we all treasured. Indeed I recall that after the war when the regiment was stationed at Colchester and I had just completed a show-jumping course without a fault, I positively glowed with satisfaction when Chesty told me that my performance had not been too bad. As might have been expected, on the battlefield he was always to be seen near the front line, immaculately turned out, with a cheery word for everyone and an absolute certainty that we would succeed in the particular mission with which we were then engaged.

Pat Uniacke commanded B Squadron. Tall, handsome, with accomplishments varying from playing the piano to piloting a single-seater aeroplane, skippering a sail boat or taking part in a full dress mounted parade, he was as much at home in the company of Tallulah Bankhead and Noël Coward as he was at a levée in St James's Palace, wearing that extravagantly frogged Hussar uniform, which we rather unkindly christened lion tamers' kit. He was cultured and kindly, but seemed always to prefer the trappings and display of life in a cavalry regiment than the business of schooling horses, hunting, other field sports and the sense of achievement to be found in commanding, training and leading men into action. When it came to organizing and running an Officers' Mess function, editing the *Regimental Journal* or making sure that wherever his squadron was stationed, its presence was known to the nobs of the neighbourhood, he reigned supreme.

Our relatively brief sojourn in Cyprus was taken up with further training of tank crews, a few simple squadron manoeuvres, map reading exercises, umpiring a major test of operational readiness, skiing in the Troodos mountains, swimming and inevitably – how could it be otherwise with Englishmen? – cricket. C Squadron received a further troop leader, Kenneth Hedley, who became a great friend, and who was an excellent cricketer. So we played mostly against various other regiments stationed there until, in the spring of 1943, the 4th Hussars were ordered back to Egypt to re-equip with Sherman and Stuart tanks to become the armoured reconnaissance regiment of the 1st Armoured Division. And so we sailed from Famagusta to Beirut, then by train to Cairo and on to Beni Yusef camp.

Porgy went off to the Staff College at Haifa and Peter Crichton took over command of C Squadron. He was a very different man; tall, elegant, always beautifully turned out, with a great love of horses, fishing, music and playing poker. It was not long before he had met, fallen in love with and become engaged to the beautiful daughter of the Swedish Ambassador to Egypt, and had acquired a small car with a dicky seat. He would, on most days when the military part of it was over – that is midday, drive into Cairo to see his lady love, dropping us troop leaders off at Gezirah Sporting Club on the way. At the same time we did a lot of serious training in the desert, particularly with regard to shooting the guns of our newly acquired American tanks. As I had received a good report from the Gunnery School at Abassia, I was appointed, in addition to my troop leader's duties, Regimental Gunnery Officer, and set up a range in the desert some ten miles north, just off the road to Alexandria.

The 75mm gun of the Sherman tank fired both armour piercing and high explosive shells and with a team of assistants I set up a series of targets consisting of weighted tar barrels at ranges varying from 1,000 to 3,000 yards, the nearer ones to test our skills with the armour piercing missiles; the further targets for HE. When one of these shells hit a tar barrel at the maximum range there was a most gratifying glow of flame on impact, so that there was no doubt about accuracy of shooting. As Gunnery Officer, I was required to attend and sometimes supervise the range practices of not only my own squadron, but others too, and I recall receiving a blistering rocket from Major Paddy O'Brian, who had taken over B Squadron from Pat Uniacke – posted to Iraq where he successfully practised his diplomatic skills – when I cast doubt on the standards of his tank commanders and gunners. But perhaps the most bizarre feature of our desert range was that as soon as one of our shooting programmes was over, there would appear on the range, as if by magic for there had been no sign of them before, a group of fellaheen who would proceed to gather up all the armour piercing solid shot whose value to some unknown metallic merchant clearly justified the risk of being hit by one of these deadly missiles.

Missiles may vary in form and we must not overlook the devastating effect that Cupid's darts may have in Egypt or elsewhere. If such men as Caesar and Antony could find themselves in thrall to a serpent of old Nile, it was hardly to be expected that a mere lieutenant of the 4th Hussars should be immune to the wiles of an Egyptian daughter of the game. Her name was not Cleopatra, but it might just as well have been.

Chapter 3

The Petticoats

'But the things you will learn from the Yellow and Brown,
They'll 'elp you a lot with the White!'

Rudyard Kipling

I feel sure it will be no surprise to learn that from an early age, I found myself not wholly indifferent to the charms of two-legged fillies – and mares! And as Captain Boodle explained to Captain Clavering in Anthony Trollope's *The Claverings*, the managing of these two categories is quite different. When you're trying a young filly, for example, your hands can't be too light. A touch too much will bring her right back on her haunches. She should hardly be aware of the bit in her mouth. But a trained mare must be wholly conscious of your presence. Mares' mouths are not so fine; they need to be brought up to the bit. And at their fences, give 'em their heads. Boodle's final point was uncompromising. 'Look here, Clavvy; ride her with spurs. Let her know they're on, and if she tries to get her head, give 'em her. Yes, by George, give 'em her.' Sound advice, I would say.

What should perhaps have surprised me was that my partiality for females of the species was quite often met with encouragement from the creature in question. Not that the path of love always ran smoothly. But the recollection that even such great men as Napoleon and Wellington had trouble with the petticoats was a consolation. Josephine could be tricky. Refusal to join him during the Italian campaign, despite pleas from the all-triumphant General Bonaparte; gross extravagance in equipping herself with fineries; liaisons with handsome young cavalry officers – small wonder that the First Consul and then the Emperor turned to such cosy armfuls as Mademoiselle George and a string of other high-stepping fillies. The Iron Duke was no less selective. Indeed he shared the attentions of Mademoiselle George, who pronounced his performance as *plus fort* than the Emperor's but Wellington had honourably married Kitty Pakenham. Despite her family's earlier rejection of a relatively unknown soldier, they changed their tune when confronted with the victor of Assaye. And although Wellington had trouble with the notorious Harriet Wilson, he found Mrs Arbuthnot a more comfortable *bonne amie*.

So it is clearly part of a soldier's life to get mixed up with the petticoats. I will pass over a teenage inclination to become better acquainted with gym-slipped schoolgirls – one of whom saw it as her wartime duty to become a chorus girl – and I was awarded full marks by two of my fellow OCTU cadets when successfully demanding her presence at the stage door of the Piccadilly Theatre. She repaid this attention of mine by flirting with my companions, taking little notice of me, and I was obliged further to demand that she produce two of her colleagues to balance the confrontation. We will pass over also other early wartime contenders who became elegantly attired in Wren uniform or more sternly kitted out as members of the so-called Land Army, who were left in no doubt about the four-legged facts of life. Nor will we dwell on the attractions of a tawny-eyed blonde who was a star performer in a beauty parlour, but will leap straight to the more momentous – shall I say – close encounters.

When the Regiment was stationed at Beni Yusef camp, not far from Mena House Hotel and the Giza pyramids, most of us were members of Gezirah Sporting Club, where even in the middle of the war, there was no shortage of enthusiasm for polo, golf, tennis, squash racquets, swimming and poodle-faking. It was there that I was introduced to two Egyptian sisters, friends of an Egyptian Air Force officer, and we would regularly meet for a game of mixed doubles. One of the sisters, Bessina, was much prettier than the other, and I ventured to invite her to dine and dance at an agreeable establishment, called, if my memory does not fail, Dolls. It was not long before I discovered that Bessina enjoyed other games as well. What is more she had access to the modest dwelling of a former nanny of hers, and to this love-nest we would from time to time withdraw. She was both keen on the sport and skilful and although during these sessions of horizontal exercise, Bessina did not actually teach me what Flashman learned from Fernah – the ninety-seven ways of making love – she did her best with the result that I became quite attached to her. Moreover, as Kipling so aptly put it 'I learned about women from 'er'.

But Bessina was not the only filly to catch my eye in Cairo. There was also Helene Rioche. French, soft-natured, clinging and romantically inclined, intoxicated with the idea of having a British cavalry officer as an admirer, our clinches did not amount to more than a few chaste embraces. She was an admirable counter to the more demanding Bessina and, being limited to her own language and a smattering of Arabic, my own lack of fluency in French was partially compensated for. Had we not sailed for Italy when we did, Helene and I might have become closer, but as it was she wrote charming love letters to me for the first few months of our Italian campaign and then, no doubt, despairing of my ever returning, switched loyalties.

Italy, of course, was another matter. Not that there was much time for dalliance while we were actually engaged with the *tedeschi* but out of the line and after the war was over, it was different. When one thinks of Italian women, one pictures at once a creature like Tosca. Passionate, full-blooded, single minded, stunningly attractive and, if necessary, murderous. To bring the whole thing down to earth a bit more in view of the company one was likely to find amongst the *contadini* of the operational zones, as opposed to the more sophisticated circles of Rome, Bologna and Trieste, it would be hard to better Eric Newby's record of *Love and War in the Apennines*. He finds himself torn between the attentions of Rita, Dolores and Wanda in the farming community of Fontanellato. At one point he is being pursued by Nero, a savage guard dog, and only escapes by being hauled up into a barn by Dolores who has been working there. As they fell back in the hay together, quite spontaneously Dolores enfolded Newby in her arms and begins to subject him to passionate kisses. We must allow Newby to take up the story:

> Because it was a warm evening...she had taken off the tight sweater which she usually wore and was now dressed in nothing but a faded, sleeveless, navy blue vest which displayed her really superb upper works to great advantage, a short skirt and boots...She turned over until she was more or less lying on top of me which, unless I had something like seven feet of hay under me would probably have done me an injury. Now I was drowning in long auburn hair. She smelled delicious...Somewhere, far off, I could hear Nero howling. What an escape I had had. Out of the frying pan into the fire.

Newby is saved from ultimate surrender by frantic cries from the farmer's wife, one of the few authorities Dolores was prepared to recognize, for their help to round up Nero before he escaped altogether. I cannot say that I was fortunate enough to encounter a Dolores during the Italian campaign – of which more in a later chapter – but I do recall the gratitude with which another Rita requited my gift of soap, severely short in Italy then. She even went so far as to suggest that she should accompany me in our further advance northwards in the role of my 'laundress'. It was an invitation that I courteously and affectionately declined.

In those intoxicating days following the war's end and our adventures first in Carinthia then Venezia Giulia, I was far too occupied by mares possessing four legs rather than those who had only two but when, at the beginning of 1946, I was dispatched to Rome for an attachment to the Italian cavalry, things changed. My main task, attached to the British military mission to the Italian Army, was to assist their cavalry regiments to master the intricacies of British armoured cars; but with the additional advantage of attending riding school with the *Corazzieri,* the equivalent of our Household Cavalry, for at that time King Umberto was still on the throne. I already had two good friends in Rome – Filippo Senni, our liaison officer during the Italian campaign, and his successor, Raimondo Marini-Clarelli, who joined us in Villa Opicina. Much of my military work was done with Filippo, who was good enough to make me an honorary member of the Circolo della Caccia, a superlatively distinguished club, which might be said to combine the virtues of our own – I speak of the circumstances of 1946 – Cavalry Club, Guards Club and Turf Club. A graceful former Palazzo, it boasted beautiful rooms, an excellent cuisine at tolerable prices, facilities for backgammon on specially designed tables and, in warm weather, dining tables on elegant terraces. The Club servants were dressed in prodigiously formal livery, and among the many members of the Club were those responsible for overseeing the revived activities of the Roman Campagna's pack of foxhounds. I counted myself fortunate indeed to enjoy the delights of this wonderful Club. It was because of Filippo and his delightful wife, Giulianella, that I was introduced to what we might, in all modesty, describe as the cream of Roman society – the Sforzas, the Colonnas, the Medicis. I am happy to say, however, that all this good fortune did not go to my head.

These were, of course, the days of La Dolce Vita, and life was made particularly sweet for me when Raimondo invited me to meet the Bettoja family, whose elder daughter, Rosalinda, was very good-looking, intelligent and accomplished. Her father owned hotels, her mother was American and she was studying economics at Rome University. We went to lots of parties, rode the horses in care of the Veterinary Corps, danced at the various night clubs, enjoyed the opera and swam at Anzio. Military duty, for I was soon recalled to the Regiment, prevented things going further, but we remained good friends, and much later, when I was commanding a brigade in Ulster, my wife and I were able to look after her daughter, who stayed with us for some months to improve her command of English.

When the Regiment moved from the romantic, alluring setting of Italy to the bleaker plains and towns of Schleswig Holstein early in 1947, the scene may have changed, but not the pursuit of the weaker sex. There was at that time, as I recall, still in force the so-called non-fraternization edict, which instantly called to mind Schiller's *Mit der Dummheit kämpfen Götter selbst vergebens* – With stupidity the gods themselves struggle in vain. On the one hand you had the red-blooded cavalry cornets and troopers, all too eager to exploit the joys of the flesh; on the other hand willing Fräuleins, not to say Frauen. Yet the edict forbids fraternization. You might as well have tried to restrain Don Giovanni, Lord Byron or Casanova. I myself was somewhat too occupied by continuing to whip in to Loopy's foxhounds. In this task I was joined by a young officer in our neighbouring regiment, the 10th Hussars. His name was Henry Bathurst and it would have been difficult to find a more agreeable, competent and enthusiastic fellow whip. He had good reason to study further what Loopy was up to for, when demobilized after his two years' service, he had his own pack of hounds at Cirencester, where he was Master. We had some fine runs in the country to the west of Lübeck, and even took the hounds as far afield as Kiel and Schleswig, where the 4th Royal Horse Artillery and the 16th/5th Lancers were respectively stationed. One of 4th RHA officers, Tom Inglis, became a lifelong friend, as many years later we found ourselves living in the same part of Wiltshire.

One of the best things ever to happen to the 4th Hussars at this time was the arrival of George Kidston to command us. George was originally a 12th Lancer, the regiment which he had commanded in the desert and he had subsequently been appointed to command several other regiments. He was without doubt one of the finest cavalry commanding officers of his generation. Handsome, richly endowed, generous in heart and in sharing his good fortune, brave, devoted to those he led, brimming over with humour, a lover of reminiscence, a really fine shot, excellent horseman and skilful angler, he had really been born with a silver spoon in his mouth and, above all, he had that knack of commanding in such a way that he succeeded time after time in overseeing a contented and efficient regiment. Two of my earliest dealings with him were these. On hearing that General Dick McCreery, a fellow 12th Lancer, at this time Commander-in-Chief, Rhine Army, was coming to inspect the 4th Hussars and knowing all too well General Dick's passion for gardens, George appointed me Gardening Officer for the day. We had a team of German gardeners who had succeeded in creating a stunning display of both flowers and vegetables. I quickly reconnoitred them all and on the day was invited to show the great General round. The result: 'I must say, George',he proclaimed, 'you have one of the best gardens in the Rhine Army.' So far, so good. The next incident was less so. Invited to ride George's superb Warden, a 16½ hh brown gelding, in the intermediate class at Lübeck horse show, we cleared the first four of five fences in soaring form, but came heavily to grief at the wall, which George subsequently informed me, I had approached in far too leisurely a fashion. But we must get back to the fillies.

It has been said that no man's education in affairs of the heart is complete until he has succumbed to the lures of a mature woman somewhat older than himself. So it was with me. George had decided that I should sit the Staff College examination in the winter of 1947 and, in order to enhance my knowledge of military law, one of the examination subjects in those days, I would be attached for a few months to our local headquarters, which was composed of the former HQ Guards Armoured Division, stationed at Plön. The Officers' Mess there was run by Sergeant Weston, Irish Guards, and by stealthy bargaining of what I fear were black market desirables, such as cigarettes, soap, NAAFI goods in general, in exchange for pheasants, partridge, pigs, venison and varieties of fruit and vegetables, the table kept at the Mess was royal. There would be occasional dances, livened by the splendid little band from Travemünde Club, playing favourites from the latest American musicals, Oklahoma and Annie Get Your Gun, and at one of these I met and danced with Madame X. Before long we had embarked on a tempestuous love affair, conducted with due discretion.

The Four Seasons Hotel on the Alster was a convenient rendezvous and so prolonged was our obsession with one another that wrestling matches were resumed after I had rejoined the Regiment early in 1948, when we were stationed at Colchester, prior to setting sail for Malaya for a taste of a savage war of peace. Madame X was all that could be desired: loving, generous with her charms, seductively experienced, and blessed with a bubbling sense of humour, never taking the whole thing too seriously. I was smitten indeed. We parted with regret, but amicably when I embarked on the troopship, bound for Singapore. We continued to exchange Christmas cards until her death some forty years later. An' I learned about women from 'er!

Perhaps I should have taken Kipling's advice further when we in the 4th Hussars found ourselves in Malaya, and learned from the Yellow too, but somehow we were so busy patrolling in our armoured cars, jungle bashing and, when off duty, playing polo, going to curry tiffins, sipping stengahs at The Club, taking part in amateur dramatics and improving our golf handicaps that, in spite of the numerous, not unapproachable and frankly delectable-looking Chinese girls, to say nothing of the more voluptuous, seductive and indolent Malay creatures, I neglected my studies here, settling for a few mild flirtations with the daughters of a senior Shell representative and the wives of Telecommunications officials. The more serious side of our duties in Malaya, our part in the long, long war to defeat Communist insurrection, must await a later chapter.

Having, to the astonishment of my fellow 4th Hussars, passed the Staff College examination, I was sent home in 1950 to attend the course at Camberley, joining a number of wartime friends from other regiments, in particular Douglas MacCallan of The Bays, Robin Brockbank, 12th Lancers, Jim Wilson, The Rifle Brigade, Desmond Scarr, 14th/20th Hussars, Pat Howard-Dobson, 7th Hussars and many others. Among the instructors there, the so-called Directing Staff, were Freddie Graham, Bill Jackson, Derek Horsford, Brian Wyldbore-Smith – all first class men with whom I would have significant dealings later on.

One of our duties at the Staff College was to write an essay on a campaign which had figured largely in military history. I chose the campaigns of Napoleon and so came face to face with A.G. Macdonell's *Napoleon and his Marshals*, a treasure which never fails to please. This essay, which won golden opinions from the aforesaid Derek Horsford, was typed for me by a girl friend, Clodagh Bennet, who was to remain a great ally in the times to come. But the Staff College course allowed little leisure for poodle-faking, and the job you get at its end would depend very much on how you did, so I worked hard, while relaxing on the cricket field, the tennis court and an occasional hack. The result? I was appointed Brigade Major of 61 Lorried Infantry Brigade, commanded by the very Freddie Graham who had headed a Staff College Division, and part of the 6th Armoured Division, reformed at the beginning of 1951, together with other divisions as a result of concern over the conflict in Korea. The 6th Armoured Division was commanded by Errol Prior-Palmer, a flamboyant, daring, short-fused, polo star of the 9th Lancers. He was an ideal choice. He looked every inch a general, behaved like one and led his division with dedication, skill and panache. After a year's training on Salisbury Plain, the division moved to the Rhine Army and I found myself quartered at Minden. Our headquarters was positioned in the former Melitta coffee-filter factory, and our Officers' Mess was in Marienstrasse, where I took up residence. It was not long before I met my future wife, Baroness Wilfried von Schellersheim.

Our courtship was a lengthy one, eight years in all, and was interrupted by frequent comings and goings. We first met at a dinner party given by my Brigadier, Freddie Graham, and as a result I was invited to visit her home at Eisbergen on the River Weser, not far from Minden, where her father, Baron Harald von Schellersheim, had an estate. Her mother, Rose-Marie, was a von Oheimb; a family of some distinction in the German aristocracy. She was charming and cultured, ran the household with a firm, benevolent hand, and was tolerant of, although deeply hurt by, the Baron's indiscretions. He was a very keen horseman and was reconciled to my friendship with his elder daughter simply by acknowledgement that I could ride his horses and drink glass for glass with him without any signs of discomfort. In his keenness to teach his daughters his own equestrian skills, he had succeeded in putting Wilfried off horses for good by mounting her on uncooperative brutes, who would dash at fences, then refuse, with foreseeable consequences. Even a long-lashed whip administrated at the point when the reluctant animal reached the fence did not help. His younger daughter, Karin, however, survived his regime of instruction and became a competent horsewoman.

Early in 1953, my two years as Brigade Major completed, I handed over to another close friend, Ian Gill, 4th/7th Dragoon Guards, and returned to the Regiment, now stationed at Tidworth, and took over command of C Squadron, the very one I had joined in 1942. It would not be long, however, before the 4th Hussars were dispatched to the Rhine Army once more, this time to Hohne, on the Lüneburger Heide. We were now part of 7 Armoured Brigade, had a splendid barracks, were equipped with Centurion tanks, and were commanded by Stephen Eve. He had succeeded Richard Close-Smith, whom we will meet again when we look more closely at the Malayan campaign. We were particularly fortunate in our Officers' Mess, a former hunting lodge. Bredebeck, which was a mile or so from the barracks, had excellent public rooms, plenty of bedrooms for bachelor officers – most of us were in this category – a lake, a park, stabling for thirty horses and an excellent indoor riding school. It was a time of great activity in field exercises, visits to the Reeperbahn for those so inclined, and numerous horse shows. There was, however, time for me to renew my friendship with the Baron von Schellersheim and his family, especially so with his elder daughter, Wilfried. It may be remembered that in Daphne du Maurier's novel, *Rebecca*, Maxim de Winter bitterly reveals to his new, young, innocent wife that Rebecca had 'beauty, brains and breeding, but she was incapable of love or tenderness or decency'. Wilfried, on the other hand, had not only beauty, brains and breeding, but was wholly capable of love and tenderness and decency. No wonder I fell in love with her.

In October 1954 the Regiment celebrated the centenary of the Charge of the Light Brigade – in which we, as the then 4th Light Dragoons, had participated – by giving a Balaklava Ball in our splendid Bredebeck Mess. It was the party of the year. Pat Uniacke, now second in command, was in his element. Tasteful electric lights lit up the lake, the whole building was extravagantly beautified with flowers, the drive up to the Mess and Bredebeck's imposing front were floodlit, trumpeters and a Guard of Honour on parade to greet the principal guests, who included the then current members of those families renowned for their part in the Crimean War – Raglan, Cathcart, Brudenell, Paget, Lucan. In the hall ready to welcome our guests were the Colonel, Stephen Eve and his wife, Betty whose maiden name, Rank, spoke of Colonel Steve's sagacity, given his love of thoroughbred horses, in marrying the daughter of Joseph Rank, millionaire and race horse owner, and myself as President of the Mess Committee. My responsibilities were to ensure that the actual business of the evening – pre-supper champagne and other liquids, dance music by our Regimental dance band, supper, and at some remote time, breakfast of bacon and eggs went well. In all this I was most ably supported by our superb Mess sergeant, Mr Wallace and his culinarily expert wife. Sergeant Wallace had won great fame during the Greek campaign in 1941 when, oblivious of the Panzer and the Stuka interference with his arrangements, he had coolly served breakfast to those members of Regimental Headquarters who were about to be unwilling lodgers in a German POW camp. For every Mess dinner and other function Sergeant Wallace would appear immaculate in white tie and tails, with a sangfroid which Jeeves himself would have applauded. Nothing could throw him off balance, and on this Balaklava Ball occasion, he excelled himself. The whole thing went off without a hitch.

I was particularly pleased that Wilfried was my guest for the evening. She stayed with Bill and Ann Currie, who had a military married quarter in Hohne, and while I was performing my reception duties, I handed her over to the care of my old friend, John Paley, who had served with me in the Regiment, indeed in the same squadron, from the time he joined the 4th Hussars in mid-1943. Somehow during the evening a diamond brooch that Wilfried was wearing came detached from her dress, and it was not until the following evening that I received a distress call from Eisbergen about the loss. Happily the brooch was found in a corner of the dance floor and order was restored. Wilfried and I drew closer as we knew each other better, and even talked of marriage, but in those days a major's pay was derisory and for the time being things went no further.

The immediate future was resolved for us. I had commanded C Squadron for two years and was vulnerable for an extra-regimental appointment. During one particular manoeuvre I was standing in the turret of my Centurion, wet through from constant rain and was attempting to show some enthusiasm and appreciation for the plate of sodden bacon and fried bread which Sergeant O'Connor, my radio operator, had just handed me. At this point the Adjutant, Hugh Marrack, arrived in a jeep and put a question to me. 'How would you like to go to Fort Knox in Kentucky as British Liaison Officer at the Armored Center there?' A picture of glorious sunshine, the Blue Grass country, Kentucky Derby, the stud farms at Lexicon, glamorous girls and bourbon whiskey floated before me. Recollecting Polonius's view that brevity is the soul of wit, I replied: 'Very much.' And so it transpired. I will say more of my two years in Kentucky later, but it will be fitting to deal with the petticoats now.

As the sole representative of the British Cavalry in those parts, it was clearly my duty to behave with decorum, so no deep intrigues featured in my dealings with the southern fillies. But from time to time it was *de rigueur* to sport a female companion at some function or other, and in the course of several months I acquired three girl friends. Variety is said to be the spice of life and I stuck to this dictum. They were very different. One was a southern belle, dark-eyed, decadent and, I fear, dipsomaniacal, with a 'yew-all' drawl and that look between the lines; number two was a prematurely grey-haired, matriarchal iceberg, tall, prim, direct and clearly in need of being de-frosted; third and last was a pretty, sweet, soft-natured creature of the girl-next-door category. With such a stable to choose from I was well placed to attend social affairs of any kidney. Over confidence, however, nearly led to my downfall, for in order to enliven the cocktail party, which I gave to the visiting Director of the Royal Armoured Corps – Major General Foote VC – I invited all three of them to attend. At one stage that evening I was concerned to see that the three of them had their heads together and were shooting unprepossessing looks at me. It required all my diplomatic skills to reconcile them to my good intentions.

About halfway through my time at Fort Knox, I was interviewed by a female reporter from the *Louisville Courier*, who was writing a series of articles about 'The Six Most Eligible Bachelors in Kentucky', and she requested that I should allow my name to go forward as one of them. In agreeing to submit to her questions, I determined to set a very high price on my own head while keeping my tongue firmly embedded in a nearby cheek. Thus in responding to her main point as to what sort of woman would tempt me to abandon bachelorhood, I spun a tale of one who would be wealthy enough to maintain my standard of living; good-looking enough, so that I could lower *The Times* at the breakfast table and contemplate her features with real pleasure, but not so stunningly beautiful that I would be compelled to repel Lotharios; appreciative of the arts, of sporting activities, willing to follow the drum; taking a leaf from Benedick's book, wise, virtuous, mild in temper, her hair of what colour it please God and, of course, like Cordelia with a voice 'ever soft, gentle and low, an excellent thing in woman'. The *Courier* reporter did not make use of all of my suggestions in her article, but she was sufficiently considerate to make me sound like a paragon, and the fan mail flowed in. I reflected that any creature answering to my description in even a mild way would long since have been snapped up by a discerning native of Kentucky, and so decided that it would be prudent not to respond.

After handing over my duties at Fort Knox to my successor, I was posted to Latimer for a few months' course in joint service matters. Among my fellow students were my old friend in The Bays, Douglas MacCallan, Roly Gibbs of 60th Rifles and Parachute Regiment fame, and the most intelligent, cultivated, witty, accomplished and clubbable naval officer it has ever been my good fortune to encounter – John Templeton-Cotill, of whom more later.

At the end of the course I returned to regimental duty. The 4th Hussars were still at Hohne and now commanded by that great man, Loopy Kennard, who invited me to combine a number of duties – training, President of the Mess Committee, some administrative changes, and also to undertake liaison with the now reformed and active German Army, the Bundeswehr. He also loaned me to our Divisional Commander, General Shan Hackett, to assist him with some tactical exercises. But all these various tasks still gave me plenty of opportunities for renewing once more my friendship with the von Schellersheim family. The Baron had parted from Rose-Marie and had married again somewhat to the dismay of his daughters. But this event did not affect my affection for Wilfried nor hers for me. We were still undecided about what future we might have together, although it would not be long before we realized that neither of us wished to be married except to one another. Before we took this step, however, and after I had been back with the Regiment for some eighteen months, I was appointed to the Staff College as an instructor and in the autumn of 1958 found myself at Minley Manor.

Minley Manor, a Division of the Staff College, but a few miles from the main building at Camberley, was a large Victorian mansion, architecturally undistinguished, but convenient for instructional and bachelor-accommodating purposes; it boasted a beautiful avenue of Wellingtonia trees – up which we would sometimes drive golf balls – a spacious paddock (where Bella, my faithful bay mare would spend happy days from April to September), a lovely cricket field and some houses for married members of the Directing Staff.

When I reported to Colonel Douglas Darling, the supremo of Minley Manor, in August 1958, he had no questions to ask me about my military background. He simply said that he wanted me to help him exercise his horses that afternoon, play squash raquets with him after tea, and make up a four at bridge that evening. Douglas was one of the most highly decorated members of The Rifle Brigade, having commanded battalions in the desert and Italy; a keen hunting man, forceful, likeable and extremely able. What could I do but comply with his three requirements?

There were several other members of The Rifle Brigade who were members of the so-called DS – Mark Bond, Hew Butler and Dick Worsley, all of whom became great friends, as did Stuart Watson, 13th/18th Hussars, Tim Creasey, Royal Anglian Regiment, and Bill Cooper, a witty, Mahler-loving, fly-fishing and generally accomplished sapper. I had not been long at Minley before Rollo Pain, 4th/7th Dragoon Guards, who was Secretary of the Sandhurst Foxhounds and Staff College Drag, together totalling some thirty-two couple of hounds, persuaded me to take over from Robert Ferguson, another great friend, a Northumberland Fusilier, a loveable man, distinguished at all field sports, a Sandhurst instructor, and about to give up being Master of the Drag on account of being posted to Norway.

I will later recount my adventures as a Master of Drag Hounds, but it is time now to bring the saga of petticoats to an end by saying that what with my immediate military duties, Bella and the foxhounds, it was not until some two years later in December 1960 that Wilfried and I finally married. It was, as I said at the outset of this narrative, the greatest stroke of good fortune ever to befall me.

In *Madame Bovary* Flaubert has some unkind things to say about cavalrymen. 'Keen brained for all their fatuous looks', he wrote, 'they spent their days in the hunting field, riding horses until they dropped, dawdled away the summer months in Baden, and, round about the age of forty, married heiresses.' But my

Regiment had another maxim: 'Captains may marry, majors should, colonels must.' As a DS at the Staff College, I was a lieutenant colonel. The devil fly away with maxims, however. Wilfried and I married for love. An' I'm still learning about women from 'er.

Chapter 4

Four Legged Friends

> 'Where in this wide world can man find nobility without pride, friendship without envy, or beauty without vanity?'
>
> Ronald Duncan

Those of us fortunate enough to have owned, ridden and loved horses will be in no doubt when we emphatically endorse the answer to Ronald Duncan's question. Among those to lead this endorsement was one of my fellow troop leaders in C Squadron, Claud Thompson. Before the war he had been Joint Master of a famous pack of foxhounds – The Scarteen (The Black and Tans) and he taught me more about horses, hunting and horse-mastership than anyone. Shortly after the outbreak of war, he had enlisted in The Blues. It was said that when a young recruit was first interviewed by a Corporal of Horse in the Household Cavalry, he would be asked if he knew how to ride. But a wise recruit would not be deceived by the seeming innocence of this question. Should the newcomer be dupe enough to return a confident affirmative, he would be invited to see 'whether he could ride this one' – at which a renowned near-unrideable animal would be led out from his loose box, with foreseeable results. If, on the other hand, he denied any such equestrian skills, only for it to be observed later that he had actually fibbed, it might be that one of the rough-riding instructors would, later on, subject him to a regime not notable for being 'full of the milk of human kindness'. The answer to make in order to avoid these pitfalls was something on the lines of: 'Well, Sir, I have been on a horse before, but I wouldn't say that I can ride.' It was this reply that a forewarned Claud Thompson made when the question was put to him. He enjoyed his relatively short term of service with The Blues; short because he was rapidly plucked out for officer training, and found himself commissioned into an infantry regiment. Then, in 1943, he transferred to the 4th Hussars and, happily for us, joined C Squadron. And having the entrée to the Royal Army Veterinary Corps at Abassia Barracks near Cairo, he generously undertook to initiate me into the secrets of having a good seat on a horse and, moreover, how to look after horses. After the war he even went so far as to arrange for me to hunt with The Cambridgeshire, but before that when we found ourselves in Austria in May 1945 as an epilogue to our successful completion of the Italian campaign – of which more later – Claud actually found for me the first horse that I was to own.

When the German armies in Italy surrendered at the beginning of May 1945, the 4th Hussars were ordered to Austria. C Squadron was detached to Mölzbichl, a village in Carinthia roughly between Paternion and Lienz. Our task was to set up a prisoner of war camp for various units of the *Wehrmacht* and their allies, including Cossack and Hungarian cavalry brigades. It was decided that a separate camp would be established for the horses and the obvious choice for the running of the four-legged POW camp was, of course, Claud. It was one of my duties to visit him from time to time to ensure that he had all he needed in the way of forage, veterinary items, straw, shoes for the horses and supplies for his Cossack and Hungarian soldiers. Sometimes I would accompany him on his tour of inspection, and it was noteworthy that although Claud spoke no foreign language and his prisoners little English, somehow they communicated with horse-like grunts and signs.

On one such visit one of the Hungarian officers, who, like myself, spoke German, had momentous tidings for us. The Colonel's charger, a magnificent animal, it seemed, which they thought had gone astray, had somehow turned up and now they wanted to show it to Claud. It was duly led up and as Claud clapped eyes on it he drew in his breath in open admiration. He was a beautiful animal, a bay gelding about five years old, not quite 16 hh and by all accounts from our Hungarian friend, bold, tough, good over fences and fast. Claud said nothing at the time except to make arrangements to try the horse out himself. Shortly after this, on my next visit, we once again did our tour of inspection and this time Claud had the Hungarian wonder for me to ride. We got on famously and it was then Claud recommended that I should take charge of him. This move was strenuously opposed by the Hungarian Colonel, who even went as far as to offer his wife to us, if only we would let him keep the gelding – clearly a man who knew his priorities. But we were adamant. Once established in our own stables, we decided to change his curious Hungarian name, but bearing in mind his native country and his near insatiable appetite for oats, hay, carrots and apples, we named him 'Hungry'.

So Hungry and I became partners, and when the Regiment was ordered back to Italy in September 1945, he went with me. We then found ourselves at Villa Opicina, an Italian Army cavalry barracks north of Trieste. It was about this time too that a number of pre-war 4th Hussar officers returned to the Regiment, having been guests of the Third Reich after the ill-fated campaign in Greece. It was not long before they bagged all the best horses that we amateurs had acquired during our time in Austria. As expert horsemen and connoisseurs of horseflesh, they took one look at Hungry and made it clear that my own horsemanship was not of the calibre that Hungry deserved. So Hungry was usually ridden by the Colonel or by the legendary Loopy Kennard – of whom more later.

I was however permitted to rejoin forces with Hungry on two occasions. First, in the threesomes at a hunter trial organized by The Queen's Bays at Palmanova, I was invited to perform, wedged between the Colonel and Loopy, respectively riding Bounty, a beautiful thoroughbred mare, and Max, a tough, steeplechasing bay gelding, and sandwiched as I was between two such bold and competent horsemen, we went round at a cracking pace and had the time of our lives. Furthermore, so impressed was the Colonel by this event that, although I was not authorized to ride Hungry in steeplechases, the Colonel allowed me to partner him in a six-furlong scurry at Aiello race course, roughly between Trieste and Udine and established there by the great General Dick

McCreery, last commander of the Eighth Army.

Ours was the first race of this particular meeting and there were fourteen starters. There were no bookmakers at this essentially British Army racecourse, but the Tote did operate, with a healthy proportion of profits going to welfare projects for former soldiers in need. As I mounted Hungry in the collecting ring, proudly wearing the Regiment's colours of primrose and blue, I congratulated his groom, a former Cossack, whom we had brought with us from Austria, on how beautifully he had turned him out. A friend of mine in The Queen's Bays wished me luck and asked if he was worth a bet. I shook my head, not in doubt as to Hungry's ability, but rather as to my own jockeying skills. Needless to say my own Regimental friends had not even bothered to ask.

We cantered down to the start, came under starter's orders – I must confess to some stomach butterflies, for it was my first race – and we were off. To my surprise and delight, Hungry shot straight to the front and stayed there for all six furlongs. Flushed with pride and making much of Hungry, I rode him back to the unsaddling enclosure, there to be greeted with sour looks from my brother officers and a bitter reproach from my friend in The Bays. Hungry's groom, on the other hand, appeared overjoyed. He had reason to. His beautiful charge had been victorious, but even more gratifying he had bought the only Tote ticket in favour of Hungry. The payout was tremendous. This was not the only race I took part in at Aiello. The next one was a far more serious affair, something that the Colonel had long planned and now put into effect – a Regimental steeplechase.

I should here explain that during our time at Villa Opicina, there had been added to the Regimental strength, apart from all the horses we had acquired, a pack of foxhounds, transported in an aeroplane, courtesy of the Royal Air Force, via Rome airport, where they had rioted, to Trieste. I will have more to say about this later, but it will be enough to explain here that we had been forced to stop hunting proper, as the fox, hounds and horsemen were constantly finding themselves on the other side of the frontier with Yugoslavia, much to the fury of their officials, and we had been obliged to satisfy ourselves with drag hunting which, in fact, turned out to be ideal over the stone-wall country of Bazovizia, north of Trieste. For the steeplechase, therefore, the

Colonel had decreed that those who had qualified by regularly going out with the drag hounds were eligible to enter. Moreover he excluded the pre-war regular officers in order to give a chance to us relatively inexperienced horsemen. It may also have been, of course, the case that those pre-war regulars preferred to absent themselves from riding over fences in such manifestly dangerous company.

There were, as I recall, eighteen starters. None of the horses had been round a steeplechase course before, although, of course, we had been schooling our animals over comparable fences. Similarly none of the riders had raced over fences before, although a few had taken part in hunter trials. At the start, the butterflies were even more active but we all got away in fine style. The approach to the first fence was, to say the least of it, unnerving. If the great Duke of Wellington had been there to observe it, he would have seen nothing to reverse his criticism of the British Cavalry in the Peninsular campaign. He would, rather, have been confirmed in his view that the cavalry relied too much on mere speed of movement, that there was no control of the advance and that no reserve seemed to be kept in hand. And yet we all got over it.

The really astonishing thing was that, with the exception of two animals which were prudently pulled up after climbing over the open ditch rather than clearing it, we all completed the course. I was riding a reliable, but not particularly speedy animal named Summer Star, and finished seventh, roughly in the middle of a field spread out over half a dozen fences. The whole thing was a fitting finale to our tour of duty in Venezia Giulia, for shortly afterwards the Regiment was ordered to Schleswig Holstein, and we took ourselves, our horses and hounds – the military train required several extra wagons for these indispensable four-legged friends – and once there set about the serious business of hunting. There were foxes about, but the hounds would normally chivvy roe-deer from the numerous coverts, which would give us a fine chase and, happily, rarely a kill.

I will not offer here a description of all the horses that figured in our lives in Germany at that time or during our subsequent service in various theatres, but there are a few of cherished memory. Barman, a chestnut gelding, carried me so well when whipping-in to Loopy Kennard, undisputed Master of our 4th

Hussar pack of hounds. In Schleswig Holstein there were relatively few hedgerows or post-and-rail fences, but lots of wire, with fortunately stout gates in and out of the fields, and Barman would soar over these gates with a readiness and spirit that brought words of praise even from Loopy. Then some years later when we found ourselves in Malaya during the so-called emergency, how can I forget Arthur, a tough little Waler, who took to the polo field with joyful enthusiasm and assisted me in out-pacing my opponents to score goal after goal. Back in Germany in the 1950s, I had a great show-jumping partner in Jasper, a dark bay gelding, whose idleness and occasional reluctance to give of his best, made it clear that it was not only for mares that the presence of spurs could be providential. As soon as he knew I was wearing them, Jasper needed no more persuasion, but would fly round the show-jumping course.

But of all the horses that I was fortunate enough to have, the star was Bella, who carried me when I was Master of the Staff College Drag Hounds. Bella in appearance, Bella in nature, Bella in performance, she deserves and will have a chapter of her own, but before we meet her, I must introduce some other four-legged friends of a totally different make.

Chapter 5

A Fox and One and a Half Couple of Foxhounds

> 'He [a Master of Hounds] should be assured that of all human pursuits hunting is the best and that of all living things a fox is the most valuable. The time which other men gave to their wives and families he [Mr. Harkaway] bestowed upon his hounds. To his stables he never went, looking on a horse as a necessary adjunct to hunting, expensive, disagreeable, and prone to get you into danger...But he was always with his hounds, and when anyone said a kind word as to their doings, that he would take as a compliment.'
>
> Anthony Trollope

We are back at the 4th Hussar barracks at Villa Opicina, and one morning in September 1945, as I strolled towards the stables to have a word with and feed a carrot to Hungry, the handsome bay gelding you have already met, the Regimental Orderly Corporal appeared in my path. Immaculate in shirt-sleeve order with cross-belt superbly blancoed, boots like glass and cap badge gleaming, he saluted, eyes tilted skywards as if regarding heaven, and spoke: 'The Commanding Officer's compliments, Sir, and could you spare him a few moments?' In other words, the Colonel is in an implacable rage about something, is tolerably certain that you are the culprit and wishes instantly, or at any rate when you reach his office, to strip you of all regimental accoutrements and dispatch you to be OC Troops, Mogadishu, never to be seen or heard of again.

Having arrived at the Adjutant's office in answer to the

Colonel's summons, I now waited apprehensively before being ushered into the presence, unaware that I was about to be dispatched, not to Mogadishu, but on a mission of far greater consequence. The Colonel's first words did at least put my nagging conscience of guilt to rest.

'Ah, John, sit down.'

'Thank you, Colonel.'

'You speak Italian, don't you!'

It was not a question, but a statement. I acknowledged some superficial acquaintance with the vernacular.

'Right. I want you to go and buy a fox. Loopy is flying back from England with seven couple of foxhounds and I've decided that we should start off by having a drag hunt round the Bazovizia country. So we must have a smell. Understand? The Equitation Fund will go up to twenty odd quid.'

In fact, as explained earlier, we started by hunting properly, but had to switch to drag hunting. I saluted and withdrew to the Officers' Mess where I consulted a map and a glass of Cinzano. Here was a challenge that was going to demand all my powers of persuasion, cunning, resolution and fluency in Italian. There was only one thing for it. I would have to do what all soldiers were supposed to do when confronted with a seemingly impossible mission – make an appreciation of the situation. First I had to run a fox to earth, then somehow or other capture it, transport it back to the barracks and find some suitable accommodation for it, then ensure its welfare as far as victuals were concerned and finally arrange for the collection of its *orina*. And then the whole idea of confining a wild animal to some sort of cage revolted against all sporting instincts. But orders were orders and having established that the fox, if and when acquired, would be housed near the stables and that someone else would look after that side of things and the animal's welfare, I set off in a 15-cwt truck with a good reliable driver, 25,000 lire [in those days the exchange rate was about 1,000 lire to £1], haversack rations, brewing up kit and an Italian dictionary.

My first port of call was at the house of a Gorizian farmer, Maurizio, with whom I had had dealings in the purchase of forage for our horses. When I had explained somewhat haltingly that we needed a fox in order to store its offerings so that we could subsequently invite foxhounds to follow a scent supplied by soaking a pad in such offering, which would be dragged along by a runner in order that we, mounted on willing steeds, could then follow, negotiating stone wall obstacles as we went, Maurizio, a true countryman, shook his head and made it clear that while hunting proper, *la caccia*, was something of which he entirely approved, he could not support the idea of catching a wild animal in order to store its *orina* so that we could have some fun with horses and hounds. I fully saw his point of view, and after a glass or two of roughish Marsala, I moved on to another acquaintance, Giuseppe, some fifteen kilometres further west. My initial statement, that I wanted a fox, produced an instant response. He reached for his shotgun and a bag of cartridges. I did not dare repeat my explanation about drag hunting, but asked him whether he knew where I could buy a live fox. '*Mi scusi, No.*' Two coverts drawn, both blank. Third time lucky? We would see.

We drove to Maiello where, during the war, I had met the local partisan leader, Giacomo, now respectably running a bank. When I explained my mission, he exuded confidence. '*Una volpe? Si, naturalmente. Andiamo!*' We climbed into the truck. '*Dove?*' I asked. '*Sempre diritto.*' Straight on. Straight on, we drove – to Udine, to Pordenone, to Treviso, to Mestre. I had to fork out lots of lire for *benzina* and glasses of Soave, but it was worth it. At Mestre we went straight to the Piazza Centrale where the great caravans and lorries of a circus were all parked together. *Il padrone* was summoned and the three of us invaded a *trattoria*. Wine was called for and the situation once more explained. A fox, a live fox, was instantly required by *il Capitano* Strawson. Never mind why. *Il Colonello* demanded a fox. But the circus owner was insistent. He had to know why. In a flash of irritation – or was it inspiration? – I snapped a quick reply: 'The Colonel liked roast fox for supper.'

'*Magnifico!*' My hand was seized and pumped. Only the English cavalry could produce such men, who overcame the *Wehrmacht*, rode the wildest of horses, hunted and ate foxes. '*Bravissimo! Ancora una bottiglia!*' I was beginning to be worried about my store of lire. Would there be enough left? Triumphantly we returned to the piazza. Orders were bellowed, underlings began running about, and ten minutes later a huge cage was produced and inside it was a big, reddish dog fox, snarling, leaping, frantically seeking a way out of his dreadful prison. It was then that my heart sank. Could I really be a party to such violation of nature? But duty was duty. I handed over the lire, the *padrone* bellowed at a vast mountain of a woman – his wife or the circus's fat lady? – to bring *una bottiglia*. I could not refuse, but thanked heavens for my driver.

Then back we went, returning Giacomo to Maiello and set off for Opicina, which we reached at midnight. The guard commander flatly refused to allow the fox into the guard room, so I sent for the Orderly Officer, who arrived twenty minutes later with every sign of having dressed hastily and in poor humour.

'Giles,' I asked, 'have you had dinner?'

'Of course!'

'Well, in the back of this truck, you will find a fox who has not yet dined. He wishes to. What is more he requires accommodation which I understand has been arranged by the Adjutant in that little hut near the stables. See to it.'

Happily there was a most agreeable end to the story. Quite quickly an adequate store of smell was collected and the Colonel then agreed that we could release Freddie Fox. We took him out one night and set him free. With one last look back he headed for the Yugoslav border. So my mission to Mestre had after all been beneficial.

In the spring of 1946, after a most successful season of drag hunting, during which I was allowed to whip in to Loopy Kennard, I was permitted to enjoy a week's leave at home. The week was hardly over when I received a dramatic telegram from the Colonel. It seemed that our pack of drag hounds was to be reinforced in readiness for further sport and some bitches were required for breeding. 'An extra week's leave granted', read the telegram, 'if you bring back Thankful, Vital and Sapphire from ...'. The name of a well-known pack of Buckinghamshire hounds followed. When the Colonel offered to do something for you provided some condition was fulfilled, you knew that this apparent open-handedness concealed a requirement that you did as you were told. I thus had little choice. The challenge had to be accepted. Last time it had been one fox. This time it was to be one and a half couple of foxhounds. I determined to make full use of my few days' extra leave. It was just as well that I didn't know what was in store for me.

The first thing to do was to alter my travel arrangements for my passage to Villach in Carinthia, via Victoria station, Dover, Calais and thence by the military MEDOC train to Austria. At Villach I would be met by regimental transport. Next, after telephoning the hunt kennels I agreed a time to pick up the hounds and agreed also to bring some couples with me, that is, sets of leather collars joined by a chain, so that the hounds could be 'coupled' and thus easier to manage. I had warned my mother that on the evening before my journey, I would be arriving at her London flat with three foxhounds, who would require accommodation and sustenance, and enable me to get to Victoria station early on the following morning. Thus on the afternoon before D-Day I set off for the kennels in a hired car complete with driver.

The kennel-huntsman was obviously reluctant to part with his hounds.

'Where be they going?' he asked.

'To Trieste.'

'Eh?'

'To northern Italy.'

'Ah! Be there foxes there?'

I had every reason to know that there were, but rather than disillusion him by admitting that we were drag hunting there, I assured him that the three bitches would be in good hands with plenty of sport ahead of them. He gave the three hounds an affectionate farewell pat, to which they responded with vigorous stern wagging, but he did not tell me that he had fed the hounds some hours previous to my arrival.

We all climbed into the car; me in front with the driver, the three foxhounds on the back seat. Before we had driven far along what was a bumpy pot-holed country road, the most appalling thing happened. Thankful, Vital and Sapphire deposited the nourishment recently received at the kennels all over the back seat and were now huddled in the space immediately behind us. I reflected that this might entail a devastating addition to the fare and began to express profound apologies to the driver. To my relief and surprise, he was smiling. 'This isn't my car,' he chortled. 'It's the governor's.'

We spent that night at my mother's flat in London, unusual quarters for foxhounds at any time. Fortunately there was a small garden to her ground floor flat to which they could retire from time to time. I kept them carefully coupled or, to be more precise, tripled for this purpose. At that time there was, of course, a shortage of meat in England, and rationing was still very much the rule. When the hounds had demolished a whole fortnight's rations, they reported to me, and I was then able to sympathize with Mr Bumble's outraged dignity when confronted with Oliver Twist's preposterous demand.

Next morning a taxi to Victoria station passed off without incident. The Railway Transport Officer in charge of the military train was enchanted by the notion of accommodating foxhounds – he was a keen follower himself – and allotted us a compartment, myself on one side, my three charges sitting on the opposite seat. At Dover, however, hard-hearted officialdom placed the first real obstacle in our progress. The Embarkation Officer refused absolutely to allow us on the military boat. None daunted I purchased one human and three canine tickets on the Golden Arrow boat, and away we sailed to Calais. On board I was greeted as something of a hero. It was not every day that foxhounds sailed for the Adriatic coast. A retired cavalryman, who looked as if he might have hunted with Wellington's Peninsular pack, pronounced it to be a jolly sporting show. A pretty woman, who had clearly observed the iron hand with which I had maintained discipline over my three charges, invited me to bring my hounds to Paris. I regretfully declined.

The customs and immigration officials at Calais were at first incredulous. There was a good deal of gesticulation, shoulder shrugging, torrents of incomprehensible French and consultation of the next senior man. I could understand only too well what Pierre Daninos' Major Thompson had meant by the sweet land of mistrust. The situation was saved by my putting across the point that Italy, not France, was to be the future home of my protégées.

I now had a stroke of luck. It happened that an empty train was returning to Villach and I was given permission to travel on it. Things were looking up. We had a complete train to ourselves. I settled down comfortably. The worst was over. The railway staff had been generous with their provision of meat and biscuits and my three charges were content. I could look forward to the approbation of the Colonel and the Regiment. Such sanguineness was premature. The climacteric moments of my journey were still to come.

Late that evening the train halted at some minor station in eastern France to take on water and fuel. It was not a scheduled halt. But I decided to take advantage of the train's equilibrium and refresh myself with a good wash. Taking my tunic off, with soap and towel in my hand, I cautioned my hounds to be on their best behaviour and advanced along the corridor. Almost at once I was startled by a commotion behind me. An inquisitive official had opened the door of my compartment and before he could close it, one of the hounds was in the corridor. In front of my horrified eyes she leapt out onto the platform and set off down it at a fine hunting pace. As she ran she gave tongue, but to my ears it was not the musical discord, the sweet thunder that Hippolyta recalled – it was the voice of doom.

There are, as we know, moments when contemplation is out of place and every circumstance cries out for action. Yelling a terrible curse at the official and slamming my compartment door, I sprang wildly to the platform and launched myself in pursuit. Here, I thought to myself, was a drag hunt in reverse. Down the platform we went and as we approached the barrier I shouted exhortations to ticket collectors to stop the runaway. No good. They withdrew in our path with all the dexterity of a matador evading a bull. We then scattered a few natives in the main station area, and my quarry, perhaps conscious now of being hunted, made for the exit. As I dashed down the steps of the station into the road, I heard the guard's whistle blow, echoed by the train's shrill emission of steam. I was trapped – not by two pursuers but by two escapees.

Yes, that was the position. On the one hand, my hound – I could see now that it was Thankful – eagerly hunting some imaginary scent, whom to abandon in a country barbarous enough not to honour fox-hunting as a calling, would be to write finis to my career as a cavalryman; on the other the train, on the point of leaving with my other two charges, my luggage and my identity card – in France the only acceptable proof that a man is alive –

and in the middle myself, coatless and thus moneyless, breathless from running, surrounded by hostile and suspicious strangers, not particularly fluent in the vernacular, with the single consolatory thought that as my soap and towel were still in my hand, I would at least be able to wash myself without incurring expenditure of any sort.

A hopeless situation, one might think. Perhaps so, but if there were no reinforcement to be obtained from hope, think what resolution I could gain from despair. Outside the station was a road junction and Thankful faltered. A moment later it became clear that those who hesitate are saved. My hand closed like a vice on her stern. I heaved her into my arms, soap and towel scattering, and ran for it. The train was about to move off, but I gained the corridor to be greeted by the train conducting officer. He patted the bitch.

'A nice girl,' he pronounced. 'What's her name?'

'Thankful,' I croaked, 'and by heavens, so am I.'

After this stormy scene the rest of the journey was something of an anti-climax. But as I handed over my three companions to the kennels I was able to make my way to my quarters with the satisfaction of having earned my extra week's leave, and having assisted the 4th Hussars' pack of hounds to resume their hunting duties in the coming season.

All this talk of hunting puts me in mind of Jorrocks' well-known cry about the sport – 'the image of war without its guilt and only five-and-twenty percent of its danger'. The memoir of a soldier would hardly be complete without some mention of war itself, so we will transport ourselves briefly to the field of battle. A few glances at the Italian campaign will suffice for our purpose here.

Chapter 6

The D-Day Dodgers

O Death be kind to the swaddie
The man with the load of bull -
Be kind to the muscled body,
Thumbs up and belly full.

Browned off with the bints and boozing,
Sweating on news from home,
Bomb-happy and scared of losing
This tent of flesh and bone...

Jocelyn Brooke

Those men of the Eighth Army who had fought in the Western Desert and who were not sent home with their regiments to prepare for the invasion of Normandy were known as the D-Day Dodgers. There was even a ditty of this title sung to the tune of Lili Marlene, joint favourite of the Eighth Army and the Deutsches Afrika Korps. But being left behind in the Mediterranean theatre did not mean that these men would be illustrative of Rosenstock-Huessy's point that 'three-quarters of a soldier's life is spent in aimlessly waiting about'. On the contrary it was clear from Churchill's declaration that in no circumstances would he allow the powerful British and British controlled armies in the Mediterranean to stand idle. His determination to make use of these armies was consistent with his long held view that the establishment of a Second Front would comprise both the Atlantic and Mediterranean coasts of Europe 'and we can push either right-handed, left-handed, or both-handed, as our resources and circumstances permit'. Thus was born the so-called Mediterranean Strategy, which meant pursuing the offensive there in 1943, while accepting that the invasion of France could not take place until 1944. In other words to get on with an assault upon Italy as soon as possible after finishing off the Axis powers in North Africa.

In one of his talks with Stalin, Churchill had referred to the soft underbelly of Europe. For the D-Day Dodgers, amongst whom were the 4th Hussars, it turned out otherwise. The underbelly of Europe proved to be uncomfortably hard. That this was so was clearly demonstrated by the battle for Sicily when the way in which General Hube handled his hard-pressed Panzer Corps in what was ideal defensive country should have sent a clear signal to Allied strategic planners. Already in September 1943, with the Sicilian campaign finished only a few weeks earlier, Kesselring had disarmed the Italian Army as a result of the Armistice, and had begun to prepare the formidable Gustav Line based on a feature immortal in the history of the British Army – Monte Cassino. The fears of a long, protracted campaign on a relatively narrow front, leaving only one alternative to frontal attacks – amphibious landings, over country characterized by repeated mountain ranges and rivers, with rain and impassable mud for much of the year, where the advantages of Allied air power and armoured strength could not be exploited, against fanatically brave and skilful German veterans, with little hope of break-through or decisive manoeuvring and the prospect of ending up trying to storm the Alps – all these fears were about to be realized.

To most of us who took part in the Italian campaign it seemed an endless repetition of trying to go forward against obstacles, whether natural ones like rivers, mud and mountains or those arranged by the Germans, such as mines, anti-tank guns, mortars and blown bridges. The country was simply made for defensive operations. Every time one river or mountain had been crossed, another one blocked the way. Plains were scarce and even when they existed they were frequently far from firm enough to accommodate armoured manoeuvres. In short, far from resembling Churchill's soft underbelly, for tactical purposes Italy was more like 'a scaly pachydermatous backbone'. Moreover the Germans had developed a pattern of operations eminently successful and designed for endless repetition. It went like this. The enemy would defend a position until it was seriously threatened, then withdraw to another already prepared and thus readily defended place, leaving behind them blown bridges, minefields and demolition. It would then be our job to mount a night attack, crossing the river to seize the high ground beyond, dig in by dawn, trusting that the sappers would by this time have cleared the way for tanks to join the assault infantry and so consolidate the position to see off an enemy counter-attack. Even during this phase, the Germans would be raining down artillery and mortar fire on the attacking force.

In order to bring all this down to a personal level, I will describe two battles in which the 4th Hussars took part; the first one of confusion and frustration; the second of clarity and success. We had done a good deal of Rosenstock-Huessy's waiting about although, I trust, not aimlessly, but shortly after Churchill's visit to us near Ancona, we were launched into the prolonged, bitter and ultimately disappointing battle for the Gothic Line. A word as to the strategic circumstances will be fitting here as it helps to explain why things did not go according to plan. Alexander, Supreme Commander, had intended at first to attack with both Fifth and Eighth Armies in the centre of the Gothic Line, and having thrust through the Apennines to destroy Kesselring's forces south of the River Po. But General Leese, Eighth Army Commander, persuaded him to change the plan. Leese, having lost his French mountain divisions, was averse to mountain operations and wished also to exploit his great strength in armour, and therefore favoured a main thrust on the Adriatic side of the front. It was ironic that Alexander's deception measures, designed to assist a central attack, had sought to persuade the Germans that the main thrust would be on the Adriatic side. That is precisely where Leese did, in the end, attack. No wonder we met the opposition we did.

'Old men forget,' declared Henry V before Agincourt. I will, however, try to remember, without advantages, what feats we did that day. Before doing so, however, it will be fitting to describe what we did – and did not do – before taking on the *Wehrmacht*.

Having sailed from Port Said to Bari and collected our tanks and trucks from Brindisi, we established a tented camp at Altamura, but did very little to prepare ourselves for what was to come. Looking back on it all after sixty years it seems to me most strange that we in the 4th Hussars did not spend more time and effort adapting to the new conditions of warfare. After all, the mountains and valleys, farmlands, rivers and vineyards, woods, roads, villages, towns, indeed the whole nature of this country, to say nothing of the Italians themselves, were as different as could be from the environment of the Western Desert. Yet apart from some shooting practice with our 75mm guns, a few minor exercises and camouflaging our tanks with the ample foliage of tree branches, we seemed to spend most of those weeks before going into action in swimming, playing bridge and going to the opera. It would have been wiser to have dispatched some of us to regiments in the front line to learn something of the form, or to have persuaded those already experienced in the conditions of fighting in Italy to come and talk to us. But no such measures were taken.

We were quite near to Bari, where there was an opera house at which a kind of repertory company would regularly give their versions of the old favourites – *La Bohème, La Traviata, Lucia di Lammermoor, Pagliacci* and so on. They put on a spirited performance, although there was one unfortunate aspect of it which at times occasioned inappropriate mirth. The principal players were ill-matched, not vocally, but physically, in that although the baritone was of average stature, the soprano was a vast creature, tall, with formidable frontal works and an altogether generous build, while the tenor was a small, thin, weedy person. The result, of course, was that in the passionate love duets over which Puccini, Verdi and Donizetti had expended so much of their genius, we were treated to the sight of a towering female, wilting with passion while her ardent lover cast up his eyes and sometimes stood on his toes in order to pour forth his requital of her precious vows. It was all most entertaining and our enjoyment was further stimulated by the behaviour of the conductor, an actor in his own right who, every now and again, during a particularly moving passage of the music, would turn to one of the boxes and bestow on its occupant, a beautiful woman, a gesture of unrestrained devotion. This was not the only operatic joy which I was to reap during the campaign, but more of this later. Like Figaro we must now get down to the more serious business of war.

Eighth Army's attack on the Gothic Line began in the last week of August and shortly after Churchill's visit to us, already described, we in the 4th Hussars, together with the rest of 1st Armoured Division, moved north to Pesaro. General Sir Oliver Leese, Eighth Army Commander, gave us a pep talk in which he told us that we were on the verge of great events and could expect to be in Venice within a matter of weeks, then on to Vienna. His expectations, however, were not matched by events. We moved further inland to the region of Monte Gridolfo. The plan was for the 1st Armoured Division to advance through the Gothic Line, once an adequate breach had been made, to break out into the Po valley and disrupt the German lines of communication. Two conditions thwarted this sanguine design. First a proper breach was not made; second the weather deteriorated severely. The sanguine design turned into a sanguinary process.

Nonetheless we in the 4th Hussars set out on our role of reconnaissance late in the afternoon of 2 September. It was a nightmare journey of sixty miles over the narrow tracks of Monte Gridolfo. Most of the way we were obliged to move without lights and I recall finding it so difficult to see ahead that I climbed out of the turret of my Sherman and sat on the hull by Trooper Tyson, my driver, to help guide him. The wearisome ordeal lasted for some twelve hours and we eventually reached our assembly area at half past four on the morning of 3 September, exactly five years from the outbreak of war. We bedded down by our tanks, unaware that only a hundred yards or so to the front was a battery of 5.5 inch medium guns, which opened up shortly afterwards. Sleep was out of the question, and just as well for orders arrived from Divisional HQ to advance some eight miles further on to reconnoitre crossing places for the division over the River Conca. Bobby Kidd gave his orders to squadron leaders and the Regiment moved off. The 4th Hussars' historian, David Scott Daniell, has admirably summed up what then happened:

> It was a dramatic moment as the heavy Sherman tanks and the light turretless Stuarts rolled off in the light of the dawn on the regiment's first operation in its new role, for which so much training had been done. It is all the more sad, therefore, to have to relate that everything went wrong. The whole

operation, the climax to so much enthusiasm and toil, was dogged by ill-fortune and was little short of disaster.

Bobby Kidd at first invited A Squadron to lead the way for this reconnaissance of the River Conca. Unwisely they chose a cross-country route, but even in September the ground was treacherously soft and before long A Squadron was bogged down. The Colonel then ordered B Squadron, led by a splendid officer, John Ogier, to assume the lead, but they too had elected to choose some very bad going to get themselves to the head of the Regimental column. Alas, they became immobile. In desperation Bobby Kidd turned to his most junior squadron leader, Jack White, who had taken over C Squadron from Peter Crichton because of the latter's disagreement with the Colonel over certain matters. It was, therefore, up to C Squadron to restore some order to this rapidly deteriorating situation. Jack White may have been the junior squadron leader, but he was extremely astute and asked the Colonel for some more precise orders. They were not very comprehensive.

In all our former training and practice, we had been taught that in giving orders, we had to be precise about what was to be done and complement this requirement with details of the enemy, own troops, supporting arms, administrative arrangements and so on. In particular it was vital to explain the current situation. It transpired that these precious principles were on this occasion more honoured in the breach than the observance. Jack White was simply told to advance to the Conca. There was no information about the enemy or own troops, and Jack, who had chosen my troop to be in the van, was able to do no more than tell me I was to advance to the River Conca, find crossings over it and then push on to see what was going on at Coriano, a large village north of the Conca, which turned out to be of great tactical importance in that part of the Gothic Line. By this time it was getting dusk. Jack and I agreed that we would stick to the narrow road which from the map seemed to lead to a possible crossing over the Conca. As accurate map reading was essential here, I decided to lead myself. So there I was – in the leading tank of the leading troop of the leading squadron of the leading regiment of the 1st Armoured Division. What an honour! It was not one I was to enjoy for very long.

By the time I had found my way over the River Conca by use of a somewhat rickety bridge and advanced further towards Coriano, it was dark. We had no infantry with us, although a company of the 60th Rifles, the so-called motor battalion of 2 Armoured Brigade, whose principal task was to support the armoured regiments, would have been a comfort in such tactical circumstances. Nor had we an artillery Forward Observation Officer to call for supporting fire when required. In short the well-established and traditional team of horse, foot and guns had simply not been established, but instead the horses by themselves were being invited to sweep all before them.

When I had reached a point about a mile short of the ridge which overlooked Coriano, we received the order to halt. The reason for doing so was never given, but it later became clear that at this time Coriano was lightly held by the Germans. During the next few days, however, it was heavily reinforced together with the neighbouring, ideally defensive ground. Had there been a determined effort to take Coriano that first night, a fully coordinated attack by the Gurkha Brigade of 1st Armoured Division, supported by artillery and armour, a lot of bloodshed might have been avoided, a breakthrough of the Gothic Line realized, and Churchill's great vision of a strategic coup in Italy might have taken shape. What a chance was missed! What actually happened was that at first light next day we resumed the advance, deployed on the ridge overlooking Coriano, and attempted to penetrate the village itself. But our squadron, still unsupported by either infantry or artillery, was unable to make progress against rapidly improvised anti-tank defences deployed by the enemy. I remember instead standing on the turret of my Sherman in order to get a better view of the forward edges of Coriano and with a few well-placed HE shells registering some likely target areas, while giving instructions to my troop for breakfast to be served.

A bit later that morning, with my troop still deployed on the ridge, I was approached by a group of very unhappy looking Italian *contadini*, whom I tried to question as to the German positions in the village. But my command of the language was insufficient to decipher their responses so I asked for our Italian liaison officer to come forward and help. Count Filippo Senni was a captain in an Italian cavalry regiment. He had been at Ampleforth and was attached to the 4th Hussars for the very purpose of assisting us in our dealings with the local people. He possessed in great measure what Eric Linklater's Private Angelo described as *il dono di coraggio*, and would ride fearlessly about the battlefield in an open jeep. On arrival at my troop he questioned the *contadini* about Coriano, but all they could say was that tedeschi were in the village. They knew nothing of what strength or exactly where.

All this was reported back to the Colonel, who gave orders that a troop of Honey tanks from HQ Squadron would attempt to probe the enemy defences. This was the Recce Troop, commanded by Tim Slee, and with the fire support from ourselves in C Squadron, he boldly led his six turretless Honeys forward along the road and up the hill towards Coriano. As they neared the village, enemy guns and mortars opened up despite our supporting fire and half the Reece Troop was destroyed. Twenty men were casualties, three Honeys knocked out and the troop leader mortally wounded. Once again the dire lack of infantry had been tragically illustrated. During the rest of that day, we in C Squadron were still deployed on the ridge, but by now the enemy had grown bolder and we were subjected to the most disagreeable mortar, artillery and anti-tank fire, so much so that Jack White eventually reported to Regimental HQ that he considered the position untenable. Soon afterwards the 60th Rifles came forward, established outposts and took over the front for the night, enabling us to withdraw into leaguer. We had now been without sleep for some sixty hours and were in need of respite.

I remember well the leaguer area, a largish field with some scattered trees with good going for our echelon trucks to join us with replenishment of diesel, ammunition, water and rations, the latter distributed by Trooper Batey for my troop. After a meal and orders for next morning, Nobby Clark set up my camp bed next to my tank, and we settled down for much needed slumber. Or so we thought. But almost at once the unpleasant screaming of shells assailed our ears and it was clear that German mortars and field artillery were making the night hideous. Some of the explosions seemed disturbingly close, then all at once Nobby Clark appeared again at my camp bed to tell me that one of our troop had been hit. I hurried over to where Trooper Davies had been, some ten yards from my camp bed. Alas, he had received a direct hit. We wrapped what remained of him in two ground sheets and reverently laid it by his tank for burial in the morning. At this point I heard a cry from Trooper Morris, saying that he too had been hit in the leg. Clark and I applied a field dressing and I made for our regimental aid post to alert our doctor. He came at once, further bandaged Morris and dispatched him in a jeep ambulance to the divisional Advanced Dressing Station.

Shelling of our leaguer area was continuing and Jack White received orders from Regimental HQ that all ranks should get into their tanks in order to avoid further casualties. I noticed when I climbed into mine that my crew were all smoking furiously. After an uncomfortable night, the morning dawned clear and bright. No more shelling for the time being. I then conducted a brief service as we buried Trooper Davies and I wrote to his parents.

For the next few weeks the battle for the Gothic Line continued and was not made any more agreeable by the accompanying rain, mud, blood and cold. What old men, like myself, remember is not so much a precise sequence of events or a day by day phasing of the struggle at Coriano, but more a pattern of selected incidents that give the true feel, or what John Keegan might call the face, of battle. By the end of October, some eight weeks after we had so confidently advanced, conscious of the Eighth Army Commander's confident prediction of our being in Venice and Vienna before the month was out, it had become clear that the Allied armies would be required to spend one more winter in the mountains. We in the 4th Hussars lost five officers, thirty-five men and nine tanks, and gained – a battle honour. Small occurrences remain vivid in my memory.

At the O Group on the morning following our most uncomfortable leaguer, it became clear that Jack White, by virtue of endless use of the radio on the previous day, whether giving instructions to us troop leaders or reporting back to Regimental HQ, had so strained his vocal chords that the best he could manage in giving orders was a hoarse whisper. What struck me as comic at the time and later was that we, in sympathy as it were, acknowledged his instructions and sought clarification where needed in a similarly subdued fashion so that the whole conference was conducted in a conspiratorial manner. We moved off and deployed on some high ground overlooking another village, with the task of supporting a company of Gurkhas, one of whose soldiers told me that in assaulting an enemy position a day or two earlier they had had several men killed at the very last moments of their attack, so that when the defending Germans had come out of their foxholes with hands up, he had decided that the enemy had left their surrender too late and the kukri was made use of to finish off that particular dispute.

It was, of course, more common for infantrymen to close with the enemy than for us in tanks, for we tended to stand off in support or engage in duels with our panzer opposite numbers and their artillery pieces, but on this occasion with the Gurkhas, we gained a rare sight of the enemy soldiers against whom we were fighting. Jack White invited me to engage, with my 75 mm gun, a suspected enemy position and, having calculated the range from my map, I succeeded in hitting it with the first round [I was after all still Regimental Gunnery Officer] and was gratified by Jack's radio message: 'Good shot.' A few moments later at a range of about 1,000 yards, a dozen or more grey uniformed German soldiers got up from their slit trenches and began to run back towards the village. I instantly ordered my gunner, still the faithful Trooper Grigg, to switch to the co-axial machine gun and engage these fleeing figures. It was, as far as memory holds a seat, the only instance of my shooting at visible German infantry.

Looking back on it all it seems as if our little world was confined largely to what we, in C Squadron, were doing, although occasionally we would get news of the other squadrons. One tragic affair brought about the death of three B Squadron troop leaders, who had gone to retrieve kit from a knocked-out Sherman and set off a landmine which did for them all. And I recall too passing two walking wounded troop leaders of A Squadron, who were making their way back to the Regimental Aid Post. The fog of war was once more illustrated by the fact that I had no idea that A Squadron were operating on our flank at that particular time.

Here I must pause to say a word in praise of our Squadron

Sergeant Major, Geordie Hoyle, whom I mentioned earlier as being discovered dressed only in boots in a Cairo backstreet. Each evening after the day's operations, we would leaguer in order to maintain and replenish the tanks, have a meal, get some sleep and prepare for the next day's business. It was Hoyle who would arrive in the leaguer area with the echelon trucks and go from tank to tank with rations, ammunition, diesel, mail from home and the broadest, almost toothless grin on his face, with some morale boosting jests and comments that had a magical effect on all the tank crews. His confidence was irrepressible, his laughter infectious, his value incalculable. Such men were the backbone of the Regiment.

Mishaps come in threes, they say, and this was certainly confirmed on the next occasion that I took the lead with my troop to find a crossing over another river [in the Gothic Line country there was always one more river to cross] and once again I decided to be in the van myself, as Sergeant Pope's map-reading was distressingly poor. It was quite clear as my tank descended a slope towards lowish ground with a steepish hill beyond, that there might well be a fordable place between the two. So intent was I on finding the right spot to turn off the road to the river that I failed to notice a radio cable strung between two trees at the height of a tank hull. As I did turn, my tank effectively cut the cable and I was then subjected to a furious volley of invective from a gunner captain who had appeared from the undergrowth and was clearly trying to lay this line of cable to a farmhouse up on the rise ahead. My instant and eloquent expression of contrition did little to mollify him. I hardened my heart and moved on, catching sight with relief of a clear, shallow crossing of the river. Reporting this to Jack White and ordering my troop to conform, I told my driver over the IC to cross to the other side. As we reached the far bank there was a huge explosion behind me. Sergeant Pope's tank had hit a mine in the middle of the river bed while moving exactly in the tracks of my tank, and it was clear that his crew, although not actually wounded, were badly shaken. I then called for both medical and recovery support, and having satisfied myself that Sergeant Pope and his crew would be able to rejoin me later, pushed on with my two other tanks, which negotiated the crossing without further trouble. Why the mine had not gone off when my own tank went over it remained a mystery.

The third mishap was one for which I was entirely to blame. After reaching our objective later that day, and having found a ruined barn for my troop to sleep in, we had our evening meal and I went back to my tank to fetch my map which I had left in the turret. In those days our radios were the so-called 19 sets, and unless we needed longer distance communications, one 3-4 foot aerial was enough for inter-troop and squadron messages. Having retrieved my map from the turret, I placed it on the top of the tank near the aerial base, heaved myself up and then, while standing there, bent sharply down to pick up the map. My right eye came in violent contact with the top of the aerial. I could hardly believe it, and as a result my slumber that night was not as easy as I would have liked. Next day our medical orderly took a look at it, put what he described as soothing ointment on my eyelid and its surrounds and bandaged the whole thing. When I reported to Squadron HQ for orders next morning, I was greeted with cries of 'Hallo! Have you been wounded?' 'It's a wound all right,' I replied, 'but alas self-inflicted.' It soon cleared up, but I still retain a slight discolouring of the right eye.

Somehow it seems that trivial matters like these jog the memory. But also memorable is the ugly side of war. Smashed houses, knocked-out guns, burnt-out tanks, to say nothing of bodies. When, later on, I was once more ordered by Jack White to take the lead and get into a position of observation, and knowing that the enemy could not be far away, I dismounted from my Sherman tank and walked up a hill to a farmhouse, passing on my way the gruesome sight of a German soldier without a head. The stench of dead bodies assailed the nostrils, not only of men, but cattle and horses too, in their case a grotesque sight, rigor mortis causing them to be positioned on their backs with all four legs pointing skywards. I passed a few more of the *Wehrmacht*'s brave and skilful soldiers, their blackened flesh visible beneath the steel helmets. The smell was nauseating. I reached the farmhouse and found there a most gallant artillery FOO, Quentin Drage MC, asked him courteously whether I might share his OP, to which he agreed, and returned to my tanks in order to bring up a Honey so that I could communicate with Jack White.

Seated beside Quentin Drage on the first floor of the farmhouse with a long lead to my Honey tank, manned by Corporal Little and Trooper Batey, and searching the ridge ahead through my binoculars, I was once again struck by the eeriness of a battlefield. There seemed to be no movement, no activity and yet all our information indicated that we were among the forward troops. Hearing some noise of tank tracks to the right of our position I went downstairs and spoke to Corporal Little, who said that a troop of Churchill tanks had just moved up parallel to our position and appeared to be hull down on the reverse slope of a slight hill. I sent a quick message to Jack White, telling him I was going to investigate and then walked over to these recently arrived tanks to find that they were of the North Irish Horse, a splendid Yeomanry Regiment, which had won much honour and praise during the 1st Army's campaign in French North Africa. The troop leader had no more idea of what was happening than I had, so wishing him good fortune I returned to my OP. At last Quentin Drage had some news. An Air OP [the gunners had a number of Auster aircraft for spotting enemy artillery and mortars and for reporting on the fall of friendly artillery fire] had sighted what he took to be a mortar battery – I should again emphasize here that the Germans were masters of camouflage and concealment – and he, Drage, was about to call for a regimental shoot [1st Royal Horse Artillery equipped with the ever-stalwart 25-pounder gun] on this suspected target. This was done and shortly afterwards, sure enough, came the response and some of those most disagreeable Moaning Minnies crashed down, only one actually hitting the farmhouse and happily causing no casualties. So the day wore on, and Trooper Batey, whom as I indicated earlier had been appointed OC 3rd Troop's rations, produced two plates of bully beef fritters, washed down with strong, sweet tea for Drage and myself. At about five o'clock that evening Jack White ordered me to return to where the squadron was positioned. I said au revoir to Quentin Drage, although in fact I never saw him again, as he was killed a few days later in an action which I will describe.

It was on that evening that the Italian climate showed its ugly side. Although still September, when we might have expected benevolent autumn sunshine, we were, for the next week, treated to almost continuous rain and cold. My faithful tank crew always tried to rig up my camp bed for maximum comfort, but not all their skill, with ground sheets hung on tree branches, could defeat the relentless drip of icy rain just where it was least welcome. We had now been in the line for some ten days, and were all quite pleased to be withdrawn into reserve for a short time. We were able to make use of abandoned, and partially wrecked, farm buildings and had no qualms about chopping up furniture from farmhouses to enhance the warmth of fires to dry our clothes and warm the atmosphere. It was during such a pause in operations that we received some reinforcements, both officers and men, to make up our tank crews to full strength again. I remember well John Paley's concern about the inexperience of one new troop leader to replace Kenneth Hedley, who had been wounded in the eye by a mine run over by his tank when he was outside it directing its movement. Our new troop leader, Ralph Liney, was quite unconcerned at the prospect of action and assured John Paley that he need not worry.

One of the discomforts that we all experienced at this time was, of course, the lack of bathing facilities. At a later time we were able to visit the so-called Mobile Bath Units, but not during this phase of the Gothic Line battles. But John Paley and I solved this problem by finding a large trough at one of the farm houses, and discarding our uniforms, hurling water over each other with the canvas buckets which were part of our tank equipment. I remember vividly John saying to me at about this time: 'Aren't you simply longing to get back into action?' I was in fact rather enjoying our limited respite, but felt that out of sheer loyalty I was obliged to express my own urgent desire to be at them again. We soon were and again were engaged in some scrappy actions, one of which was memorable for three small incidents. The first was that during a short delay in the advance, I climbed out of my tank, spade in hand, to fulfil a certain requirement, only to be forced back into it by the most unwelcome intrusion of Moaning Minnies. But nature was not to be denied, and the urgency of the matter was such that valour on this occasion overcame discretion. Later on that day we had pushed forward on to a ridge overlooking one more river and we were subjected to another unpleasant form of activity by the Germans – air burst artillery, that is HE shells which were timed to explode in the air above their targets, and it was during this particular assault that Jack White ordered all tank commanders to don steel helmets. Although it may seem incredible today, all officers wore their Service Dress hats in action, not the far more convenient and practical beret. Our arrival on the ridge also yielded half a dozen prisoners, and being reasonably fluent in German, I was invited to question one of them as to which unit he belonged. He was very young, no more than a boy, and I got little out of him.

A week or so later on returning to the squadron leaguer from another minor reconnoitring task at which my troop seemed to have acquitted itself with credit, one of my fellow troop leaders looked at me with distaste and told me I was turning yellow. He was not, however, commenting on my possession of *il dono di coraggio*. He was referring to the colour of my skin. It took me a moment or two to realize what he meant, but a glance in the looking glass was enough. I *was* yellow. I was soon to learn, however, that to get jaundice was not a wholly unwelcome fortune of war. It is true that alcohol is forbidden, but this is a small price to pay for a period of clean sheets, regular food and respite from the uneasy feeling that the shell with your name on it, although overdue, had not decided to cut the rendezvous altogether. As, by this time, operations seemed to have settled down to a matter of holding the line until the spring, I determined to make the best of my bout of jaundice. What I had not expected was that the highlight of it would be ten days' convalescence in, of all places, Beniamino Gigli's sumptuous villa at Porto Reconati, some twenty miles from Ancona. Said to have cost an unthinkable number of lire, it was perhaps a little bizarre when eyed with the critical gaze of the classicist, but as a convalescent home it was ideal. Warm, big, bright and comfortable, it was run by the British Red Cross who, in the absence of its master, had sensibly retained his staff in the kitchen, the laundry and the gardens.

The superb *tagliatelli*, the delicate *lasagne*, the simple but satisfying *risotto con funghi* are treasured recollections even today. These delights coupled with strolls in the handsome, palely sunlit gardens were restoring my physical condition to peak form. Nor was administration to another of the senses neglected. There was a music room in the villa, spacious, well furnished and equipped with machinery for playing the most renowned recordings of one of the world's greatest tenors. Several times a week Gigli's major domo, whom we convalescents christened Malvolio, would give us a concert of opera recordings. Malvolio had two great loves – *la caccia* [he meant shooting, of course] and His Master's Voice. He would announce each piece before playing it, tell us when and with whom his master had first sung it, and sit listening as spellbound as any of us. His selection was unerring. He would follow the cynical and reckless Duke of Mantua with a few simple songs and then move on to the impassioned and noble dying fall of Edgardo. Our appreciation of Verdi, Donizetti, Puccini and the others was much enhanced by these magical concerts. I returned to the Regiment refreshed both physically and aesthetically.

It cannot be said that the 1st Armoured Division had been well handled during September 1944. There seemed to have been no proper coordination between tanks, infantry and artillery. We in the 4th Hussars had been invited to advance with our tanks unsupported against enemy defensive positions, which were models of concealment, well-sited anti-tank guns, and artillery/mortar observation posts with foreseeable results. But worse was to come; far worse, for another cavalry regiment. For far too many of the D-Day Dodgers there was to be no future at all. On 20 September 1944, after the Coriano battles, The Queen's Bays were ordered by Major General Richard Hull, commanding 1st Armoured Division, to advance on the Via Roveta axis to seize the village of Montecieco, a move which would leave intact a hill called Point 153 to the flank of the proposed advance. In spite of the concern of both Lieutenant Colonel Asquith, commanding The Bays and Lieutenant Colonel Price, commanding the 9th Lancers, that they were being invited to advance without infantry support and knowing that Major General Baade, legendary leader of the German 90th Light Division, was in front of them, the order to proceed was confirmed. The result was disastrous and compared by the Armoured Brigade Commander, Goodbody, to the Charge of the Light Brigade. Baade had sited his 88mm anti-tank guns at Point 153 and other key tactical features. When The Bays advanced – by this time they had only twenty-seven Sherman tanks, fuelled by petrol, not diesel as ours in the 4th Hussars were, and thus fatally inflammable, out of the fifty-two before the Gothic Line battles – the German gunners could hardly believe their eyes. Each Sherman presented itself to be shot at, rather like a clay pigeon shoot, and twenty-four out of the twenty-seven were destroyed; sixty-four men were killed or wounded. It had been a massacre, and The Bays never forgave the higher command for their blundering insistence.

It seems to us now inconceivable that the division's infantry brigade was not called upon to take Point 153 and the other flanking tactical features before inviting the armour to advance. Among those killed was my former companion at the OP, Quentin Drage, who had accompanied The Bays as their Forward Observation Officer. Inevitably a scapegoat was sought, and the brigade commander, Goodbody, was sacked. [It is, however, pleasing to record that he subsequently reached high rank as Adjutant General.] Hull was given another division to command after the disbandment of 1st Armoured Division. But even today the reflection haunts us that if this was the best the British could do after five years of war, it was no surprise that they did not break through quickly and reach the plains of Lombardy.

What remains astonishing to those of us who fought in and survived the Gothic Line battles was: first, the amazing optimism displayed by higher British commanders, who seemed not to have grasped, after all the experience they had had, that German soldiers were masters of defence, would never give up lightly, were commanded by skilled, determined generals and that, under Hitler's direction, the brilliant Kesselring would never willingly give an inch of ground; secondly, given the British superiority of material, particularly of artillery and air power, and given also that indispensable commodity in war – time – why it was that we did not deploy our soldiers in the way the Germans did, in teams of tanks, infantry, anti-tank guns, artillery and sappers, making use of every skill and every ounce of fire-power in coordinated and carefully prepared attacks, rather than driving forward with tanks, virtually unsupported by anything else, and simply writing them off as a result? We in the 4th Hussars had suffered from this lack of tactical dexterity. The Queen's Bays had had an even more bitter lesson.

After the break-up of 1st Armoured Division, the 4th Hussars underwent a reorganization, and it seemed as if, for once, we were taking a leaf out of the *Wehrmacht*'s book. A and C Squadron were converted from tanks to what were known as Kangaroos, sawn off Shermans and Priests, each one of which would carry a section of infantry. In other words we would now be able to launch an attack with infantry protected by armour and supported by tanks and artillery fire right up to the objective. It must still excite our wonder that we only hit on this idea after five years of war, whereas the Germans had had motorized infantry from the very outset of blitzkrieg. Although at first sight C Squadron's new role, equipped with sufficient Kangaroos to carry two infantry battalions into action, might seem less glamorous and challenging than our former one with armoured fighting vehicles, as the tank was known in the military jargon of the day, it turned out that because we were carrying infantry on to their objective, we got rather closer to the enemy than we had in the days of shooting at them from further back. The first use of C Squadron's Kangaroos was in the so-called Battle of the Bulge – a tiny affair when compared with the Ardennes counter-offensive of the same name – but nonetheless significant. An attack by a proper team of 2/6th Battalion of The Queen's Regiment, supported by ourselves and 1st Royal Tank Regiment, ensured that the German occupation of a salient south of the River Senio was brought to an end. Casualties on our side were minimal and The Queen's were full of enthusiasm for the advantages which Kangaroos afforded – speed into action, protection right up to the objective, tank and artillery supporting fire until the last moment and, on this first occasion, the achievement of tactical surprise which rapidly overcame German opposition. When Churchill heard of this, he sent a special congratulatory signal to the Regiment.

The next and final phase of the Eighth Army's operations would be crossing the River Senio, driving into the Po valley and finishing off the whole campaign. We, in C Squadron, trained hard with infantry battalions which had to master the drills of mounting and dismounting and, while preparing for battle, we were positioned at a village called Forlimpopoli, some twenty odd kilometres south of Ravenna. Inevitably our training involved cross-country manoeuvres which did little to improve the condition of the vineyards of the local farmers. When, they would ask, are you going to stop destroying our grapes and our livelihood? Jack White sent me to mollify them with cartons of cigarettes, very much a desirable currency in those days, and they in turn would offer bottles of a rather coarse red wine. In one of these farm houses my eye was caught by a dark-eyed buxom creature, who in the light of what Eric Newby had described as 'really superb upper works' might have been a double for his Dolores. But my mind was on sterner matters.

The Eighth Army was to begin the Allied offensive by attacking across the Senio on 9 April 1945, force their way to Argenta and drive on to more open ground, and then in conjunction with Fifth Army destroy German forces south of the River Po. Before the battle started Jack White had handed over command of C Squadron to the affable James Fryer, who had been Porgy Archer's second in command when I first joined the squadron. Early in April we had moved to an assembly area south of the Senio, and for this last battle of the Italian campaign I found myself in command of half C Squadron, and thus able to carry an infantry battalion into action. My two troop leaders for this operation were that splendid former MFH, Claud Thompson, and my old friend, John Paley. James Fryer had also chosen me to lead the whole advance, so I asked for an Auster aircraft to take me up to view the ground over which we would be moving. It was fascinating to observe that whereas south of the Senio all was activity, preparation, movement and bustle, north of the river there was nothing to be seen. The Germans were masters of camouflage and concealment. Having picked out my route and noted some landmarks which I hoped would be easily recognizable from the ground too, I returned to the squadron.

By this time we had joined the New Zealand battalion which my half squadron were to carry into battle next morning. That evening there was an artillery barrage of unprecedented violence and duration to soften up the enemy, together with powerful air attacks on enemy targets. Then, at first light, we crossed the river. We were further supported by a squadron of New Zealand tanks and artillery observers, and succeeded in pushing on with a few skirmishes over another river without much interference from the Germans. So confident did the New Zealand battalion commander become – he was with me in my Kangaroo – that he turned and said: 'This must be the breakthrough.' No sooner were the words out of his mouth than we were subjected to the most vicious shelling and mortaring imaginable, while my two troop leaders, carrying the magnificent Kiwi infantrymen, reported stiff opposition at a relatively small river ahead. A prolonged artillery duel followed, during which the farmhouse where I had set up our joint Battalion/Half Squadron HQ was repeatedly hit. I was fortunately in my Kangaroo reporting to James Fryer when one shell came through the roof killing the New Zealand Adjutant and wounding several others. We then organized a night attack which succeeded in dislodging the German opposition.

At dawn we resumed the advance and I found myself proceeding down a country road flanked by my two troops. The infantry were still dismounted at this time and we were going to rendezvous with them for further movement forward. Suddenly that fearsome tearing noise, like an express train going past, occurred and it was clear that someone was firing armour-piercing shot at us. I moved off the road to a large, strong-looking farmhouse, where I found the New Zealand battalion commander. I asked him what the situation was, and have always admired his answer, a splendid euphemism for admitting he had no idea. He looked at me steadily and replied: 'Fluid!' The fog of war is something often spoken of by historians and other military commentators, and I could not help reflecting that if, as was the case here, a battalion commander and his immediate armoured supporter had little or no notion of what was happening to themselves and their own front line, how much smaller would be their understanding of what was going on generally.

My own grasp of the situation was not aided by a radio message from James Fryer, my squadron leader, to the effect that a number of German SP guns were moving towards my position. Being in a vehicle without any armament other than a machine gun, I demanded by radio that these unwelcome intruders should be engaged by maximum artillery fire. No reply, but happily the SP guns did not appear. After a few more scrappy actions and struggles to get over rivers whose bridges had been blown and banks mined, we found ourselves advancing faster and faster towards the Po. At one point my anger with a New Zealand major for not producing the armoured bulldozer which I had demanded to assist us with one of these crossings produced from him a solemn shaking of the head and the comment: 'You're a hard man.' But my mood lightened when it became obvious that what we needed now were maps and fuel, not ammunition, for German resistance seemed to have ceased. It *was* the break-through at last and a wonderful feeling of freedom swept over us.

The concerted efforts of the Eighth and Fifth Armies had brought about the collapse of German resistance. Although Harold Nicolson called the Italian campaign the worst we waged, on 2 May it ended with the surrender of almost a million German soldiers. The D-Day Dodgers had beaten the D-Day participants to it by almost a week. For the 4th Hussars the war was over and now we could return to real soldiering.

Chapter 7

Real Soldiering

'Who told you to dismount, Sir?'

Sergeant Instructor to Cavalry Cornet

Once the Regiment settled down in the Italian cavalry barracks at Villa Opicina, the stage was set for the regular 4th Hussars officers, warrant officers and sergeants to reintroduce the time honoured routines of proper soldiering. The war had been a mere interlude, an unwelcome interruption to the serious business of being a crack cavalry regiment. Expressed simply this business entailed smartness on parade, proper ceremony, indulgence in field sports, daily activities heralded by trumpet sounding, superb standards of the various messes, an acceptance that on normal days, the military side of things would be over by midday and, above all, riding school.

At this time we were commanded by Tony Barne, who had taken over from Bobby Kidd during the Italian campaign, and we could not have had a finer Commanding Officer to set us on the right lines for peace time. He led by example, was always immaculately turned out, excelled at horsemanship, shooting and yachting, and understood that after nearly six years of war, provided proper standards of excellence in all military matters were maintained, all ranks of the Regiment should be allowed to enjoy themselves. To be stationed near Trieste was a reasonable guarantee that most sources of pleasure sought by cavalrymen – wine, women and song among them – were reasonably to hand. Trieste had been untouched by war between the Allies and the *Wehrmacht*, although for a worrying month or so, as the conflict drew to a close, the presence of Tito's partisans had led to some tricky negotiations, which fortunately ended in the withdrawal of Yugoslav forces and establishment of a new frontier, called the Morgan Line after its principal executor, General Morgan. Thus, in Trieste itself, the opera flourished and was often reinforced by visits from the La Scala company; restaurants were of the highest standard; the *ragazze* were numerous and on the whole *simpatico*; the wines of Friuli-Venezia Giulia were eminently quaffable and, all in all, the world was our oyster and did not need a sword to open.

There was also Venice within easy reach, Cortina d'Ampezzo for skiing, wonderful swimming and sailing and, of course, the horses. I have already introduced the drag hounds and I will have more to say of this shortly, but in order to qualify to hunt, we relative newcomers to the Regiment had to pass off riding school. How we suffered! The old cries of 'Who told you to dismount?' or 'Is the horse all right?' – the latter question usually posed after a crashing fall over some impossible fence – these cries rang out once more as we strived to improve our skill. To trot endlessly without stirrups, endure a blanket ride or go down a line of fences with folded arms and no stirrups – these were our daily fare, and we thereby learned a lot. How to sit well down in the saddle, improve our hands, drive a horse into his fences; they all added up to a gratifying gain in confidence. Perhaps the most testing of all exercises was the one when we were circling round the school at the trot with no stirrups, when the order 'Change horses one up' or some equivalent was given. It then became necessary rapidly to dismount from your own animal, who was still trotting, run forward to the horse in front and remount while your quarry was still moving relentlessly forward. But it all added to the sense of achievement in the end. There was also the matter of horse management, for there is nothing like grooming a horse yourself, mucking out, feeding and watering and seeing to the tack, to make you understand and appreciate what the grooms do for your beloved animals.

Thus trained and equipped we were able to enjoy drag hunting, and I shall always recall one particular day with our own regimental pack, when I was assigned a chestnut called Partisan. Those familiar with the works of Anthony Trollope and in particular the character of Lord Chiltern, whose entire existence was dedicated to the preservation and then pursuit of foxes, will recall that he liked to have something to do on horseback. All his horses pulled like the mischief, rushed like devils and wanted a good deal of riding. 'When a man tells me that a horse is an armchair, I always tell him to put the brute in his bedroom.' Now Partisan was certainly no armchair and did pull like the mischief. Nevertheless I was told that he would go best in a snaffle. At the meet, which was in an old farmyard of the grass and stone-wall country north-east of Trieste, it was immediately clear he was going to be a handful, for no sooner had he seen the hounds and heard the sound of the horn than – Trollope again – 'he stretched out his head, and put his mouth upon the bit, and began to tremble in every muscle'. Give him lots of room, I was advised, and I could not help reflecting that had I tried there and then to insure my life for a healthy sum, the premium would have been substantial.

But as we got going I had every reason to be satisfied with Partisan's performance. He seemed to have a passion for leaping over stone walls and, by keeping him well clear of the field, we were not giving trouble to others. It was not until the third leg that I felt any desire to change him for an armchair because until then I seemed to be just in control except when we were in sight of, and nearing, the next stone wall. But shortly after we had set off on the final leg, Partisan and I keeping well clear of the others, I heard furious voices behind me and recognized those of a bold-riding and wholly eccentric couple – the Major and his Memsahib of The Queen's Bays, respectively known as 'Crash' and 'Wonky' – who seemed to be indulging in a dispute as to whose animal would complete the run first. Wonky was the first to draw level with me, on the nearside, and then Crash on the offside, and they were still yelling imprecations at one another and at their galloping steeds. This commotion was too much for Partisan, and with a bound that almost unseated me, he shot forward with a clearly intense desire to shake off such unruly fellows of the chase and moreover to ensure that it would be he and I who finished well ahead of such an ill-disciplined couple. Somehow I stayed on board, only to receive a reprimand from the Colonel at the end of the line for not being 'well down in the saddle'. The fact was that it was only by standing up in the stirrups that I was able to stop Partisan from taking me across the Morgan Line and thus at the mercy of Tito's border guards. In spite of my explaining to the Colonel the predicament in which I had found myself, he decreed that although I had made good progress in improving my horsemanship it would be beneficial all round if I were sent off to Palmanova, another garrison town in Venezia Giulia, to be a student at a month's equitation course run by the Royal Army Veterinary Corps.

This turned out to be a blessing. The particular course which I took had as its principal instructor a rough riding sergeant of the 9th Lancers, and as there were only ten of us, both officers and men of various regiments stationed nearby, he was able to give proper attention to each one of us. We had all brought our own horses with us, the Colonel having generously allowed me to take Bounty, a beautiful Hanoverian mare with excellent manners and a kindly disposition. One of my fellow students was Douglas Macrae-Brown of the Royal Horse Artillery, who had brought a huge, grey animal, named after that gallant and chivalrous general of Afrika Korps fame, Rommel, the Desert Fox. Douglas became a great friend and we will hear more of him later. The equitation course was of special value with regard to horse management. The course very sensibly demanded that we look after our own horses and that the morning parade began with an inspection of ourselves, our horses and their furniture. The next hour or so would be spent in the indoor riding school and sometimes would be followed by a cross-country hack with a number of stiffish fences thrown in. There were frequent blanket-rides, i.e. a strapped blanket in lieu of a saddle, and at the end of the course my fellow students and I were much more competent and confident horsemen.

Back with the Regiment at Opicina I found that another great feature of the return to real soldiering was to be found. The 4th Hussar band had arrived, having been touring parts of Germany and Austria on its way back to us. This meant, apart from many other functions, that various trumpet calls now ruled our military procedures. Reveille, Stables, Commanding Officer's Orders, Parades, Last Post and so on were all sounded and the old regular 4th Hussars were content to find themselves in such familiar territory. Our bandmaster, Jigs Jaeger, was a wonderful man, a superb musician, a tolerant and enthusiastic teacher of his bandsmen, a morale-raiser for all ranks by his infectious, irrepressible good humour, and – herein lay the fame with which he endowed our own 4th Hussar band and later as Director Of Music, The Irish Guards, their already well-established musical distinction – a great showman. One of the recent failures of the Army Board is to have authorized the removal of bands from each infantry and cavalry regiment. The regimental band was an indispensable part of the soldiers' lives. For parades, concerts, dances, reviews within the regiment itself, to say nothing of the tours for recruiting purposes or simply to entertain the public at large, it contributed enormously to the wellbeing, morale and spirit of the regiment. I recall that in the 1980s, when the Kneller Hall School of Military Music made an attempt to remove the cavalry bands, it was necessary for me, as Chairman of the Cavalry Colonels, to appeal to the then Chief of General Staff, that admirable soldier, Dwin Bramall, to support the bands' retention, albeit at a lower strength. Happily he did so. Later, alas, unwise counsels prevailed, and the Cavalry of the Line now has to rely on three Bands, Hussar, Lancer and Dragoon, to serve all the regiments which have survived the equally unwise diminution of the British Army's order of battle. In the case of my own regiment, now The Queen's Royal Hussars, we have retained a band of pipes and drums, manned by members of the Regiment who are also armoured crewmen.

It was late in 1946 that we moved from Opicina to Monfalcone, about halfway between Trieste and Udine. Once again there was a splendid indoor riding school, and our principal tormentor was Stephen Eve, perhaps the most polished horseman that the 4th Hussars could boast – he had won the saddle at Weedon – and he certainly knew how to put us though our paces. The only snag was that he did not have the gift of making himself understood when mouthing his instructions to us, so that his order 'Down the centre in half sections' was totally misinterpreted. We would do something quite different, which roused him to a fury of explosive denunciations, simply causing more confusion. But such was our enthusiasm to learn from him – even at 6.30 a.m. on a cold winter morning – that we all survived.

Racing at Aiello went on and I recall witnessing another instance of Loopy Kennard's record as one of the really great cavalrymen of his day. One of his close friends in the Regiment, Francis Romney, was about to ride Partisan – yes, the same animal who had carried me so boldly out drag hunting – in a two and a half mile steeplechase when, while parading in the paddock, Partisan reared, threw Francis, who landed awkwardly and broke his collar bone. With the agreement of the stewards, Loopy, who was wearing customary coat and trousers, peeled off his coat, slipped over his shirt our 4th Hussar racing silk, rode down to the start and finished second. Francis, who in addition to being a polished horseman, was a slim, handsome, elegant and cultured man, soon recovered. Much later, when we were stationed in Germany he became an ardent enthusiast for show-jumping, not only performing himself with distinction, but designing courses for our own regimental tournaments.

Monfalcone also offered excellent shooting and in these early post-war days the local landowners had no objection to our freely shooting their game. Partridge, pheasants and even golden plover were to hand, and I recall one triumphant moment when walking up partridge with Loopy and his highly competent labrador, Duty, a covey got up in front of us, and my first shot brought down two partridge. So pleased was I that I neglected to discharge the other barrel. The incident was duly recorded in the game book as – one cartridge, a brace of partridge. Eventually our orders to quit Italy and move to the more sombre setting of Schleswig Holstein came through and off we set for Lübeck. By this time because of the demobilization of many war-time soldiers, the Regiment was at cadre strength, so that, as already recorded, the railway wagons bearing horses, hounds, saddlery and other equestrian necessities just about outweighed those for the soldiers.

Real soldiering was not quite so much fun in Schleswig Holstein as it had been in Venezia Giulia. There was still the hunting and shooting, but the gradual reduction of regimental strength because of demobilization was not exactly morale building. There was, however, one great event which enlivened our existence – the Berlin Tattoo. It was decreed by higher command that there was to be a military tattoo in the summer of 1947 at the Berlin Olympic Stadium. It would be a grand affair – massed bands, colourful uniforms, demonstrations of precise drill, physical training displays, and most important, the horses. One regiment was to perform a musical ride; another, deploying Lancers in full fig, would gallop to the rescue of gentlefolk, distressed by highwaymen having demanded their money or their lives; we, the 4th Hussars, were to present a hunting scene with the star players, of course, our own foxhounds. Getting to Berlin from Lübeck involved another bizarre train journey with some twenty horses and six couple of hounds, including my three beloved bitches, Thankful, Vital and Sapphire, who were becoming eligible to be the most train-travelled foxhounds in history. We also mustered a phaeton for the squire and his lady, saddles, bridles, rugs and other horse furniture, our blacksmith properly equipped, ourselves, and not forgetting grooms, regimental wives, friends, children. Overseeing the horse management was inevitably the Regimental Sergeant Major, whom we have already met – Chesty Read.

Once in Berlin there were briefings, rehearsals, getting the timing right, so that we left barracks to arrive at the Stadium shortly before our act. Then came a dress rehearsal with the commentary to be delivered in both English and German. Thousands of Berliners would be attending and the grand opening would be honoured by the presence of our Commander-in-Chief and the Mayor of Berlin. I am glad to say that my old fellow-whip, Henry Bathurst was with us and Loopy Kennard, as MFH, was the star of the show. In order to portray as many aspects of the sport as possible in a mere ten minutes, we had telescoped events severely. As the flood lighting came on – for the Tattoo was an evening affair – there would be revealed in the arena's centre Loopy and his hounds with Henry and me keeping them in a disciplined group. The buttons of our hunting coats gleamed, breeches snow white, boots well polished, hunting caps finely brushed – in short worthy of our beautifully groomed horses. Then in groups appeared members of the hunt, walking or trotting up, saluting the Master and positioning themselves nearby; some of the grooms, suitably liveried, would walk on, bearing silver salvers loaded with stirrup cups, just as the squire and his lady dashed up in the phaeton. Courteous cap-raising, obsequious forelock-tugging would precede the rapid emptying of stirrup cups and their collection; a note on the horn would indicate that it was time to move off, and then – with the floodlights switching to another part of the arena – Loopy's horn would give us the 'gone away' and he would lead his hounds over three well spaced brush fences, whips and field following, the squire roaring approval as we all galloped out of the arena.

After our ten-minute appearance on stage, the half-hour hack back to barracks cooled us down, before supper and a nightclub brought to a close our Thespian evening. So it went on for a week, playing to packed houses, for admission was free, and we all felt the fascination of the boards, while horses and hounds alike seemed to enter into the spirit of the thing. After this, life back in barracks at Lübeck seemed a little thin but, once the hunting season started again, we had some marvellous runs with the hounds. But before I describe my discomfort on one such occasion, there was a more sombre occurrence, which I shall long remember.

There were at this time a number of so-called war crimes trials conducted in Hamburg courtrooms by a British legal expert with the assistance of regimental officers brought for this very purpose. Hamburg still bore the scars of war, bombing and the dreadful fire-storm which had destroyed so many of its buildings and killed thousands of its people. I found myself sitting with three other officers from other regiments and guided by the legal expert. We were in short both jury and judge. The case before us concerned the alleged mistreatment of an RAF pilot, shot down during a bombing raid. The man on trial was in his sixties, worn, thin, visibly fearful of his fate, and his alleged crime was that he had beaten the pilot as he tried to extricate himself from his parachute. Evidence against him was given by a neighbour whose manner, looks and general shiftiness gave us little cause for confidence in his reliability. The eloquent German defence lawyer attacked the evidence with fluency, sincerity and conviction. He poured scorn on the credibility – *die Glaubwürdigkeit* – of the witness to such effect that my three fellow jurymen/judges and I, when required by our legal master to write on a slip of paper our finding, all wrote 'Not Guilty'. I am not at all sure that the master was entirely satisfied. He had something of the look of Judge Jeffreys. But our verdict prevailed, and I shall never forget the outburst of relief and joy that the prisoner's wife gave way to when she understood that her husband was to be freed there and then.

But back to the more agreeable pastime of hunting. Colonel George had been very good in allowing me to ride his splendid animal, Warden, for my whipping-in duties, but for one particular meet, Warden had been loaned to one of George's friends, and I was invited to make do with a horse, which we had been looking after for a German landowner, who had been called away to visit his cousins in southern Germany. The animal's name was Pacifico, and, as I was to discover, never was a gelding more ill-named. It seemed that for a normal hack he would behave well enough, yet, as we know, hunting is *not* in this category.

There are some horses who are the very essence of proper conduct under all circumstances except one – when they hear the hunting horn. Hacking Pacifico to the meet had presented no problems, but when Loopy indicated that the hounds were to be released from the hound van, and they came gambolling out, the scene changed. Rearing, cavorting, all four legs off the ground at the same time, Pacifico began behaving like a circus horse. It was a wonder I stayed on board and the two of us became the centre of disapproving attention. After a word from Loopy I steered Pacifico away from the hounds and other horses to a discreet position to a flank. This move temporarily restored some sort of order. But the worst was still to come. As Loopy blew the customary short note on the horn for moving off, Pacifico took off. All restraint was removed. He proceeded to display distinct affinity to Mr Soapey Sponge's Multum in Parvo who, it will be recalled, would not only carry his rider into the midst of hounds at a meet, but would think nothing of upsetting the master himself in the middle of the pack. Pacifico was quite up to both these tricks and I was invited to 'move off'. I did so but not, alas, out of trouble. Pacifico, having been restrained and fallen back a little from those riding behind Loopy, hounds and Henry Bathurst, suddenly gave a great plunge forward, almost unseating me, and now, with a thundering of hooves, sparks in showers coming up from the road as his shoes encountered it, was literally charging towards the hounds. Scattering those in the way, he then absolutely *leapt* over them. Terrible oaths from Loopy burned my ears as I set off in a John Gilpin-like manner for heaven knew where! At least we had not ridden over hounds. We had jumped them!

It took me the best part of a mile to get Pacifico under any sort of control. We were galloping wildly along a country road, sometimes on the verge, sometimes on the fortunately rather rough surface, and I was dreading that we should either come to a crossroads or meet some vehicle coming the other way. I had no expectation of anything, short of a racing car, catching us up from behind. But how was I to stop? 'Diseases desperate grown', observed Claudius, King of Denmark, 'by desperate appliances are relieved, Or not at all.' Quite so! It was with desperation that I applied my hands and wrists with all the strength they could muster to the reins. The trouble was that by this time most of their strength had been exhausted by my previous struggles with the brute. At length, by hooking the reins over my right arm to the elbow joint, standing up in the stirrups and heaving backwards, I managed to slow him down and turn him round. Yet Pacifico still showed no sign of living up to his name. His blood was up after all this excitement; he was quivering, nostrils aflare, ears pricking, dancing about. There was only one thing for it. I rode him into a ploughed field and sticking next to the headland, attempted to gallop the fidgets out of him. He had a mouth like a bull and the strength of ten, but he gradually assumed a more sober pace, and I was able to consider what to do next. There was no sign of the hunt, so I decided that prudence should prevail and hacked quietly back to the stables. This escapade was the exception and on most days, riding a more reliable animal, I was able to fulfil my duties as a whip, and was much gratified when Loopy told me I was a great help to him 'because you're always up with the hounds'.

Early in 1948 the Regiment moved to Colchester, and despite the austerity of post-war England, we managed to make the return to real soldiering as agreeable as we could want. Moreover in the early part of the summer, we were warned for service in Malaya, where an insurrection by Communist guerrillas was threatening the Government there. This, in turn, meant that we were made up to full strength and received high quality regular and National Service reinforcements. Among them were some first class officers, transferring from the Indian cavalry – Kenneth Bidie, Hugh Marrack, 'Sailor' Hawkins, Peter Young, and others from the Foot Guards – Michael Questier, Mark Fairfield and Tom Tilbrook. It was with these comrades in arms that I would have my first taste of a savage war of peace. In August 1948 we sailed from Southampton in the troopship *Dilwara* bound for Singapore.

Chapter 8

Stengahs and Sten Guns

'The long, long war.'

Richard Clutterbuck

What became known as the Malayan Emergency began in June 1948. Chin Peng, the Communist leader had, a year earlier, initiated a campaign of urban strikes and riots in an attempt to gain further support for his party. But he soon saw that these measures were producing hostility rather than recruits, and so he determined on a campaign of armed rebellion, of terror – murder, coercion and economic disruption. By taking his men back to the jungle, from which he had harassed the Japanese, he planned to exploit the discontent of half a million Chinese squatters who scraped a living from land near the jungle's edge. From such people he could get recruits, information, food and money. I will not give here a full account of this prolonged campaign, but simply explain my small part in it.

I was commanding A Squadron, 4th Hussars, and we were stationed at Ipoh in the northern state of Perak. Our tasks varied. We did not only patrol the roads and tracks which led to rubber plantations and tin mines – two of the main sources of revenue – but also took to the jungle on foot to seek out bandits, acquire intelligence or react to some report of terrorist activity. One of these latter operations was unique. I received the curt, but clear, instruction to travel down the railway line between Ipoh and Chemor with seven NCOs and men in two little jeeps fitted with wheels which matched the railway gauge in order to clear the line of mines and an ambush party of guerrillas who had shot up the night train to Taiping. A simple enough order, I reflected.

As we set off, I was warned to be careful and to report progress. Away we went, the leading jeep about fifty yards in front of mine, headlights on as it was a dark, cloudy night, guns at the ready, all-round lookouts, radio tuned to an armoured car patrol which would take the road to Chemor. All serene for a few miles, then suddenly as we were passing through a steep cutting, the somewhat eerie sound of wheels on tracks was shattered by a prolonged burst of automatic fire, which seemed to spray both jeeps. Lights off, we pressed on for 100 yards to clear the cutting, halted, dismounted and, leaving a sentry with each jeep, now closed up together, doubled back to the ambush area. We crawled to the top of the northern bank from where the shooting had seemed to come, and with our Sten guns fired somewhat blindly at – what? Shadows, trees, the undergrowth; no sinister figures were to be seen. My sergeant gave me a grenade, and moving back to the other bank to gain height, I drew the pin and flung it as far as I could towards where we thought the firing had come from. A violent explosion, then silence, except for the chattering of insects. There was no question of pursuing anything in total darkness. We rallied at the jeeps, unwittingly walking over wires and explosives attached to the railway line – we did not discover these devices until next morning when they had to be defused and removed. The leading jeep had bullet holes in the body, but happily none of us was wounded. I reported on the radio that we had been ambushed and were proceeding to Chemor, which we reached soon afterwards without further incident.

At the station there we rendezvoused with armoured cars and armoured personal carriers, and on the way back to Ipoh, stopped to search a village opposite the ambush site. No one there knew anything or had seen anybody. Back at Ipoh we reported the railway line clear, only to be informed at breakfast time by the police that it wasn't clear. The engine driver had seen the explosives. Out we went again, this time by train, taking with us Sergeant Jock Ferrier [later Major Ferrier MBE MM, one of the finest 4th Hussars I served with] who was an explosives expert. He removed the fuses, and then we collected up the wires and explosives, took it all back to Ipoh, and once more reported the line clear. The night train to Taiping got under way at last, some twelve hours late. All in all a tiny, minor incident, yet characteristic of the disruption to normal life that such trivial guerrilla action could cause.

When we were not engaged on operations there was plenty of opportunity for amusing ourselves agreeably in Perak – sipping stengahs in the Ipoh Club, curry tiffins with planters, amateur dramatics, improving golf handicaps, playing polo on the local airfield. All the locals were pleased to entertain us and we made good friends amongst them all. But military matters came first. Early on in my time at Ipoh, I was sent for by the local commander, told of a reported bandit camp, containing half a dozen terrorists in the jungle between Ipoh and Sungei Siput – a renowned spot for bandit activity – where numerous squatters provided them with the support they needed. It was necessary to conceal our intentions so that we did not frighten the bandits away before we got near their camp. This meant having an approach which could not be detected too readily and reported. To go by road or track would have been an instant giveaway. Twice I went up in an Auster to survey the surrounding country and decide where to put the ambushing 'Stops' out and which way to advance with the main flushing party. As always in such affairs I liaised with the police, and we decided that as the railway line passed within a mile or so of our target, we would requisition a train for what was given out as a routine changeover of personnel between Ipoh and Kuala Kangsor.

Before dawn one morning we set off. At pre-planned places the train was halted to let off first the blocking party under command of a troop leader, who was given the time to get into position, then later my own larger group which was to advance to the patch of jungle reputed to house the bandit camp. It all went according to plan – with one notable exception. My most vivid memories are of sharp cracks made by all of us as we made our way through a bamboo plantation. It was impossible to move through this area silently. Then my attention was diverted by one of my sergeants moving by my side suddenly shouting in pain, halting, stripping off his jungle green shirt to reveal red ants crawling all over his chest and back. As I assisted in their removal, I felt grateful for the ants' discrimination.

We got into position. I established a small headquarters, the blocking party reported by radio that they were ready, and the flushing group, who were understandably concerned that they would not be shot by the blockers, moved in. Anticlimax! There was no shooting at all. There was no game, in fact. The birds had flown, but there were unmistakable signs of a camp. At least we had gained a little experience in the art of ulu bashing. Of course the real work of hunting down and killing the Communist terrorists was that of the infantry, supported by the Police Field Force, their Special Branch, the SAS and the locally enlisted Malayan Scouts. The whole campaign depended on a number of strategic measures. General Briggs' plan of removing squatters from the jungle edge and rehousing them in new villages protected by local forces was a significant step in what was the key to success – isolating the bandits from their sources of support, denying them access to food, money, recruits and information. This, together with the appointment of Gerald Templer in the combined post of High Commissioner and Director of Operations, did much to seize back the initiative. Templer's Hearts and Minds campaign met with further success as he convinced the people of Malaya that he was going to win. Who, after all, likes to be on the losing side?

Meanwhile the 4th Hussars continued to play their part. George Kidston had handed over command to Richard Close-Smith early in 1949. He had been a wonderful Commanding Officer, admired and respected by all, and he would continue to feature in our lives, later becoming Colonel of the Regiment. Richard, urbane, cultured, easy-going and, with a gracious charm concealed beneath this stylish demeanour, a deep love for the Regiment and a determination that we would acquit ourselves well. He perhaps was inclined to rate the faultless turnout of our soldiers more highly than the accuracy of their shooting, but his support for his squadron leaders was always strong and undemanding. The trouble was that there was little for him to do as the sabre squadrons were spread all over Malaya and under command of the local triumvirate of Military-Police-Civil Government, which every state and every district of the country had.

Meanwhile I continued in command of A Squadron – as a captain. [Happily after I had handed over to Cliff Jones later in 1949, I was able to claim the pay of a major for my period of command.] We patrolled endlessly to keep the planters and miners happy, gave support to the local Gurkha battalion in clearing squatter camps and detached a troop for a specific task of restoring morale to an isolated village. This led to a successful attack on a bandit camp some months later, in which we called upon the support of rocket-firing fighter aircraft. We did more foot patrols in the jungle acting on police information, but made no contact with the enemy. And then came a totally unexpected contact, in which we suffered our first casualties. As recorded already, the area of Sungei Siput was a hotbed of guerrilla activity and we would frequently, at irregular intervals of course, patrol with our armoured vehicles the minor roads and tracks which led north from Sungei Siput itself to various rubber plantations. 4th Troop under command of Michael Questier, with Jon Sutro, who had recently joined us, as his understudy, and some dozen NCOs and men, was engaged in carrying out a patrol of this sort when they ran into a strong ambush, which we later learned had been prepared by the bandits to attack an expected convoy of lorries. A fierce fight ensued in which the troop leader, Michael Questier, and six soldiers were killed. Jon Sutro took command and succeeded in extricating the remaining soldiers and their vehicles from the ambush. All those surviving had been wounded. For his leadership and bravery Jon Sutro received an immediate award of the Military Cross and another member of the troop, Lance Coporal Smith, the Distinguished Conduct Medal. Moreover 4th Troop had given the enemy a bloody nose. The police follow-up party discovered six dead bandits and many blood trails away from the ambush area which indicated that others of the enemy had been wounded.

From time to time our tasks were more light-hearted. The Colonel sent for me one morning and told me to take my squadron at once to Sungei Patani in Kedah and report to the commander of the 1st/6th Gurkha Rifles, Colonel Townsend, who turned out to be the brother of Princess Margaret's group captain friend, Peter Townsend. The plan, I learned, was to do a sweep of the Dindings and search for a bandit gang that had been unpleasantly active. Some sort of cover was needed to divert attention while the main force was unobtrusively getting into position. I was therefore given a dual task – to support the main operation and to execute the deception plan, which was to take two troops and ostentatiously occupy the island of Pangkor, a small beautiful island, about six miles by three, lying opposite and two miles from the small port and fishing town of Lumut in the Dindings. [Nowadays it would cost a small fortune to stay at Pangkor, which has become an exclusive holiday resort.]

I mustered my force early one morning and, sending an officer ahead to requisition three launches, we set off in our armoured cars, pennants flying, to Lumut, where we boarded the three launches. Standing on the bridge of the central launch, accompanied by my Squadron Sergeant Major, I felt something of the destroyer captain's piratical dash. I made the proper signal and off we went, the launches leaving a fine wake behind them. Soon after, we landed at three separate jetties, and I dispatched the two troops to the northern and southern ends of the island while, with my small headquarters, I made for the lovely bay on the west coast. It was idyllic. As I lay on the beach after a brisk swim, I watched the Malabar fishermen pulling in their great nets and chanting their calypso-like songs, and reflected that but for the Dindings operation, which shortly I would have to get on with, I would never have come to this beautiful island. The troopers of my squadron long remembered our invasion of Pangkor. When, they asked, would they again participate in so indisputably successful a mission – all objectives taken and no casualties?

I fear that I have not been able to give an impression of what the more serious part of the Malayan campaign was like. Infantrymen who lived and worked in the jungle for long periods, had to learn how to move through it silently, how to build bashas of tree branches and leaves, what could and could not be eaten, how to combat the blood-sucking leeches, how to set up an ambush and patiently, motionlessly, wait for it to be sprung, how to shoot and kill fleeting targets. They had to be able to recognize, often with the help of expert trackers, when booby traps had been set by retiring terrorists. For many of them the jungle was not, as Spencer-Chapman had called it, neutral. One young officer of the Queen's Own Royal West Kents admirably described his dislike of the jungle:

It's the perpetual gloom and the smell of corruption that is so

> awful. Everything stinks of rotting vegetation. You are always wet through; it rains like hot pennies six times a day and the leaves never stop dripping. In dense secondary jungle it is good going to cover a hundred yards in an hour and you cannot see the enemy an arm's length away. But most terrifying of all is at night, when you are one of a patrol's four sentries. It is the blackest darkness and you can make no noise and certainly not communicate with your neighbours, twenty-five yards away. There is an intense loneliness. What I loathe most and have never got used to, is living like an animal, wet, filthy and hungry. But an even worse fear is that I might let my men down; *that* keeps me going.

It was with the British soldiers' perseverance, pluck and powers of command that the long war was eventually brought to a successful conclusion. We must later on pay another visit to the jungle, but with a difference. Next time the jungle will be that of Borneo; next time the enemy will be Indonesian, with Brunei rebels playing a subsidiary role; and next time I will be in command, not of a squadron, but of the Regiment itself. Before this however, we must turn our attention to what it was like to be a student at that machine for turning out General Officers – the Staff College.

Chapter 9

Staff College and After

Tam Marte Quam Minerva

Life at the Staff College broadened one's mind immeasurably. After the wholly enjoyable, but necessarily restricted experiences as a regimental soldier, to find oneself mixed in with contemporaries from all other arms of the service, together with a number of officers from Commonwealth countries and European armies was a revelation, an education and a broad levelling. I found myself in D Division of the College – A and B Divisions were at Camberley, C Division at Minley Manor – with fifty odd colleagues from cavalry, infantry, artillery and engineer regiments, and those of the supporting services – a mixed bunch of talent, wartime adventures and immensely varied tastes. D Division was in Blenheim Barracks, Aldershot and commanded by Colonel Freddie Graham, an Argyll and Sutherland Highlander, who had commanded a battalion in the Italian campaign with distinction – hence the DSO ribbon on his tunic – and was to achieve great fame by virtue of his moustache, black on one side, white on the other, and thus the best of advertisements for a well-known brand of whisky, or Highland Oil as he called it. He and his wife were great enthusiasts for Highland Dancing, and one of our agreeable pastimes on one evening of each week was to take part in their instruction – Freddie performing gallantly on the pipes – and learn proficiency at the eightsome reel, the Dashing White Sergeant and other complex manoeuvres.

Instruction at the Staff College was largely done by a system of syndicates – ten students of varying arms of the service and one

Directing Staff teacher. Most of the DS had commanded battalions or regiments during the war and knew what they were talking about, whilst conscious of the point that many of those they were teaching had commanded squadrons or companies. There were lots of stars among our DS – Crackers May, Durham Light Infantry, Brian Wyldbore-Smith, Royal Artillery, Bill Jackson, Royal Engineers, Dick Ward, Royal Tank Regiment. They had all distinguished themselves in battle and mustered countless DSOs and MCs. Another such one, Derek Horsford, in command of a Gurkha Battalion during the Arakan campaign against the Japanese became so impatient with his soldiers for loosing off their rifles at shadows that he took away all their ammunition and told them to rely on the kukri. We students learned much from these veterans during our syndicate discussions of every military subject under the sun. One of the subjects which most interested me was military history, and my study of Napoleon's campaigns led me to further studies of that unique mixture of strategic opportunism, tactical brilliance, lasting civil administration, political ruthlessness, soaring ambition and absolute inability to see when the game was up.

It was not all work and no play, however. Cricket and tennis were the summer pursuits. There were two main cricket teams – the College XI, which enlisted the cream of our players, and the so-called Owls [an owl was the Staff College symbol – for wisdom, we assumed, rather than sleepiness]. The Owls played most of their matches on the idyllic cricket field at Minley Manor. We were captained by a delightful gunner, John Douglas-Withers, whose dachshund, David, became the XI's mascot, and among my fellow players was Rowley Mans, a fanatically keen cricketer, who subsequently won great fame by persuading Jomo Kenyatta to be moderate in some of Kenya's post-independence activities. The ground sloped slightly so that if from the wicket to the northern side you connected with a powerful off-drive, the ball would race unstoppably to the boundary. Tennis too provided much enjoyment. Douglas MacCallan, my old friend from The Bays, and I entered for the men's doubles competition and were only worsted in the final by the cunning play of Michael Biggs, the Royal Engineer boss of C Division.

It was the custom in those days for the students to perform in a pantomime at the end of the year and course. Here was the opportunity to have back at our instructors and highlight their idiosyncrasies or eccentricities, and the theme chosen for our show was the Staff College in Roman times. Our Commandant, Dudley Ward, was a somewhat forbidding figure, who would address us from time to time in the main lecture hall and come out with such sayings as: 'This student's tactics would not have *surprised* the enemy; they might have astonished him, but that is hardly the same thing'; or: 'They say you must try to get into the mind of your commander – there is usually plenty of room.' Equipped with a handful of comparable one-liners – as they are now called – Dan Read, an admirable field-sporting 3rd Hussar – took on the role to perfection. The Owl was played by Rowley Mans; Robin Brockbank, a 12th Lancer, renowned for his courage in action, his outstanding ability with gun, rod and horse, his deep love and knowledge of the country life, and his charm, presented an Ancient Briton. I, together with several others, was dressed as a Roman Centurion [we had borrowed the costumes from the recently made film, *Caesar and Cleopatra*] and strutted about the stage spouting witticisms. It was, as became a pantomime, equipped with a musical score – all written by a fellow student – and the love interest was maintained by the hero, a modern Staff College student, dreaming that he was in Rome, pursuing his lady love.

We all worked hard, took pleasure in meeting old friends and making new ones. Shortly before the end of the course, the annual Staff College magazine, fittingly called *Owl Pie* was published. All contributions by students; the editor, another valued friend – Alun Gwynne-Jones, later Lord Chalfont who greatly distinguished himself as Defence Correspondent of *The Times*, Foreign Office minister, historian, television presenter, spokesman on military matters in the House of Lords, and never forgot his old friends from soldiering days. He knew a lot about soldiering and had been awarded the Military Cross for his courage and perseverance during the Malayan campaign. I recall with pleasure one evening when Alun was still with *The Times*, he, John Templeton-Cotill [the witty, urbane and clever naval officer I mentioned earlier] and I, together with our wives went to some curious restaurant in Queen's Gate and partook of what was advertised as an Elizabethan dinner with wenches serving all sorts of unlikely dishes, washed down by mead and sack, which encouraged Alun to stuff £5 notes down the bosoms of these wenches while goosing them with the other hand. It reached the point where no serving wench would dare to come near our table. 'We have heard the chimes at midnight, Master Shallow.' We then all repaired to Alun's house in Chelsea and were unwise enough to crack a bottle of champagne with foreseeably dire results.

Apart from *Owl Pie* there were other publications as the course ended. We were all told what jobs we were going to get as a result of our efforts. The outbreak of the Korean war was, in this respect, timely for it was decided to resuscitate three former divisions – 6th and 11th Armoured and the 3rd Infantry. This, in turn, meant that innumerable staff appointments at divisional and brigade headquarters would be created. As already indicated Freddie Graham was given 61 Lorried Infantry Brigade to command, part of the 6th Armoured Division, and he had chosen me to be his Brigade Major. As the essential tactical employment of an armoured division involves the close cooperation of infantry and armour, with artillery and engineer support, it clearly made sense for an infantry brigadier to have as his chief of staff a supposed expert in the use of tanks. I must confess that I found my task both demanding and agreeable. As a bachelor still I was able to devote long hours to mastering the job. The priorities were clear. First, get Brigade HQ to function smoothly and efficiently, both in the field and in barracks. We were housed at Rollestone Camp, a hutted affair roughly between Larkhill and Shrewton, just the right size for our Staff and Signal Squadron. And, most important for the next requirement within easy reach of our infantry battalions, for whom we were responsible and whose officers and men I had to get to know together with, at a later stage, those key figures of the armoured brigade, the artillery, engineers and supporting services. There was also the little matter of winning and keeping the confidence of Divisional HQ. Happily many of the staff there had been my fellow students at Camberley, so that we knew and trusted one another. Among them stand out Christopher Thursby-Pelham, Welsh Guards, Dan Read – the pantomime commandant – 3rd Hussars, Peter Body, Royal Horse Artillery, Desmond Scarr, 14th/20th Hussars. My opposite number in the armoured brigade was John Medlicott, 12th Lancers, whose principal pleasures seemed to be riding in point-to-points, going to nightclubs and pulling the legs of senior officers. One regiment in the armoured brigade was that famous bunch of death or glory boys, the 17th/21st Lancers, commanded by a legendary cavalry figure, WAC Anderson. There was one other cavalry regiment in the division, the 3rd Carabiniers, led by Joe Fishbourne, and containing some very clubbable men like Oliver Horne, another steeple-chasing fanatic, of whom it was sometimes said that he had endured so many crashing falls that there were no bones in his body which had not been broken. Other memorable members of the regiment were Jim Ashton, Toby Alexander and John Compton. I was always welcomed by them on my frequent visits. The two Royal Horse Artillery colonels were exceptionally able and good-natured – Jock Mcneil 1st RHA and Henry Peck 5th RHA, while the sapper regiment was commanded by Jim Shepherd. It was a formidable team, strongly and dashingly led by Errol Prior-Palmer and, during our first year, deployed on and around Salisbury Plain, we trained hard, got to know each other and prepared for our move to the British Army of the Rhine.

But there was time for relaxation too. Freddie Graham was a very keen shooting man and ably assisted by the administrative expert of Brigade HQ, Louis Hargroves, he was fully occupied by the various military shoots which flourished at Tidworth, Larkhill, Netheravon and Warminster. I was able to go out with the Royal Artillery foxhounds. Although I had no horse of my own the Larkhill Saddle Club would provide a mount. Later in the year there were innumerable cricket matches and Brigade HQ mustered a team to play against the other headquarters and various regiments. One of my fellow staff officers was the young Richard Parsons – subsequently our ambassador in Madrid – whose inclination for amateur dramatics found him cast in a production of *Pride and Prejudice* at Salisbury Playhouse. When Richard, who was doing his national service, told me first that he intended to join the diplomatic service, second that his part in the play was to be that of the unspeakable bounder, George Wickham, I was able to congratulate him, pointing out that playing the role of so devious, smooth-tongued and hypocritical a character would be the most fitting preparation for the career he had in mind.

Of course, I went to see the play in the company of Desmond Scarr, and we enjoyed it immensely. The girl playing Elizabeth was just right – tolerably handsome, suitably prejudiced and a cool deliverer of the wittier lines. Mrs Bennet was every bit as loquacious and vulgar as one could wish, and Jane strikingly good looking. Darcy gave a fair imitation of Laurence Olivier and Mr Bennet relished his teasing of Mr Collins and his own brand of irony. But my favourite was, like Mr Bennet's, Wickham, for Richard Parsons played him with all the bogus charm, flashy arrogance and innate shallowness that the part demanded. Afterwards Desmond Scarr, Richard and I gave a supper party at the Haunch of Venison [still going strong, I am glad to say] for Elizabeth, Jane and Lady Catherine de Bourgh, the last named having shed her required guise of snobbish grandeur, and turned out to be young, articulate and comely.

Part of our table talk during supper turned on the relatively, at that time, recent publication of *Pemberley Shades*, DA Bonavia-Hunt's praiseworthy shot at presenting the lives of the Darcys after their marriage. We agreed, of course, that excellent though it was, nothing and no one quite had, or could have, the touch of Jane Austen herself. This truth has not, however, deterred many others from trying their respective hands. *Sanditon* and *The Watsons* have been laudably finished by 'Another Lady' and Joan Aiken's sequel to *Mansfield Park* has considerable merit. Emma Tennant though struck a false note with her attempts to prolong the Pemberley story.

Towards the end of 1951 the whole division moved to Germany and was widely deployed in the general area of Nord-Westfalen with garrisons at Minden, Osnabrück, Herford, Lübbecke and Münster. Individual and low level tactical training continued, but once spring arrived the manoeuvre season got going in a big way, and one of my particular tasks was to ensure that the frequent moves of Brigade HQ were carried out swiftly, smoothly and with the assurance that communications would be maintained throughout and that the HQ would be admirably camouflaged and concealed. We developed a drill for such changes of position and more or less perfected it. I found that much of the work in deploying the brigade, issuing appropriate orders and keeping divisional HQ informed of the situation fell quite properly to me, aided by my excellent staff and a team of liaison officers from the various regiments and other units under command. I was able at times to flatter myself that *I* was commanding the brigade and was finding it a relatively easy thing to do. It would, as I was to discover some years later, be much more demanding to command a regiment.

Happily for us the sporting calendar still played a major part in our affairs. Skiing was well organized for all of us, irrespective of skill. The horse featured large throughout Rhine Army's regiments. One of my colleagues, Brian Holdsworth, DCLI, shared with me the purchase price and upkeep of a splendid 17 hh chestnut gelding called Lofty, who took us round the show jumping and hunter trial courses in fine style. Freddie Graham was able to get his fill of shooting, although on one occasion overstepped the mark. It was during a major manoeuvre during which we in 6th Armoured Division were required to force a crossing of the Rhine against a suitably deployed opposition. Just before the exercise really got going, Louis Hargroves, who had discovered that in a large wood near our Brigade HQ there was an inviting pheasant population, took Freddie, who always had his gun and gun dog – a magnificent spaniel called Bruce – with him on manoeuvres, in pursuit of these tempting targets only to be challenged by the local *Forstmeister*. This dignitary, totally unmoved by the rank, imposing front and two-tone moustache of the Brigade Commander, was so furious that his pheasants were being disturbed that he seized Freddie's gun and sent for the police. Result – the entire manoeuvre programme was halted until the matter could be sorted out, apologies made, compensation offered and an amicable settling of the affair reached.

So the year 1952 passed rapidly. The pattern remained much the same according to the season. The spring, summer and early autumn months filled with field training at levels rising from simple platoon and troop exercises, then company and squadron manoeuvres, rising to all arms training at regimental and brigade direction, and culminating in some huge deployment of all the armoured and infantry divisions in the later autumn after the harvest. There were, of course lots of parties, including formal dinners in regimental messes; soccer, hockey, cricket, tennis matches were played; horse shows galore; regimental balls to mark special historical events; parades of great variety, including one which we with our Brigade HQ at Minden were required to conduct – it was a farewell to General Eisenhower, who was about to return to the United States to run for President. He won. Yet before this he lost a bet made by our Divisional Commander, Errol Prior-Palmer, to the effect that he, Errol, could with his division extract it from one part of a defensive deployment, move it a certain distance and redeploy it ready for action in such and such a number of hours. This wager led to a paper exercise in which we were all involved to see who was right. I, with my fellow brigade major, now that most excellent of men, Allan Taylor RTR, and other staff officers, was given the task of testing whether the movement of the division to conform with the requirements was practical. It was a most interesting calculation. We had to know four things. What had to be moved, when it could be extracted, where it had to move to and by when it had to be in its position ready for action. The key to it all was sound planning. One route for wheels, another for tracks, traffic control of the highest order, repair and recovery, speeds which could be maintained, reconnaissance, advance parties, assembly areas and so on – all rather ordinary, unromantic drills, yet vital to military competence. Our plan, which was presented to General Errol and the brigade commanders with their respective commanding officers and staffs, convinced even the most sceptical, including a senior representative from General Eisenhower's headquarters, that Errol had won his bet. We planners were thus able to bask in his unqualified approval.

Soon after this my two years as Freddie Graham's Brigade Major were up. I handed over to Ian Gill and returned to England, there to rejoin the 4th Hussars, stationed at Tidworth. During my year at Minden, I had been shown much kindness by the von Schellersheim family. Wilfried and I had become very close, and I was able to assure her that my regiment would be joining the Rhine Army late in 1953, so that our parting would not be prolonged. Her father, the Baron, while not overjoyed at his daughter's friendship with a British officer, was to some extent mollified by the fact that I was at least a cavalryman and could ride with confidence his not always easily managed horses. I learned later that the Baron had in the past often tested the mettle of other aspiring suitors to his daughter's affections by filling them up with drink during the evening's festivities and then inviting them to join him in an early morning hack the following day. He soon discovered, however, that such tactics did not work.

On arrival at Tidworth to find that Stephen Eve was now commanding the 4th Hussars, I was welcomed by him and many of my old regimental friends, and told that I was to take over command of C Squadron, the very squadron that I had first joined. My second in command was Tony Harrison, who had been in the Yeomanry and had joined us before the Malayan campaign. One of my troop leaders was David Vetch, who was to remain a life-long friend and who in the year 2004 brilliantly organized and conducted a celebration of the 150th anniversary of the Charge of the Light Brigade at Balaklava. What is more it all took place on the spot. My Squadron Sergeant Major, Kelleher, was a tough, determined and hard-drinking man, whose loyalty to me and C Squadron was absolute, but who could turn nasty if thwarted. The Regiment was equipped with Centurion tanks, new to me so that I had rapidly to familiarize myself with its intricacies.

In the summer of 1953 my squadron was tasked with assisting a Territorial Army brigade with its gunnery training of the year, and this resulted in our taking charge of three Yeomanry Regiments' worth of tanks and preparing them for the yeomen's use. The brigade contained, amongst others, that celebrated bunch of madcaps known as the Cheshire Yeomanry, who got up to every trick in the game and thoroughly enlivened affairs at Lulworth Camp where one of the ranges for tank gunnery was positioned.

C Squadron HQ was at Park Camp, an agreeable spot requisitioned from the local landowner and Lord Lieutenant of Dorset, Joseph Weld, who was the kindest and most tolerant host we could have wished for. Before long I was to serve under the direction of his cousin, Colonel Humphrey Weld of The Queen's Bays, who became a very dear friend. We enjoyed great days both in the United States and later in Dorset, where Humphrey's estate at Chideock Manor lay, and by whose kindness I was able to hunt with the Seavington and shoot the Chideock pheasants. We all greatly enjoyed our summer at Lulworth. Tony Harrison took a house there for his family; David Vetch pursued with success a fox-hunting heiress; Gordon Strachan, another of my troop leaders, showed how fast and inaccurately he could hurl balls down on the cricket field; the bathing in Lulworth Cove was a delight; and the Yeomanry Brigade expressed their satisfaction at our care for them. The Cheshire Yeomanry burnt down only one wooden building, so we felt that we had escaped lightly.

There is something very special about command of a squadron – or, for that matter, a company or battery. It is probably the last time that you really know *all* the men under your command, and to be far removed from Regimental HQ gives a further stimulant to your notion that you are monarch of all you survey. But our summer of independence came to an end; we returned to Tidworth; and soon afterwards received our orders for the 4th Hussars to move to Hohne, a military garrison on the Lüneburger Heide, to join 7 Armoured Brigade. It was, as I recall, during the last month of 1953. I was put in charge of the train party, that is the bulk of the Regiment, and I remember well our march from Assaye Barracks in Tidworth to the entraining point at Ludgershall with myself at the head of the Regiment. I remember too being greeted at the railhead near Hohne by the Brigade Commander, Ralph Younger, originally 7th Hussars, but recently commanding The Greys, and his Brigade Major, Hew Butler, Rifle Brigade. We were all wearing greatcoats in view of the winter weather greatly to the approval of Ralph Younger, who, I later heard, commented to Hew: 'Did you see how smart their greatcoats were?' We had clearly got off to a good start. Such are the idiosyncrasies of senior cavalrymen!

And so the old routine of life in Rhine Army started all over again, but this time at the level of commanding C Squadron, rather than an entire brigade. Training at all levels was the order of the day, and once more we familiarized ourselves with Soltau Training Area, over which we had so frequently manoeuvred before. Gunnery plays a large part, and I was delighted to renew my acquaintance with a sergeant of The Greys, who had been my instructor in those far off days at Abassia in 1943 when we were getting to know the Sherman Tank. Now we had the Centurion and a fine piece of kit it was, probably the best tank that the British had yet produced. Reliable, fast, with an excellent gun, and a high reverse gear, which might be put into useful service if the Red Army did decide to cry havoc and let slip the dogs of war. As usual there was a grand Army manoeuvre in the autumn, called *Battle Royal*. We all got very tired after days and nights without sleep, and the most memorable incident was the one when Loopy Kennard, commanding A Squadron, decided to have a kip at a vital moment in the 4th Hussars' role in the exercise, was then kicked awake by Stephen Eve, still commanding the Regiment only to be told by Loopy to 'remove himself'.

But as usual we found plenty of amusement and enjoyment. Our splendid Officers' Mess, Bredebeck, was a haven of comfort, with stabling for all our horses, and an indoor riding school. It was there that we celebrated the 100th anniversary of the Charge of the Light Brigade, described earlier. From there we went off to the numerous horse shows and hunter trials; the shooting parties departed for excellent sport amongst the duck and geese; evenings in the Mess itself were enlivened by playing bridge, backgammon and piquet – skill and luck at cards was a most agreeable way of reducing one's mess bill at the expense of others. Stephen Eve again appointed me as President of the Mess Committee. We gave and went to cocktail parties and regimental balls. And I continued to find that command of C Squadron was immensely satisfying. It was all an admirable coalition of working hard to achieve military efficiency combined with high morale and relaxation in the sporting and social world of Rhine Army. One inspired idea of the C.-in-C. was that during the colder months of January, February and March, we should spend 'Three Nights Out' in the countryside. We did so, but my squadron somehow or other found a congenial *Gasthaus* to pass some of the time, and to indulge in an impromptu 'Smoker' during which those who fancied themselves as entertainers were able to display their wares. As squadron leader I was, of course, given no choice, but absolutely obliged to perform.

My second in command at this time was John Paley, of whom I have spoken already. He had joined C Squadron in 1943, having transferred from Skinner's Horse. He became my closest friend. He was a born soldier, knew more about the British Army than anyone else, was bold and thrusting in action, full of mischief as far as pulling generals' legs was concerned, and a man of total loyalty. We would enjoy long hacks together when off duty. When on duty he was a model of what second in command should be – a rock of support, full of ideas for improving our tactical and field craft skills, administratively sound and always ready to throw a lighter note on whatever problem we were struggling with.

During this time I was able to visit the von Schellersheim family. Wilfried and I would dine and dance at the various officers' clubs, which had been established at Hanover, Bückeburg and Bad Oeynhausen. Loopy had kindly lent me his oldish, but stylish, Bentley for one of my weekends at Rittergut Eisbergen, and after an excellent dinner at the 21 Club, we were making our way back to the house when an ominous jarring revealed a flat tyre. There was no spare, but we limped home and next morning the Baron took charge, made a brief telephone call and the local garage man – it was Easter Sunday morning – was instructed to put it all to rights. He did so and I was able to make my way back to Hohne without further mishap.

There was one final manoeuvre after *Battle Royal*, and it was on this occasion, when wrestling with a sodden breakfast, that Hugh Marrack, as mentioned earlier, gave me the option of posting off to Kentucky to become the British Liaison Officer, Fort Knox. And it is to Kentucky that we will now go.

Chapter 10

Blue Grass Country

> 'I don't care what you call me or the race, but the hat is a bowler.'
>
> The Earl of Derby

I spent two years at Fort Knox which, apart from the gold, was the United States Army's Armored Center, the equivalent of our own RAC establishment at Lulworth and Bovington. The task of the British Liaison Officer there was to report on American developments in armoured warfare, both as far as equipment and tactical doctrine were concerned, and also to observe manoeuvres. My introduction to it all was made easy by my predecessor, Peter Sutton, like myself a bachelor. I took over his so-called Bachelor Officer Quarter; he assisted me in buying a car, introduced me to the people I would have to work with and, above all, took me to Oxmoor, the home of the Bullitt family, where I met Tommy Bullitt. He became a great friend and it was through his kindness and overwhelming hospitality that my time in America was so enjoyable. Peter Sutton had greatly endeared himself to his American colleagues' families by his skill as a conjuror. And when they learned that I could boast no such accomplishment, they felt badly let down.

One of the problems for a bachelor like myself, living on an American military post, is that there is no Officers' Mess, as we understand it. There are clubs, where you may feed and small cookhouses designed to serve those living in the BOQs, but none of the agreeable companionship, comfort, good food and close friendships, to say nothing of the ceremony, formality, style and social well-being of a British regimental mess. I made little use of the BOQ cookhouses, but sustained myself when not lunching or dining with friends at the various Officers' Clubs.

The British Liaison Officers at US Army posts throughout the country reported to the British Joint Services Mission in Washington, headed by my former Divisional Commander, Errol Prior-Palmer, who being the man he was and married to a sister of the Earl of Linlithgow, went down well with both the US bigwigs in Washington and also at the military establishments he would frequently visit. My own immediate master was Colonel Humphrey Weld MC, The Queen's Bays, who had commanded his Regiment and whom I had met during our Venezia Giulia days. He came to see me at Fort Knox once I had settled down. I found him a kindred spirit. A proper cavalryman with a love of horses, of music, history, literature, field sports, Dorset, where his family estate lay, and of good living. We became close friends.

In Kentucky, of course, the horse was paramount. The Blue Grass country of Lexington with its innumerable stud farms which boasted beautiful stabling, huge paddocks with immaculate post and rail fencing, owners and breeders for whom the prize of winning the Kentucky Derby was the ultimate goal. I was lucky enough to attend this famous race twice, thanks to the generosity of Tommy Bullitt. On the second occasion we were accompanied by Errol Prior-Palmer and his wife Doreen, better known as Bunty. We were all staying at Oxmoor for this event, and our time there included a hack round the extensive Oxmoor estate. There were many gates to be opened and closed during this prolonged hack, and as the junior member present, I was obliged to dismount and remount at every gate – they could not be unlatched from the saddle. All quite fair, of course, except for the inclination of my companions to get moving while I was about to remount.

Then there was the hunting. Friends of the Bullitts lent me horses to follow one of Kentucky's pack of foxhounds, and we had one or two notable runs, although the fences between fields were disappointing – mere triangular shaped chicken coops which required little more than a lengthening of stride to clear. One dramatic incident stays in my memory. Hacking alongside the Master who was taking his hounds to a hitherto undrawn covert, we were suddenly confronted by a clearly furious farmer, who was wielding an ugly looking shotgun. The Master drew up, his hounds obediently clustered round him. The farmer then spoke. 'If you bring those dogs onto my land, I will shoot you and them.' I have always admired the Master's sangfroid when thus challenged. Without hesitation or the least sign of displeasure, he blandly replied: 'In that case, I'll take them somewhere else.' The lesson must have sunk home, for a year or two later, when I found myself Master of the Staff College Drag Hounds, I always made a point of ensuring the goodwill of farmers and landowners before taking my hounds anywhere near them.

There were also some horses at Fort Knox itself, and one of my American colleagues introduced me to the stables there. I had several hacks with him and it was quickly apparent that the Kentucky horses were not familiar with what one might call English aids. They seemed to prefer a very loose rein and one pace only – the canter. I persisted, however, and managed to make them walk-march and trot. One of my early morning hacks – the plan was to have breakfast with the dark-eyed southern belle, whom we met earlier – went badly awry. Having reached her house, I dismounted and tied the reins to a suitable post in the style we have so often observed Gary Cooper and John Wayne to perform on the screen. I settled down to a breakfast of eggs easy over and ham, washed down with some excellent, strong coffee, – no doubt a daily necessity for my female friend with her over indulgence in dry martinis and bourbon whiskey. The meal over, I returned to the post where my gallant steed should have awaited me. Not a sign of the animal. It was clear that he had got tired of waiting, wanted his own breakfast, had wrenched himself free of the post and returned, no doubt at a more than leisurely canter, to his loose box. My southern belle kindly got her car out, drove me to the stables where I discovered that a posse had been dispatched to find me, presumably thought to be lying helpless on some track, grievously hurt and in need of rescue. The Fort Knox Riding Club manager was unamused at my explanation and made it plain that I was not to try such tricks again, if I wished to avail myself further of his precious animals. I was all contrition.

A relatively minor affair, not to be compared with a later transgression which cast a long shadow on my reputation as a clean-living, honourable British cavalry officer. It has long been a cliché that the British and Americans are two nations divided by a common language, and it was this incident which brought home to me the absolute veracity of this sentiment. The place? The residence of a pretty senior Kentucky matriarch, a friend of the Bullitt family, owner of a string of race horses and one whose approval was more than desirable. The occasion? A somewhat formal dinner party.

I was sitting two away from my hostess, the matriarch, and opposite a man whom I knew to be equally interested in equestrian sports. On my left was a forbidding-looking female, the wife of the man opposite, and on my right an entirely different proposition, who afforded me some difficulty in concentrating on the food set before me. The meal was almost over when the fellow opposite began to talk about riding to me. As he was enormously fat and clearly out of condition, I could not resist asking him a question. As I spoke there occurred that momentary conversational pause which lent to my remark the characteristics of a clarion call.

'Tell me, Sir,' I said, 'When were you last in the saddle?'

The momentary pause became a dramatic and for me inexplicable silence. The fellow opposite turned puce, his wife fidgeted in a most disconcerting way, and the bombshell on my right appeared to await his reply with interest, but not much confidence. My hostess looked like thunder.

At this point I must make clear something that was later explained to me, and which may already have become clear. In the particular community where I was dining, the expression 'In the Saddle' referred quite uncompromisingly to a sport conducted, as it were, with a two-legged rather than a four-legged mare. But at the time of the dinner I did not, of course, know this. Before the fellow opposite could answer, however, my hostess had taken the reins into her firm, capable hands.

'Perhaps you would like to tell us, Colonel,' she said with a slight edge to her voice, 'when you were last in the saddle.'

I looked round the table. Everyone was mentally on tiptoe, awaiting a reply. Either Southern courtesy or real interest, I thought to myself, gratifying in either case.

'Well, as a matter of fact,' I answered, 'this afternoon, but unfortunately the old girl threw me.' I was referring, of course, to a normally well-mannered chestnut mare.

'Threw you!' repeated my hostess in a shocked but fascinated voice.

By this time the female on my left hand had edged away from me slightly, while the bombshell on my right was gazing at me with renewed respect. The interest of the table had clearly reached fever pitch, and my explanation of being thrown was awaited with the utmost eagerness. Did some suspicion of peril enter my mind? Did the electric silence of the table flash a warning to me of misfortune's approach? Perhaps, for I hesitated momentarily, then rushed forward to my doom.

'Yes,' I said, 'as I cast my leg over her, she turned her head and bit me and... .'

But the rest of my explanation was lost. My hostess had risen and, in a voice of ice which cut through the confused exclamations and ill-suppressed laughter, declared:

'Ladies, we will withdraw. I can see that the Colonel imagines himself to be in his Club in London.'

It is hardly necessary to add that I was never again a guest for dinner at that particular house.

Horses were not the only four-legged friends I had in Kentucky. After I had been at Fort Knox for about six months, a senior American Colonel asked me if I would be good enough to look after his official residence and his dog, Peter, an Alsatian, for the two months that he and his family would be away. As the Colonel's house was in the Fort's exclusive 5th Avenue and as I was assured by him that Peter was well-disciplined, gentle with children, good in traffic and with only one fault – traditional it seemed in America – a marked aversion to the mail-man, I was happy to accept the role of house and dog sitter. Peter and I got on well from the start, and all seemed set fair for an agreeable relationship. When sorrows come, however, as Claudius has reminded us, they come not as single spies, but in battalions, and there were, I fear, three occasions when my command of the situation left much to be desired.

First came the question of giving Peter enough exercise. Walking is not a great feature of American life, and there was far too much vehicle activity on the post for pleasant dog walks, so I hit on the idea of Peter's accompanying me for a hack on one of the Fort Knox horses. In England most dogs enjoyed nothing more than jogging along at heel while their masters exercised their hunters. Alas, I miscalculated. On arrival at the stables, Peter got out of the car and seemed at first to view the horses with favour – until, that is, I went to mount mine. Whether it was some sort of disaffection for my paying attention to another animal, I cannot say, but as I put my left foot in the nearside stirrup, Peter leaped at the poor creature from behind and seized its tail. There followed an absurd fracas. My steed revolved, kicking furiously, taking with it the cowboy-groom, who was still holding his head, while I, having grabbed a besom, ran round, vainly trying to get behind the horse in order to swipe Peter away, and Peter himself, barking away, tried to keep pace with the horse's gyrations and jumped up and down at his tail. At length my horse managed to connect his off-hind with Peter's rear, which sobered him sufficiently for me to sweep him back to the car and imprison him there. My somewhat delayed hack therefore took place without Peter, and I was obliged to exercise him on foot along the trails where I had hoped he would lope obediently behind a mounted British Liaison Officer.

Round Two of the battle for supremacy between Peter and me was played out on the large central grass square which was positioned between the quarters of the Fort Knox general officers and other senior men. The house I was looking after was one of them, so that we had a very good view of this green expanse, on which some of the golfing generals liked to practise their approach shots. In the American Army everyone plays golf. At Fort Knox there were two courses, on one of which much of my time was spent with my fellow liaison officers from the Canadian Army and the US Marine Corps. One evening while reading in the drawing room of my 5th Avenue house, I was startled to see Peter, who had been sitting quietly with me, dart through the open window, tail going furiously and crouch on the grass some fifty yards in front and slightly to the flank of the Commanding General, the keenest of players who, equipped with some golf balls and an iron club, had emerged from his house and was about to enjoy half an hour away from his military responsibilities. He cast a look of irritation at the lurking Peter, whose tongue was hanging out in anticipation of the game, but proceeded to drop the golf balls on to the turf and squared up to the first one. At once, Peter, a picture of alertness, tensed and half rose on his haunches. The shot was played, Peter raced after it and carried it off to the furthest corner of the field, chewing hard. Well, I thought, the general can now hit the other balls without interruption. Not at all! Peter came roving back, eager to continue the game. The general saw two more of his golf balls retrieved and removed, and then gave up in disgust. I waited until dusk had fallen and then – for golf balls are expensive in America – with Peter's aid recovered his prizes. There were some teeth marks on them, but they would do for me. The second round had indubitably gone to Peter.

The third incident was the repetition of an old, old story. I have never really understood why dogs should take such an exception to postmen. Is it because they are never asked into the house for a drink? Or is it that as your faithful friend gazes up at you while you sort the letters, he sees your face darken as you encounter a sheaf of bills, and so marks down the deliverer of them as an enemy? I had been warned of Peter's dislikes, and had taken measures to ensure that when the Fort Knox mailman was due, Peter was secure in the drawing room with doors and windows closed. Even so he would sit on a chair and look out of the window at the mailman as he walked up to the front door. He would wear a wistful expression, as if to say, one day, they'll forget to lock me in. Sure enough, one day when I was escorting Major General Foote VC – the very man for whose entertainment I had invited my three Kentuckian *bonnes amies* to an evening party – it happened. I had left Peter in the care of the cleaning woman, who had clearly been careless in respect of doors and windows. During my tour with General Foote, the military police came to tell me that the mailman was in hospital and Peter with the veterinary officer. Later I heard about it. As the mailman, blithely whistling, trod towards the door, a thunderbolt shot from behind it, and, getting the poor fellow down, proceeded to try to extract from him that debt which Shylock so cunningly and unsuccessfully had planned should be forfeited by Antonio. I visited Peter in his vet's quarters. We exchanged reproachful looks. Soon after his owners returned. I wondered whether Peter should not have been in kennels instead of with me. But think of all the fun we would have missed.

Leaving all the four legged friends aside, it was, of course, the people of Kentucky who made my time there so agreeable. Tommy Bullitt's kindness enabled me to meet many of his friends who lived near Louisville. One of the problems I had was that of reciprocating their endless hospitality. I was, however, able to give small dinner parties at the Pendennis Club – my membership again thanks to Tommy – and I also found a delightful country hostelry, the Doe Run Inn, not far from Fort Knox, where I could entertain both military and Louisville friends. Shortly before Humphrey Weld departed from Washington, the two of us gave a huge dinner party there. It was well received.

I was delighted to learn half way through my time at Fort Knox that my brother, Peter, philosophy don at Oxford, was to teach at Duke University, North Carolina, for one semester. We therefore arranged a meeting, toured Virginia together, and he came to stay at Fort Knox for a week or so. Once again my Louisville friends rallied round, as they always did when Humphrey Weld came to visit me. I shall long remember two particular couples – Jack and Mena Doyle, he square and squat, she a bean pole, both full of fun and laughter. Also Floyd and Olivia Smith, he addicted to what he called hunting – shooting and fishing to us – and addicted too, I fear, to Old Crow bourbon whisky; she brimming over with good nature and a dedicated giver of parties. The sheer thoughtfulness of my American friends took some beating. On hearing, for example, that Humphrey and I had to observe some military manoeuvre in Louisiana, Olivia instantly rang up some friends of hers in New Orleans to arrange that we should be looked after by them when off duty. When somewhat tentatively I telephoned these unknown New Orleans people, they instantly responded and our leisure hours were filled with activity. This extraordinary concern for one's welfare extended even to my final days in America, when, with a few days to spare in New York, before on embarking on the *Queen Mary*, I was looked after by friends of one of my Fort Knox colleagues. The looking-after included a visit to the theatre on Broadway, where Rex Harrison and Julie Andrews were performing in *My Fair Lady* before it came to London. They even provided me with two copies of the record.

When Humphrey Weld returned to England, he was succeeded by Peter Arkwright, 11th Hussars, who had commanded the Regiment, and while doing so made it clear to all that instead of the original 'Prince Albert's Own' title, it was now 'Peter Arkwright's Own'. We went together to Mexico, where we were admirably cared for by our Military Attaché and his wife. They took us to a bull fight. I did not care for the sport and never went to another. Soon came the time for my own departure. My successor was Robin Chater, who was married, so my first task was to find a good house for him and his wife.

I was fortunate. About a month before the Chaters were to arrive, a married quarter for a Lieutenant Colonel in a pleasant Fort Knox avenue became available. I grabbed it, arranged for its furnishing, and with the help of the Canadian Liaison Officer's wife planned for suitable provisions of victuals and, even more important, adequate supplies of the hard stuff, so that on their setting foot in their future home, there would be no immediate need for foraging. Robin Chater and his wife were delighted with the arrangements I had made, and were even more appreciative of my introducing them to the Bullitts and my other Louisville friends. Although not addicted to fox-hunting, the Chaters were enthusiastic beaglers, and were quickly embraced by the beagling community of Kentucky. My principal task done, I was able to throw one final cocktail party for the many friends I had made, handing over the Chaters to their care and make my plans for returning to England, taking with me the Plymouth automobile, which, because I had now owned it for two years, would be importable without tax. There was, however, one snag.

During my last few months at Fort Knox the horizon had been clouded by the Suez adventure of October and November 1956. My American military colleagues were most unsympathetic and I came in for some harsh criticism of HMG's foreign policy. I could but counter it by pointing out that it was not the military men in Whitehall who had sponsored so ludicrous an attempt to revive Imperial illusions, but the men of politics. Indeed it became clear that Mountbatten himself was strongly opposed to the idea, and

Templer, then Chief of General Staff, had shown up the barrenness of the plan by putting the case thus: 'We can take Cairo all right. But what do we do then?' It all ended in tears, of course – British withdrawal, Eden's resignation, Eisenhower's displeasure, our name in the Middle East as low as could be.

There was a further setback for me. Petrol rationing in England at the very moment that I set foot in the country accompanied by a large, petrol-hungry American car. Undaunted I set sail for Latimer for a short course in joint service matters, before rejoining my Regiment at Hohne, now commanded by that legendary cavalryman, Loopy Kennard.

Chapter 11

Farewell to the 4th Hussars

'Field-Marshal Templer announced the amalgamation of the 4th Hussars and the 8th Hussars.'

Autobiography of George Kennard

Six months at Latimer's Joint Services Staff College passed agreeably enough. There was not much work to do and some very pleasant people to do it with. I remember particularly Douglas MacCallan of The Bays; Roly Gibbs, 60th Rifles; Bill Cheyne, a Highlander, who greatly distinguished himself in command of a brigade in Borneo years later, was destined for great things until struck down by a debilitating disease; Rowley Mans, the Owls' cricketer who had played the Owl's part in the Staff College pantomime and Patrick Pollock, Irish Guards, elegant, urbane with an ever-ready good natured quip on his lips. And, of course, there were all the naval and RAF officers with whom we worked to learn something of their activities and to impart to them something of ours. The Directing Staff were composed of competent and likeable members of all three services, led by the Commandant, Major General NAP White – inevitably saddled with the nickname – Napoleon – who had one habit which has stuck in my memory. At the end of each lecture by some distinguished fellow – the standard was high and would include such men as Duncan Sandys, Mountbatten and General Horrocks – Napoleon White would try to extract some gem of wisdom from what had gone before, earnestly tell us what it was, and end by saying: 'And I'll leave that thought with you.' As he spoke these words his eyes would rise to the ceiling of the lecture hall as if to glean some inspiration from the heavens to bless the profound gift of knowledge that he had just bestowed upon us.

One of my fellow students was Commander John Templeton-Cotill RN, whom I introduced earlier. He was – and indeed still is – a man of exceptional quality. Clever, witty, well-read, personable, as fluent with the spoken as with the written word, with a taste for the upper set, a fine appreciation of the arts, a keen country sportsman and, as far as I could tell, professionally able. We became friends and remained so for the rest of our lives. He lives in France and we exchange letters regularly. His are colourful, witty and amusing.

My former master in the United States, Colonel Humphrey Weld, had retired to his estate in Dorset, and was now, amongst other things, Joint Master of the Seavington Hunt. Early in 1957 he wrote and invited me to Chideock for a day's hunting. The problem was petrol, now severely rationed, but the good nature of my fellow students came to the rescue for they provided me with sufficient coupons to get my large American car to Dorset and back. We had a splendid day. It was a dawn meet at Chideock Manor, bright, but not too cold, and after the stirrup cups had been consumed by the mounted and dismounted supporters, off we went, resplendent in our scarlet coats, in the wake of the huntsman, Jack Dark, and his hounds. There was quite a good field, some forty men and women mounted, and a few followers in Land Rovers. We found in the first covert drawn and had a fine run of some twenty minutes with some goodish hedgerows and post-and-rail fences to negotiate, but Monsieur Renard evaded us somehow. There was then some hanging about while Jack Dark vainly tried another covert and then, advised by two stalwart members of the Seavington – John Cole-Fox and his sister, Bridget, took his hounds off to some gorse on the Cole-Fox land. Another find and another exhilarating run, but again no kill. It was now getting dusk and Humphrey decided to call a halt to proceedings. We hacked back to the kennels and on to Chideock. Among the guests staying at Chideock Manor was a 9th Lancer and his wife, who had not long before given birth to a bouncing boy. I was much impressed when as we all arrived back at the Chideock stables, she said to him: 'You go and deal with the boy. *I* will look after the horses.' There seemed little doubt as to which category she regarded as the more important.

During the last week of the JSSC course there were presentations by the students of what they had thought of it all, not unlike the Staff College pantomimes. Called upon to think of something suitable, I penned a short play for my own group, entitled 'Leave it with Jeeves'. The players assembled in Bertie Wooster's flat to discuss strategic matters. Present were a Royal Naval Commander – Douglas MacCallen aping John Templeton-Cotill, a Wing Commander RAF, Captain Bertram Wooster, played by Patrick Pollock and, of course, the mastermind, Jeeves, played by myself. Into this discussion bursts General Sir Napoleon Bumble, intent on discovering and then punishing which of these young officers has been attempting to seduce his daughter, Daffodil – gallantly played by another naval member. He fails to do so, but becomes heavily immersed in the strategic dilemma posed by nuclear weapons. All is resolved by Jeeves, who produces a masterly appreciation of the situation – needless to say all the best lines and epigrams are spoken by Jeeves himself – and the play ended with me, now equipped with a silver salver on which rested a well-mixed dry martini, descending from the stage to present this offering to the Commandant, Major General Napoleon White, with the words: 'And I'll leave that, Sir, if I may, with you.' Thunderous applause!

Next stop – the 4th Hussars, still stationed at Hohne with a somewhat different Loopy Kennard in charge. During former Commanding Officer's regimes Loopy had been the first to challenge orders from above and to pursue his own line. Now that he was commanding himself, a more sober and responsible figure emerged. Not that he had lost any tendency to flout instructions from on high, but that which happened within the Regiment was of infinite import. It was as well that he had assumed this new way of looking at things, for there would shortly be far-reaching and grave matters to be confronted.

To rejoin the Regiment after two years' absence is, of course, a great thing. It is homecoming of a different sort. Here are the officers and men you have soldiered with, campaigned with, ridden horses with, trained with, laughed with, played backgammon with. Here are those you have led in action, been commanded by, have competed against in point-to-points, partnered at the bridge table, on the tennis court and in the pairs event of a hunter trials. As I drove up to Bredebeck, our splendid Officers' Mess at Hohne, I was greeted by a young officer unknown to me [he had joined the Regiment while I was at Fort Knox]. His name was Rodney Martin, and he was as fine a young cavalryman as you could find anywhere. Full of energy, brimming with laughter, keen as mustard and lion-hearted, he was a most valuable addition to the 4th Hussars' regular content [it should be remembered that at this time, 1957, national service was still in full flow and many of the young officers we received served for two years only]. Rodney showed me to my rooms in the Mess – as the senior bachelor then with the Regiment it was axiomatic that these were the best ones – and while my old soldier-servant, Murray, dealt with my kit, I drove to the barracks to report to the Commanding Officer, Loopy Kennard. It was decided that as I had already twice commanded squadrons, there was little point in my doing so again – better give the experience to those who had not – but that I should oversee training matters, keep an eye on messing arrangements for the men, assist with administration generally and – once more – become President of the Mess Committee. This settled, I looked in to see Francis Romney, the second in command, who was now passionately dedicated to show jumping – the blackboard in his office was covered with potential courses – who told me of the plans he had for a forthcoming 4th Hussars Horse Show to be staged in the park at Bredebeck. He was concerned about the problem of changing the heights of fences between one class and another to ensure that it would be done both quickly and accurately. I made a suggestion which he welcomed and we will attend this Horse Show later.

In order to be effective, training must both be imaginative and enjoyable. I recalled that the former Cavalry Training pamphlet had made much of so-called Sword and Lance competitions, which, simply put, required a mounted soldier to ride down a prepared course which contained both obstacles and targets, which had to be surmounted and engaged within a certain time. Bringing this all up to date, it seemed to me that an amusing and competitive exercise could be organized whereby a number of young officers, each mounted in a Land Rover or scout car, would be invited to map read the way round a course of minor roads and tracks, with a series of halts at which the competitor would be subjected to some military test. It might be a map-reading question, a judgement of distance, repair of a faulty vehicle, a tactical conundrum, an historical reference to be identified and so on. The competitors would start and finish at Bredebeck, where the first and last stands would be – respectively to persuade one of our more tricky animals to clear two fences in the riding school and to engage two clays released from the roof of the Mess with a shotgun loaded with two cartridges. The mileage of each competing vehicle would be measured and extra marks would be given for the lowest recorded. At each stand would be an officer who would mark up each competitor's efforts, and at the end of it all, each competitor would be asked a question to test his observation of the countryside over which he had travelled. Colonel Loopy thoroughly approved of such things, and the first time we tried it, all went swimmingly. Of course, those who were competent horsemen and good shots had an edge, and it was no surprise to me that the winner turned out to be Rodney Martin, who celebrated his victory by ordering champagne for all and throwing his fox terrier, Drum, into the air to be caught again in his master's arms.

There were, before long, serious things afoot. The Duncan Sandys White Paper of 1957 presaged an end to national service, a reduction in the British Army's strength and a number of regimental amalgamations. Among these was to be that of the 4th and 8th Hussars. Loopy at once sent a signal to the 8th Hussars, stationed nearby at Lüneburg, commiserating with them that they were to be amalgamated, but at the same time congratulating them on their good fortune that they were to join us. He did much more. As there would inevitably be redundancies, particularly in senior ranks of the Sergeants' Messes, Loopy wrote a letter to *The Times* inviting prospective employers to apply to him in offering positions to 'men to whom pride of service and loyalty mean more than higher pay and shorter working hours'. The response was most gratifying. Furthermore a joint 4th/8th Hussar committee was established to plan the whole process of amalgamation.

Before tackling the issue of amalgamation, however, I will say a word about two missions on which Colonel Loopy dispatched me, which both broadened my outlook and tested my versatility.

The first of these was a few weeks' attachment to 7th Armoured Divisional Headquarters at Verden in order to assist and advise the Divisional Commander, no less a figure than that renowned soldier, Shan Hackett, who stood head and shoulders above all his contemporaries for sheer intellect, leadership, fluency with pen and voice – in many languages – range of accomplishments and what Dr Johnson would have classified as clubbability, in planning and conducting a forthcoming field exercise. My work here involved first reconnoitring the ground over which this manoeuvre would be staged, second to study the terms of reference given to Shan Hackett, and third to suggest how he should deploy his division in such a way as to ensure that the other side got the worst of it. In order to balance this advice and to ensure that it was logistically feasible, a most likeable and laughter-loving sapper, Eric O'Callaghan, was also posted in to work with me. We produced a plan – the essence of it was that given the preponderance of the mythical exercise enemy [the Soviet Union] there would have to be an initial fighting withdrawal, followed by a deadly counter-stroke at the very moment of dispersion and logistic weakness brought about by the enemy's broad front assault. I gave it a name – the Recoil Battle, to be likened to a powerful spring which, at first, yields to intolerable pressure and at the critical moment with all the power induced by compression strikes back with irresistible force. This concept went down well with Shan and his staff, and I was released back to the Regiment.

But I was to have many more dealings with Shan Hackett, one of which followed hard upon the Recoil Battle. One of his pet subjects was that of fostering good relations between the British Army and the German people. Fluent in German himself, he encouraged his subordinates to learn the language and when he heard that the *Bundeswehr*, the newly raised German Armed Forces, had established a new leadership school and had invited the participation of officers from the British, French, Belgian and American armies, he pounced and instructed Loopy Kennard to nominate a German speaking officer to attend the forthcoming course. As my somewhat varied duties did not necessitate my constant presence and knowing that I spoke German, the short straw was mine, and I duly reported to the *Bundeswehr*'s *Schule für Innere Führung* in Koblenz, which was in the former French Zone of occupied Germany. It was an interesting experience to be a student surrounded by German officers of all three services, many of them sporting gallantry decorations won in battles against the countries of those Allied officers now attending the course.

I cannot say that I greatly enjoyed it. My command of German was adequate for casual chat and social gatherings, but was severely tested when it came to following the philosophical meanderings of academics mustered from various universities. The expression '*Innere Führung*' – literally inner leadership – was designed as a counter to the former harsh, fanatical, inexorable command methods of the Third Reich, and to foster a new concept of command, amenable to a now democratic regime, and based upon an inner conviction that activities resulting from the new sort of leadership now in vogue were right and proper. The German Army had always had a political dimension – think of General von Seeckt's definition of it as 'a state within the state' – and it was clearly one of the aims of this course to clarify the non-political nature of the new *Bundeswehr*.

There was one aspect of the school at Koblenz that found little favour with me – the standard of messing. I found I could not face the evening meal, but happily – and here it was France I had to thank – the French Club in Koblenz was still going strong, and night after night, my Belgian colleague and I would drive into town and sit down to a well-cooked dinner, washed down with some decent wine. Conscious of the need to write a report about all this when the course ended, I made the necessary jottings, including a recommendation that should it become customary to send more British officers on future courses at the school, they should be properly prepared by polishing their mastery of the German language. One of the customs which the new democratic regime had not eliminated among my German fellow students was that of clicking heels when saluting, and I must confess that I very nearly fell into the habit of doing it myself. One further surprise awaited me. Having returned to the Regiment and written my report, which went both to Brigade and Divisional Headquarters, as well as Loopy himself, I found that General Shan had forwarded it to the C.-in-C. British Army of the Rhine, now General Sir Dudley Ward, who had been the Staff College Commandant in my student days. He demanded that I report to him personally to tell him more about it, and on doing so I only just restrained myself from clicking heels as I entered his office and saluted.

Back at Hohne I became immersed in assisting with the plans for the 4th Hussars to amalgamate with the 8th Hussars. The most important thing about it concerned, of course, the people. Joining two regiments would mean that only half their combined numbers would be required to man the new regiment. Who was to go, who to stay? There would be some volunteering, officers, NCOs and men, with appropriate compensation, but there would also be some compulsory redundancies. All this had to be carefully considered and resolved. Then there was the question – who was to command? And to command what? What was to be the new regiment's official title? My own suggestion here was rejected.

The 4th were Queen's Own Hussars; the 8th were King's Royal Irish Hussars. The Queen was now on the throne; the Irish connection was desirable for both traditional and recruiting reasons. It was also important, in my view, that the origins of the new regiment should be instantly recognizable by its title. Hence my suggestions: The 4th/8th Hussars (Queen's Royal Irish). To my dismay there was irrevocable opposition to this proposal from the 8th Hussar representatives of the amalgamation committee, who pointed out that there would be a tendency to drop the 8th part of the title, so that the regiment would simply be known as the 4th. I countered this by reminding the committee that no such dangers had been encountered by the 4th/7th Dragoon Guards, the 13th/18th Hussars, the 16th/5th and 17th/21st Lancers. But I was overruled and the final title was settled as The Queen's Royal Irish Hussars with no numbers at all. For some years afterwards when asked the name of my regiment and I replied, a puzzled look would follow and it was not until I elaborated and explained that our regiment was the result of the 4th and 8th Hussars joining together that my audience was enlightened. Other matters, such as dress [there was no disagreement about hanging on to the 8th Hussars' striking tent cap or Green Suit for informal dining apparel], badges, mottoes, accoutrements presented no difficulties. Compromise guided the plot. The cap and collar badge, which incorporated the 4th Hussar garter and motto, together with the 8th Hussar harp in the hands of a female, did, however, evoke from our Colonel-in-Chief, Prince Philip, the query as to why the female concerned was fashioned to resemble the Duke of Wellington with udders.

As all these preparations for amalgamation proceeded, Loopy Kennard did a most generous thing. It had been agreed that George Butler, an 8th Hussar, formerly of Guides Cavalry, with whom he won a DSO and MC, was to be the first Commanding Officer of The Queen's Royal Irish Hussars. He already knew the officers and men of the 8th Hussars but not, of course, those of the 4th. Loopy therefore relinquished his right to remain in command of the 4th Hussars until the last moment so that George Butler could command the 4th for eight months before amalgamation and so get to know the officers, NCOs and men of the 4th Hussars, particularly those who would be helping to form the new regiment. Whilst sad to see Loopy go – he had been an inspiring, dedicated and loveable Colonel with that priceless gift of persuading the young to try their hand at every sort of sporting and adventurous activity, and setting an example of leadership which many might aspire to but few attain – we all saw the point of it and counted ourselves lucky that George Butler was a true cavalryman – shrewd, able, brave, authoritative, a great horseman, with a sparkling sense of humour and a way with all ranks. We could not have had a finer man to weld the two parts together and to give the new regiment a character and charisma all its own.

It was not until after George Butler had taken over that the grand 4th Hussar Horse Show, referred to earlier and which Francis Romney had been so meticulously planning, took place. The park at Bredebeck was ideal for what Francis had in mind. It was not to be a trial of what we now refer to as eventing, but purely show jumping with three classes – novice, intermediate and open. The ring itself was spacious enough for – if my memory does not fail me – some sixteen fences, and outside the ring plenty of room for spectators, gathering paddock, judges' box, and fence repairers and adjustors. Away on the other side of the drive up to Bredebeck itself was a large area for horse boxes, grooms, veterinary officers, watering troughs, spectators' cars, refreshment tents and so on.

At this point I must introduce a 4th Hussar I should have featured earlier – our Quartermaster, Major Ronnie Pitt. He had been appointed QM during the desert battles in the early 1940s and had won golden opinions from all who knew him. A pre-war regular soldier, he was intelligent, articulate, fiercely proud of his regiment, industrious, imaginative, equally at home with the newest joined trooper or the Corps Commander, his administrative skills constantly tested and never found wanting, Ronnie Pitt was what my friend in the 4th/7th Dragoon Guards, Ian Gill, would have called 'straight gold'. It was, of course, on his shoulders that all the necessary arrangements for ensuring that no item of kit, whether a curry-comb or a giant marquee, required for the perfection of Francis Romney's affair would be found wanting, fell. He did not disappoint us. On the contrary, letters of appreciation for the administrative management of it all flowed in during subsequent weeks.

I referred earlier also to my own contribution to the smooth running of the show jumping events. Compared with today's sophisticated ways of doing things, it will sound tamely elementary, but I am talking of something which took place fifty years ago. I suggested to Francis that I would put together a team of fence handlers, two men to each fence, whose tasks would be – first, to put back knocked-down poles, bricks, gates, or other parts of the fence involved; second, when it came to changing the course from, say, novice to intermediate with a minimum time lag, this would be done by a colour code for each class in the interests of speed and accuracy. Further to this, fence repair teams would be on hand with spare material to mend any broken parts and in some cases, for example a gate, be able to effect a replacement. It would also be necessary, I suggested, to rehearse all these activities so that on the day, no one would be in doubt as to what was to be done. Francis approved of all these measures and we proceeded accordingly.

There was, however, one other matter of concern to me. I had at this time reason to be dissatisfied with one of my four-legged friends. I referred earlier to a dark bay gelding called Jasper. I had entered him for the novices' class in our forthcoming event, and for some time had been endeavouring to persuade him to see things from my point of view. I had been told by his former owner that Jasper could jump anything when he wanted to, but the old question persisted: would he do so when *I* wanted him to? So far I had not been having much luck. We had, of course, some schooling fences at Bredebeck, but in my efforts to induce Jasper to take real pleasure in clearing them, I was conscious of that depressing slowing of his paces as we would approach these obstacles. No amount of leg pressure seemed to help and I have always been a reluctant wielder of the whip. One of my fellow officers, Jock Colman, a keen and competent horseman, then suggested that I might consider donning a pair of spurs. I did and the effect on Jasper was magical. It seemed that as soon as he realized that I was spurred, he became a different animal. There was no need for me to apply them. Conscious of their presence when once more I took him to the schooling fences, he surged towards them as if he intended to eat them and cleared one fence after another with never a fault.

The day of our horse show dawned. There was a wonderful turnout, with full entries from many other regiments – cavalry, artillery and infantry, and some star turns included. That great man, Monkey Blacker, commanding The Skins, brought a team, as did Ronnie Coaker, 17th/21st Lancers. My old friend, Ian Gill, commanding 4th/7th Dragoon Guards was there. Our new Commanding Officer, George Butler, was one of the judges. Francis Romney had put all the finishing touches to the show ring, all the fences beautifully painted, flowers galore, officials in place, loudspeakers to announce results tested. It was a lovely day and at 10 o'clock sharp, the show began. Jasper and I were the first to perform, so that I could then attend to my duties with my team of fence menders and course adjustors. Jasper was splendidly groomed and I had done my best to be a credit to him in service dress tunic, breeches and boots – with spurs – 4th Hussar cap badge gleaming.

'First entry in the Novices' Class,' announced the loudspeaker, 'Major Strawson riding Jasper.'

I rode into the ring, saluted the judges, earning a friendly grin from George Butler, cantered to the start point and away we went. Jasper, ever aware of the spurs' presence, went like a dream.

Clear round! Well satisfied, I rode out of the ring, handed Jasper over to his groom, and joined my team of fence-men to pursue my duties.

The whole affair was a triumph, much to Francis Romney's gratification, for it was he who had designed the courses, master-minded everything, and devoted hours of study and preparation to what was after all his principal sporting interest. His efforts certainly illustrated how rewarding can be an infinite capacity for taking pains. The one disappointment for Francis was that he and his carefully schooled mare had not won first prize in the Open Class. Nor for that matter had either Monkey Blacker or Ronnie Coaker, despite their acknowledged skills and superior mounts. This event, to the surprise yet approval of all, was won by a relatively junior officer of the 17th/21st Lancers, whose clear round – one of many – was achieved in the fastest time. It is pleasing to record also that my team of helpers was later congratulated by Francis on the dexterity with which they had put up knocked down fences and re-rigged the courses for changes of class.

The next great event was the amalgamation itself. A magnificent parade involved the marching on of two regiments – the 4th Hussars commanded by George Butler and the 8th Hussars by Henry Huth, their marching off again to allow those selected to form the new regiment to come together, and then the marching on of The Queen's Royal Irish Hussars, Colonel George at their head, a consecration of the new Guidon, inspection by the Colonel-in-Chief, Prince Philip, advance in review order, General Salute, a short speech by Colonel George, and a march past. It was all highly emotional, but a spectacle long to be remembered. One most pleasing feature of the new regiment's future was that Winston Churchill had agreed to become Colonel, and he sent a suitably eloquent message about his confidence that The Queen's Royal Irish Hussars would 'do and dare' with the best of them and bring further fame to add to the former regiments' illustrious past. Shortly before all this I had been informed that I was to become a member of the Directing Staff at the Staff College, and was to report to Minley Manor, and, as noted in an earlier chapter, I became, not only an instructor of young ambitious Staff College students, but, far more important and demanding, a Master of Drag Hounds.

1. Three cheers for the Colonel. Churchill with 4th Hussars, Cairo, November 1943. *(IWM E26688)*

Churchill inspects 4th Hussars, Italy, August 1944, with Lieutenant Colonel Bobby Kidd. *(IWM NA 18013)*

3. Churchill with Leese and Alexander, Italy, August 1944. *(IWM NA 1804)*

4. *Top:* 3rd Troop, C Squadron, 4th Hussars, Beni Yusef 1943.

5. *Centre:* Gothic Line country.

6. *Bottom:* Coriano.

Montecieco.

8. German anti-tank gunners.

4th Hussars were equipped with Sherman tanks.

10. Piazza del Unita, Trieste. The author is decorated with the US Bronze Star.

11. 4th Hussars greeted by General Ritchie, Singapore, September 1948. *Left to right*: Hugh Marrack, Gordon Smith, author, Peter Young, Ritchie, Lieutenant Colonel George Kidston.

12. and 13. 4th Hussars patrols, Malaya, 1949-50. *(IWM MH29464 and HU 9500)*

14. Fort Knox 1956. Handing over to Robin Chater.

15. Churchill at Hohne in 1957 with Loopy Kennard, Robin Freemantle and Sergeant Baxter.

16. *Top:* Bella.

17. *Middle:* A meet at Arborfield. Tom Hickman, *left;* Michael Festing, *right*; author riding General. A few minutes later the hounds rioted.

18. *Bottom:* The barren rocks of Aden. *(IWM 64/198/10)*

19. Our marriage at Eisbergen, December 1960.

20. With Reiterverein (Riding Club).

21. Regimental support: Tim Pierson, Jock Colman, Kenneth Bidie and Rodney Martin.

22. In command, Malaysia 1963.

23. Queen's Royal Irish Hussars river patrol, Sarawak.

24. Long House bashing, Sarawak 1964.

25. Queen's Royal Irish Hussars road patrol, Borneo. *(IWM 28247)*

26. Borneo – on foot.
(IWM R33174)

27. Funeral of Sir Winston Churchill – the Lying in State. Captain Cramsie, Captain Kenny and Major Wright.

28. *Above:* The Regimental Insignia Party opposite the entry to Horse Guards.

29. *Centre:* Insignia Party. *Left to right:* Major Tilbrook, Lieutenant Colonel Strawson, Major Bidie and Major Sutro.

30. *Bottom:* The Bearer Party at Waterloo Station. *Left:* RSM Holberton, *right:* Captain De Morgan.

31. Brigmerston farmhouse.

32. The mini-château, Brittany.

33. *Above:* The Old Rectory, Boyton.

34. *Centre:* Old Comrades' dinner, Lord's Tavern. *Left to right:* The Colonel-in-Chief, Stephen Eve, author, Steve Daniell, Jon Sutro, John Paley, Cliff Jones, Roy Vallance.

35. *Bottom:* We attend an evening party, HQ UKLF: RSM Ayres in charge.

36. With Douglas MacRae-Brown at Ascot.

37. Viola and Carolin.

38. *Left:* In Cairo with my driver, Mustafa Kema and Lord Aldington.

39. Tercentenary, Münster 1985. Major General Brian Kenny and General Sir John Hackett are on the right.

40. Mounted escort for the Colonel-in-Chief: Lieutenant Colonel Daniell, Commanding Officer, is behind the driver.

Chapter 12

Master of Drag Hounds

'The 'oss loves the 'ound, and I loves both.'

Jorrocks

Before accepting the appointment of master and huntsman of the Staff College Drag, I felt it would be expedient to consult my favourite novelist, a great hunting man, Anthony Trollope. I was on the whole encouraged by what he had to say. A master of hounds, Trollope has told us, must be strong in heart, in health, in purpose and in purse. I was able to reassure myself that my heart and health were in good order and that strength of purpose was, after all, an essential ingredient of a proper soldier. When it came to the purse, however, I was on weaker ground, but happily the Hunt was able to help here. Further investigation as to other qualities which Trollope prescribed added to my confidence that I would be up to the job. Diligent, eager, watchful – yes, I thought I could comply with this; the exercise of unflinching authority combined with good humour and forbearance – exactly my way of doing things; the need to impress everyone that decisions taken would always be right – again the very essence of command. So far, so good.

Yet there was still one serious deficiency in my inventory. Hunting kit I had; horse furniture I had; a hunting horn, property of the Hunt, would be handed over by my predecessor. There was but one pressing requirement. I had no horse. While it was true that the very nature of drag hunting means that you can hunt without a fox, it was equally certain that you cannot hunt a pack of drag hounds without a horse. It was when I made good this deficiency that I also made my first acquaintance with Bella, of whom I earlier made special mention. One of Trollope's hunting characters, Mr Harkaway, while conceding the need for a horse in order to hunt, looked upon that animal as costly, disagreeable and inclined to get you into trouble. But for me the horse has always been the joy of following hounds, and Bella reinforced my conviction a thousand fold.

She was a bay mare of nearly 16 hh, alert, friendly and bold, with a serene and steady look which appealed to me. When I asked how old she was, no one seemed to know. More than ten, less than twenty was the best guess. But her age did not matter. Her legs were sound, her wind good, her spirit undaunted, and she had that priceless quality, which every hunting man seeks in his horses and few find. Except for one instance when in danger of jumping on a hound, she never refused. Surtees told us that there is no secret so close as that between a rider and his horse. There are some horses which, as you approach a formidable obstacle, let you into their secret early: 'Just try and get me over this fence' is their message. Not Bella. 'Try and stop me getting over it', was her form. The mere sight of a fence in front of us was enough to spur her into action. I had to acknowledge lack of personal control at the fences and content myself with being reasonably in control between them.

On the first occasion that I rode her I was a member of the field. It was in February and as I had agreed to take over the pack before the end of that season, there was no time to lose in learning the job. I therefore went out several times to study how things were done, and as Bella had been recommended to me as a likely mount, it was agreed that I could try her out. 'She takes quite a hold,' I was informed 'but jumps like a stag.' What I had not been told was that in any such event as drag hunting, Bella firmly believed her rightful place was in front. It was something I soon learned on this first occasion, for no sooner had we set off on the first leg of the line, Bella, treating the fences like hurdles, made her way to the front of the field and even threatened to draw level with the Master, who made clear in a few sort, sharp phrases that it was not appropriate for me to usurp his position. I did my best to conform, but finished the day with aching wrists. What would happen, I wondered, when as Master myself, I would be in command not only of Bella but the hounds, the whips and the field.

I need not have worried. On the second occasion of my probation, as it were, we encountered some heavy going, big fences and a long gallop. As we soared over some tricky post-and-rails with ditches, leaving a number of frustrated followers behind us, my respect and affection for Bella knew no bounds, and my confidence in her, and thus myself, was enhanced still further when at an end of the season meet for the local Pony Clubs, I hunted the hounds myself for the first time, I found that out in front she stopped pulling uncontrollably – except at the fences that is – and settled down to a good, fast hunting pace, as contented to be the Master's mount as I was to be riding her.

Negotiations between the Hunt, the Saddle Club, which at that time owned Bella, and myself then proceeded, and the best-loved of my four-legged friends was mine. I was never to regret it. She was beautifully behaved in the stable, loved the hounds, and except for a cut knee which put her off the road for a week or two was never lame. She was, in short, the perfect huntsman's horse and carried me superbly for the whole of the next season. Her only fault, if fault you can call it, was that she had an impish sense of fun, which would appear when something unusual occurred or when she thought I was not paying sufficient attention to the task in hand. Her method of recalling me to my duties was to put in a terrific buck, throw me over her head, and then to gaze quizzically down on me. She never did it out hunting, but on a few less urgent occasions, I was seriously discomforted. One of them brought home to me the truth of that old maxim – pride comes before a fall.

Hound exercise, although routine, is by no means one of the least pleasing aspects of a Master's responsibilities. One morning I took the hounds out with two of my whips to assist me. It was one of those mornings when it was not just a pleasure to be up early, but almost a duty. I drove to the stables at Camberley where Bella awaited me, admirably groomed, saddled and accoutred by Trooper Tedbury, Household Cavalry, who was devoted to Bella. Things proceeded well. The hounds behaved themselves, Bella was on her toes, the whips were doing their stuff. I felt some pride in the superlative control which I seemed to be exercising over my band of quadrupeds. I congratulated myself too soon. As we rounded the corner of a copse on Barossa Common, pandemonium broke out. There in front of us was a well-known local character who had, countless years earlier, appointed herself champion and guardian of all stray dogs in the area. She was pushing a kind of wooden go-cart made of box planks, in which were perched three or four cheerful mongrels and from which a number of leads allowed further assorted strays to roam a little further from her kindly hand. Camberley Kate was taking her dogs for their regular walk. This appetizing sight was too much for the, until now, well-disciplined pack of hounds I had with me. Their hunting instincts were thoroughly aroused. Giving tongue with a harmony that would have warmed Peter Beckford's heart, they surged forward. Far from being dismayed, however, Camberley Kate's charges seemed to welcome the prospect of a pitched battle. The two commanders-in-chief thereupon endeavoured to restore some order to a situation pregnant with danger. The mistress of strays, unbowed, had drawn a whistle from her raiment and was producing from it a series of high-pitched notes which seemed rather to urge her troops to greater bellicosity than to quiet them. Meanwhile I, with an oath entirely appropriate to my new calling, had plunged into the midst of the struggle, whip poised, intent on showing who was Master in fact as well as name. At this critical juncture, my faithful Bella decided to take a hand in the affair, and with a buck that would have unseated Murat, deposited me in the very midst of the mêlée.

Remarkably enough this intervention had the very effect required. The stray dogs rallied to their benefactress, who led them soothingly away, and the hounds lavished their affection on me which left me in no doubt as to the texture of their tongues. Bella and the whips surveyed the scene with ill-concealed satisfaction. With a brittle grimace I hoisted myself back in the saddle and led my re-concentrated forces back to kennels. But I had to concede that Bella had saved the day.

I will not weary you with a full account of the duties which a Master of Drag Hounds undertakes. I have recorded this elsewhere. (*On Drag-Hunting*, J.A. Allen, 1999) But this section of my memoirs would be incomplete without mention of what a day's drag hunting could actually be like. Here are two such examples.

It was on these occasions that Bella came into her own. She had already shown how she liked to play a leading role at hound exercise, but what she really relished was the real thing. She would always know which was which. The extra grooming she received, with her mane admirably plaited, the sight of me in proper hunting kit, the hounds coupled for hacking to the meet – all these were unmistakable signs. And her unfailing courage, good manners and perseverance were qualities which endeared her to me.

At the meet we enjoyed the centre of the stage, Bella standing quietly, surrounded by the hounds to whom I threw a morsel of bread and biscuit, and sipped a stirrup cup, while telling myself that I was monarch of all I surveyed. An admiring matron came up to me, and tried to draw my attention to the ravishing prettiness of a Pony Club member who, the matron claimed, was gazing at me with the same raptness that Desdemona contemplated the Moor. I recalled Trollope's recipe that a Master of Hounds should be somewhat feared; should be a man with whom others will not care to argue and, glancing down at the suddenly restless pack, growled that I had enough bitches to look after already.

The field had assembled and it was time to move off. Bella stirred excitedly as I put the horn to my lips and sounded an appropriate note. What should then have happened is that the hounds quietly jogged along behind me, flanked by the whips until we reached the place where the scent was laid, and then, released from my iron discipline, gave tongue and got on with their business of hunting the line to the first check. But sometimes with an enthusiasm misguided but not wholly reprehensible, they anticipated my executive order. So it was on this occasion. They had, for some time, been standing like greyhounds in the slips, straining upon the start, and then at the sound of my warning toot, before I announced to them that the game was, in fact afoot, they were, to put it briefly, off. With no precise purpose, mind you. Waiters with silver salvers swerved out of their way, hard-faced women clutched Boxers to their bosoms, knowing members of the field mocked my unsuccessful efforts to quell the riot.

There was only one thing to do. I rode quickly to where the line began and gave Bella her head.

Now, surely, all would be well. Drawing my horn again I blew the 'gone away' – in confirmation of what had already taken place and hoped for the best. Sure enough, my charges appeared from all directions, picked up the scent, spoke with reinforced volume and overtook me. I heaved a sigh of relief and settled down to assist Bella in negotiating the fences which were between us and the end of the first leg. Bella went like a dream. As I jumped into the last field of this leg, the hounds should have rallied round me with the whips' help and waited until it was time to move off to the next leg. But to my horror they began to hunt a heel line, that is the original one in reverse. Oaths, further use of horn and dispatching of whips eventually restored order. Bella remained unmoved by the fuss.

We moved off to the next leg. Trouble behind me, I thought, as we galloped on behind the hounds. Half way along this particular leg was a brook, which Bella had soared over many a time. As we reached it, however, an idle hound was just struggling out onto the far bank, and although I felt sure we could avoid it, Bella disagreed and the sharpest refusal imaginable took place. The field was then rewarded with the sight of the Master, ejected from the saddle, but happily holding on to the reins, rising to his feet and unsmilingly remounting to ride on to the line's end. It was Bella's only refusal, but further evidence that Jorrocks was right when he maintained that the 'oss loves the 'ound'. The final leg went without a hitch, as indeed normally the whole line did. Jack, the kennel huntsman, was waiting, held Bella when I dismounted, handed me the worry which I threw to the hounds, sounding the kill. I then exchanged courtesies with those who had taken part, and took to the road with hounds and whips for the hack back to kennels. Another day with the drag was soon over. But I told myself at the end that it was Bella, not I, who was the hero, or rather the heroine, of it all. And the cosseting which she received on arriving at the stables, after hounds had been delivered into Jack's hands, made this thoroughly clear.

A few weeks after this I was again preparing for the following Wednesday's meet of the Drag. It was a particularly good line. About three-quarters of an hour's hack from kennels – which settled hounds down much better than a short hack or going in the van and horse-box to more distant meets. And this line was in an excellent piece of country, three legs, each of about two miles, with an interesting, demanding variety of obstacles – some stiffish posts-and-rails with ditch one side, some splendid brush fences, a few gates and one marvellous uphill open ditch which never failed to thrill. By this time I knew all the farmers pretty well, but in arranging a future meet, I would always call in to see them. On this occasion, with my two companions, the runner and the chief of our fence-mending team, we were walking each leg, checking on fences and the red-and-white direction signs, calling on each farmer to remind him that we were coming. Although they all got the meet notices, they liked a chat as well. As we walked, our driver took the Land Rover to meet us at the end of one leg to take us to the start of the next one. All seemed well – fences in good order, the going just right, farmers happy. We should have a successful day.

I was very much hoping so as my old friend, Colonel Humphrey Weld had agreed to come and have a day with us, and I had the loan of a goodish animal for him. There was only one fly in the ointment. My beautiful Bella had cut her knee while jumping a fence on the previous week's line – an accident I referred to earlier – and was not fit. I had a call on a large grey gelding called General, who went well enough in a group, but I was not sure whether he would lead over all the fences – an absolute necessity. In the Staff College Drag the Master, who also hunts hounds, must get out in front and stay there without having trouble making his horse jump. Well, we would see.

Shortly before 1 o'clock on the Wednesday we were at the kennels, me on General and Humphrey on Charlie. My two whips, both Sandhurst cadets, were already there, and after having a word with Jack and putting some pieces of bread in the pocket of my hunting coat, I signalled him to let the hounds out. We were taking five couple – among them Flyer and Driver, both lean, wild and mean. Hounds were coupled. I was taking no chances on the hack to the meet. We moved off just after 1 p.m. Hounds always met at 2 p.m., and there would be ten minutes to spare after getting there. All went smoothly to and at the meet. Hounds were uncoupled, there was a good field, nearly thirty, not surprising as it was one of the best lines we had. We met at the drive entrance to a large country house. To reach the start of the first leg, we would turn left out of the gate. The runner with the 'smell' had had his instructions and would, by this time, have laid scent for the first leg and be on his way by Land Rover to the start of the second.

I blew the customary short note on the horn and we moved off. Imagine my consternation when, after we had jogged a few hundred yards down the road towards the laying-on point, a fox, yes, a large brown dog fox, slunk across the road without so much as a glance at me or the hounds, down into a ditch and up again into the adjoining field. I was speechless with amazement and apprehension. Behind me members of the field, however, were less inarticulate. Every form of oral encouragement was hurled at the fox, at the hounds and at me.

There are those who will tell you that the natural instincts of drag hounds have been blunted by strong, false scents and that they are no good for anything but following a smell. Be wary of such assurance. My drag hounds, with Flyer and Driver to lead them, would hunt anything. Certainly they had no doubts about our uninvited guest. Giving tongue with unaccustomed vigour and volume, they surged forward in full cry. What was I to do? Let nature take its course or try to proceed with our planned jaunt across a prepared piece of country? Trollope's words nagged at me – 'he must condescend to no explanation and yet must impress men with an assurance that his decision will certainly be right'. Now, if ever, was the moment to make the right decision. In the event it was made for me.

It was made by Monsieur Renard who re-crossed the road and, wonder of wonders, began to follow the laid line, seduced perhaps by a scent even more powerful than his own. There was no hesitating now. With a feeling of deep relief, accompanied by mounting excitement, I blew the 'gone away', turned left into the field where the line began, and galloped off after my hounds who were streaking in the wake of Monsieur Renard. Just what he did while we were negotiating the next few fields and fences I never knew, for when we got to the end of the first leg, the hounds checked, just as on a normal day. It seemed that Monsieur Renard had made his escape. A pause while we got the hounds under control, then we moved off again.

There was about a mile to hack between the end of the first and the start of the second leg. All went according to plan until I released hounds into the field. Hounds immediately got on to the scent and were away. In the act of raising the horn to my lips, I saw out of the corner of my eye a herd of cows about to stampede across my bows. Was it possible? Mr Bellamy was the most reliable of farmers. He never forgot when we were coming, never failed to take wire down, or remove his cows to another field. Yet there they were in the very act of putting up a wall of beef between the Master and his hounds. I aimed General for the corner of the field, hoping to reach the post-and-rail fence before the leading heifer. Until then I had no idea that cows could move so fast. It was going to be a tight thing. In the event General did something he and I have never done before or since. We jumped both cow and fence. The rest of the second leg was almost dull by comparison. Nothing untoward happened. The heifers had obligingly remained in the far corner, allowing the field to negotiate that first fence elsewhere. At the check, Humphrey Weld dryly observed to me that he had no idea drag hunting could be so dramatic.

What can I say about the final leg? Only that we did not encounter an elephant during it. No circus riders or highwaymen or Cossacks appeared to disturb us. It was, in terms of what had gone before, uneventful. Yet General took the open ditch in fine style. As we hacked home later, I noticed that even Flyer and Driver were somewhat subdued. Had they too been aware that we had just ridden an historic drag line? Humphrey, hacking along beside me, told me how much he had enjoyed it. I was pleased that on this rare occasion, when I had been able to arrange a day's hunting for him – as opposed to the many days he had given me with the Seavington – it had all been rather special.

During the summer following this hunting season Wilfried von Schellersheim and I decided that it was time we got married and we did so that winter. It was all wonderfully well laid on by her father, the Baron and his second wife. The ceremony was in the small church at Eisenbergen, the reception in their lovely house overlooking the River Weser. My Regiment rallied round. Lots of fellow officers attended, the warrant officers provided a Guard of

Honour, my old comrade in arms, John Paley, was best man, the bride looked beautiful, and after jollifications which went on until the evening, Wilfried and I left for our honeymoon at Königssee, an enchanting lake not far from Berchtesgaden where Wilfried's aunt had a villa. And so I got married and lived happily ever after.

Chapter 13

From Minley Manor to Malaysia via Whitehall

'You have been selected to command The Queen's Royal Irish Hussars.'

War Office Posting Order

We returned from Königssee to Minley where a married quarter awaited us. It was a small but pleasant cottage just outside the main gate of the manor, called Crossways. We settled in happily there. Wilfried soon mastered the intricacies of housekeeping in England and I returned to my duties of turning the aspiring captains and majors, who were students, into potential generals. My fellow members of the Directing Staff, as indicated earlier, were a fine bunch. Colonel Bill Jackson was now in charge at Minley, a most gallant sapper who was also a military historian of distinction. Some years later he put me in the way of writing military history myself and capped this with several most generous reviews of my publications. One of my fellow instructors was Geoffrey Collins, an artilleryman and Auster pilot, who lived with his family in a nearby, somewhat larger house. It had to be larger because, as I soon learned, when you entered it, you were likely to find a sheep, who thought he was a dog, having been brought up with the Collins' spaniel and labrador, stretched out on a carpet in front of the drawing room fire. On moving into their kitchen you were as likely as not to meet a large pony, either chewing a carrot or drinking water from the sink. Next to their house were the stables, which accommodated among other horses one belonging to Vivien Wallace, wife of Colonel Tommy

Wallace, Rifle Brigade and one of the most knowledgeable racing tipsters I have yet encountered. Vivien asked me to exercise her animal in the mornings – she was busy in Camberley – so I would ride out for a hack, accompanied by the Collins' elder daughter, mounted on the large pony who had been extracted from the kitchen.

We had not been many months at Crossways when it became clear that the first of innumerable moves of house was imminent. I was to take up a War Office post as General Staff Officer 1 of Staff Duties 4, a branch concerned principally with manpower and its distribution throughout the Army. What is more I would be taking over from my former Staff College companion, Alun Gwynne-Jones, who was leaving the Army to become Defence Correspondent of *The Times*. Wilfried gallantly volunteered to reconnoitre parts of London not too distant from Whitehall to find a suitable flat, and was instantly successful in hitting upon a first floor flat in Holland Road, to which we moved in June 1960.

This change of employment and location meant, of course, that I had to give up being Master of the Drag. Since the season ended Bella had been happily at liberty in a large paddock at Minley with a gelding companion, belonging to Charles Taylor, The Skins, who was a whipper-in with the Sandhurst Foxhounds. Obviously I could not take Bella to London, but most fortunately Mick Close, former 9th Lancer, Joint Master of the Sandhurst Foxhounds wanted a mare to breed from and, judging Bella not to be too old for such a purpose and aware of her skill and courage in the hunting field, made a generous offer for her and she went to the best of homes. It is gratifying to record that Bella had a foal in 1961, a filly who turned out to have her dam's qualities of boldness and enthusiasm, and further in her turn produced another comparably superb hunter.

All this talk of Bella's offspring brings me to a supremely important event. Wilfried was expecting our first child in the latter part of September. September passed without result, so on 2 October 1960, I took her to see a matinee performance of *Macbeth*. This did the trick and that night in the military hospital at Woolwich, Viola, our elder daughter, was born. The first floor flat in Holland Road was less attractive for the manipulation of a perambulator, and we moved to a quieter, ground floor flat in

Putney, which had the added advantage of a garden and nearby Putney Heath. This addition to the family obviously restricted our social activities to some extent, but the arrival of a German au pair enabled us to accept some invitations to dine and occasionally to enjoy an evening at the theatre.

My work in the War Office was of particular interest as the Army at this time was under-manned, recruiting having become sluggish, while commitments both to NATO and our still considerable obligation east of Suez were as demanding as ever. All this meant that the manning problems loomed large and the determination of priorities was a source of disagreement amongst the various claimants for preferential treatment. There were several soldiers with whom I worked who greatly impressed me with their intelligence, dedication and sheer ability. Among them were Victor Fitzgeorge-Balfour, Coldstream Guards, whom I had met briefly during the Malayan campaign, and who was to go on to great heights both in Whitehall and Brussels; George Cole, Director of Staff Duties, who knew how to stroke the Whitehall machine to his advantage and combined great perspicacity with a shrewd sense of humour. He was also a sportsman of considerable skill. In short he was just the man to work for. During my time at the War Office, I met for the first time Nigel Bagnall, then a major in the Military Operations branch. He was very outspoken, holding strong and usually sound views on military matters and I came to know him very well in some of our subsequent appointments. He eventually became a field marshal and Chief of the General Staff. I shall have a word to say about some other field marshals and lesser brass hats later on.

The Secretary of State at this time was none other than John Profumo, who was shortly to get into trouble with Christine Keeler, and I was twice required to report to him in his rather grand set of rooms to assist in preparing him for parliamentary questions. I found him courteous, quick to grasp the point and charmingly appreciative of the efforts made to help him. It was a pleasure later on to observe him from the box in the House of Commons competently dealing with the opposition's attempts to confound him.

I had always had an inclination for writing and as I was living in London on a lieutenant colonel's pay, bearing in mind also Dr

Johnson's advice that only a blockhead wrote except for money, I decided to enter a piece for the annual Bertrand Stewart Prize Essay, a competition run by The Army Quarterly. Happily my essay won. The £100 prize was more than welcome. As the summer months arrived Wilfried and I took great pleasure in going to the Open Air Theatre in Regent's Park to see a Shakespeare play, leaving Viola in the safe hands of Renate, our au pair. As time went by, I was able to earn more with my pen. But, of course, my profession as a soldier came first.

After some two years as GSO 1 of Staff Duties 4, I received the most wonderful news, that I had been appointed to command the Regiment, at that time – it was 1962 – stationed at Aden and Sharjah. I was fortunate enough to get permission to visit them there for although I would not be taking over from Tim Pierson until the beginning of 1963, it was four years since I had been with the Regiment and it was important that we should renew our ties. I flew to Aden to be met by Peter Sturges, then a most effective Adjutant, and spent just inside a week talking to old friends, meeting new members of the Regiment and playing polo at Khormaksar airfield. One of my fellow players was Brigadier James Lunt, commanding a brigade of local troops, with whom I was to have further dealings later. At this time the Regiment had a flight of Auster aircraft, and in one of these I flew to Dhala in the north of the Protectorate, where I met Colonel Sandy Thomas, who was commanding a battalion of Federal troops and whom I was to meet again years later when my brigade made up part of his division. Flying to Dhala enabled me to observe the hazards of the road from Aden to the north, ideal for ambush in scores of places. The Regiment with its Saladin armoured cars and Ferret scout cars was responsible for escorting convoys along this road to and from Dhala. I noted too with much pleasure that many of the officers had cultivated the most impressive gardens in front of their hutted quarters, for even the sandy soil of Little Aden would respond to constant watering. The Regiment was to serve one year there and then move to Malaya and Singapore towards the end of 1962 and I would assume command early in 1963. The jungles and rubber plantations would, I thought, be a more pleasant environment than the Barren Rocks of Aden, although I had not anticipated that no sooner did I set foot in

Singapore than another savage war of peace would get under way.

Back in England we made our plans. As Wilfried was expecting our second child in the summer of 1963, we decided that initially she and Viola would not accompany me to Malaya, but spend the months before the next birth at her family home in Eisbergen. Having handed over my War Office job to Bill Scotter, a former DS colleague at the Staff College, who later became a most effective Vice Chief of the General Staff and C.-in-C. Rhine Army, but alas died in office, and having completed the travel plans for Wilfried and Viola, I flew courtesy of the Royal Air Force to Singapore.

Command of one's own regiment is the goal of every soldier, particularly if the task in hand is varied, challenging and adventurous. I was lucky therefore in that when I took over at the beginning of 1963 the Borneo campaign was just getting started. An abortive rebellion in Brunei which broke out in December 1962 was quickly suppressed, but was followed by Indonesia's President Sukarno declaring a policy of 'confrontation' aimed at disrupting the newly formed federation of Malaya, Sarawak, North Borneo and Singapore. Sukarno was set upon putting an end to Malaysia before it even got off the ground. One of his earlier moves therefore was to exploit trouble caused by the Brunei rebels and also to plan incursions into North Borneo and Sarawak. As Commander British Forces West Sarawak and Commanding Officer, The Queen's Royal Irish Hussars, I was required to ensure the security of the 1st, 2nd and 3rd Divisions, a huge area which had some 750 miles of border with Kalimantan or Indonesian Borneo. The threat to West Sarawak was twofold – external, that is incursions from Kalimantan by Indonesian guerrillas, some of whom were the remnants of Azahari's Brunei rebels and others were Indonesian soldiers; and internal, from the so-called Clandestine Communist Organization, which numbered anything from 10,000 to 20,000.

To do this I had one squadron of my Regiment equipped with armoured cars, a company of infantry supplied by the Royal Marines, a few administrative elements, two Royal Naval minesweepers, two Auster aircraft and – most important – a squadron of the SAS. My headquarters was in the Police HQ Kuching. With so lengthy a frontier and so few troops, the SAS squadron was invaluable for surveillance and intelligence gathering, enabling me to conserve my limited infantry and armoured cars for the tasks of securing communication centres and patrolling widely, by road, by river with long boats – for Sarawak is a country of rivers – and by penetrating the jungle on foot. In this way we hoped to reassure the local people and, together with the police intelligence system, learn enough about what was going on to deter those who might have ideas about turning threats into hostile action. I also thoroughly endorsed a proposal by the administration and the police to re-establish a force of Sarawak Rangers for patrol and intelligence activities.

The SAS squadron deployed itself near the frontier and began its task of surveillance, gathering intelligence and the so-called 'Hearts and Minds' campaign, designed to win the loyalty of Sarawak's people, a campaign dear to the heart of the Director of Operations in Borneo, the famous and expert jungle fighter, Major General Walter Walker. This campaign was waged to bind the local people to our way of thinking with hoops made of kindness, medical supplies, radios, moving people and things about, and generally giving help in a hundred ways.

Having visited all my outposts, taken the invaluable advice of that great man, Tom Harisson, who was curator of the Kuching Museum and who had led Dyak and other tribesmen against the Japanese during the war [he knew more about Borneo than anyone else I met], made myself known to the various civil administrators and policemen of Sarawak's 1st, 2nd and 3rd Divisions – the Austers were invaluable for getting round the country – and attended regular conferences held by the Governor in Kuching and General Walker in Brunei, I put in an eloquent plea for helicopters. In a country with few roads, helicopters could transform the military capability of a small force by sheer speed of reaction and ability to land and take off almost anywhere which boasted a small clearing in the jungle. My plea was turned down on the grounds of non-availability. I could do little except await the moment when their indispensability would be made clear.

It was not long in coming. Early on the morning of 12 April 1963, Good Friday, as I was shaving in my room of our Officers' Mess – a villa belonging to the Sarawak Steamship Company – my Borneo Adjutant, Rodney Martin, burst in and announced that a group of some thirty guerrillas had crossed the border at Tebedu, a village twenty-five miles from Serian in the 1st Division, had killed a few policemen and generally looted and terrorized the place. Had I, Rodney asked, any immediate instructions? After ensuring that the proper messages had been sent and the proper people alerted, I sensed that this was one of those moments to say something for posterity: 'Tell them to bring my breakfast to the Operations Room!'

The situation in Tebedu was restored by dispatching a troop of the Royal Marines there, yet never was the lack of helicopters so keenly felt, for it was a long drive over very poor tracks. What could have been done in a mere twenty minutes took more like four hours. But soon after the Tebedu raid, intelligence from the SAS, the police and other sources as to the likelihood of further incursions by Indonesian-led guerrillas concentrated my mind. It was confirmed by Sigint – information we received from radio transmissions picked up and processed by special signal units. Moreover there were disquieting indications from the police and civil administrators that 'the natives were restless', in other words that the Clandestine Communist Organization were about to make their grievances and their presence felt. Having by this time persuaded General Walker to let me have a few naval helicopters – the skill, courage and commitment of whose officers and men were beyond praise – we were able to step up our patrol activity in the sense of covering far more ground and making each platoon seem like a company.

But the imminence and the measure of further enemy action seemed to be such that with the few hundred men we had to secure so vast an area, it was unlikely that any successful counter could be managed. Fortunately the police fully supported my view and together we were able to persuade the Governor that substantial reinforcements were necessary if he were to continue to govern the first three divisions of Sarawak. For the first time and only time in my military career, I sent a FLASH signal. It was addressed to General HQ Far East and read:

> In view of likely further incursions from Kalimantan and probability of C.C.O. insurgency, I have recommended to H.E. The Governor, who agrees with me, the instant dispatch

of a brigade of troops from Singapore to ensure the security of Sarawak.

Like an eagle in a dovecote this signal had the gratifying effect of fluttering a number of staff officers in GHQ Singapore, and next day a posse of generals and other senior fellows arrived in Kuching courtesy of the Royal Air Force to talk the matter over. It was swiftly agreed that HMS *Bulwark* would bring a substantial part of 3 Commando Brigade, Royal Marines, and the rest would follow by other means. So began a gradual escalation of military activity by either side, the Indonesians using more and more regular units, our forces being strengthened until we eventually had some 15,000 troops in Borneo, infantry mainly, but supported by armoured cars, light aircraft, gunners, sappers, signals and all the logistic units, to say nothing of huge, indispensable support from the Royal Navy and Royal Air Force.

It was, in many ways, a most satisfactory campaign – plenty of excitement and interest, not too many casualties and military success which led to a political result greatly welcomed by all those of right mind – the fall of Sukarno. The Regiment played its full part. We maintained one sabre squadron in Sarawak throughout our tour of duty and one half-squadron in Brunei and North Borneo, now renamed Sabah. During our eighteen months of Borneo operations, each sabre squadron was deployed for six months in Sarawak, six months in Ipoh and six months divided between Singapore and Brunei/Sabah. Although this involved lots of movement, including families, it ensured that officers and men were all able to feel that they had their fair share of the fun and the danger. One changeover of squadrons presented a unique problem. B Squadron was about to hand over to A Squadron, the latter having arrived at Kuching docks by LST. The plan was for A Squadron to move with all its Saladin armoured cars and Ferret scout cars to take over all B Squadron's positions, and then for B Squadron to move to the LST for the voyage back to Malaya. During the night before this planned handover, however, the heavens opened and widespread flooding made such movement impossible. As the LST had to sail forthwith, there was but one thing for it. A Squadron took over all B Squadron's equipment in situ, and vice versa. Needless to say each squadron regarded the other one's kit to be vastly inferior to its own.

Once I had handed over my own command of West Sarawak to Brigadier Barton, 3 Commando Brigade, I returned to our main headquarters in Ipoh, where my Adjutant, Barry De Morgan, an officer of the highest possible calibre, had kept things on an even keel during my absence in Borneo.

Life in Ipoh was very agreeable. We played polo both within the Regiment and against visiting teams; we even organized a polo tournament to which, among other senior people, Brian Wyldbore-Smith, now a general and Chief of Staff at Far East HQ, came; we would also take polo ponies and teams to other tournaments at Penang, Johore and Singapore, where I renewed acquaintance with Lieutenant Andrew Marx RN, a keen polo player, who had commanded one of the naval minesweepers in Borneo and with whom I had shared an adventurous expedition up the River Rajang. There was also golf at the Ipoh Club, one of my opponents being the celebrated Dr Reid Tweedie, who throughout the Malayan Emergency had somehow survived in his isolated house at Sungei Siput – it was rumoured that he had agreed to attend wounded bandits in exchange for not being murdered. Whether true or not, he was a delightful companion and a generous host. His curry lunches were renowned, preceded by Singapore Gin Slings – he was one of the few men I knew who made them properly and I still have the recipe on the very piece of paper he gave me more than forty years ago.

I still visited Borneo frequently to see how the Kuching based squadron was getting on and also to visit the troops we had in Brunei and Sabah. On the way there I would normally look in at Nee Soon camp, Singapore, to talk to the half squadron based there. Sometimes on one of the Borneo trips I would visit a Dyak Longhouse in company with my soldiers. Longhouses were often in remote parts of the jungle reachable only by river – until, that is, helicopter landing pads had been cleared and, on arrival at a Longhouse, with an interpreter to help, we would exchange courtesies and information with the chief, who was suitably presented with gifts of cigarettes and whisky, and he would then propose that we had a party. This involved the consumption of quantities of *tuak*, a kind of rice wine, and individual dancing to the accompaniment of a string and pipe band provided by the family.

The girls suitably dressed – that is not bare-breasted, as they often were – would perform first and then the guests, including myself, were invited to show their own dancing skills. It was a time when the Twist was in fashion and somehow I succeeded in winning their approval. The ceremony for sleeping was then enacted. A bed was prepared for me with mosquito net and other comforts, such as a jar of drinking water, a ceremonial sarong was handed to me, and with the entire Longhouse family in positions of observation, I was required modestly to disrobe, don the sarong and compose myself for slumber. It was all part of the Hearts and Minds campaign, and much fun was had by all.

In August 1963 Wilfried had given birth to our second daughter, who was subsequently christened Carolin. At her wedding many years later, I explained that I had initially pressed for another name from one of Shakespeare's heroines, but had been unable to convince Carolin's mother. My proposal of Perdita was dismissed on the grounds that we were not intending to lose her; my next shot at Cordelia simply led to my being reminded of what frightful sisters she had; while my final effort – Cleopatra – was spurned from the point of view that we would not be over-pleased if she behaved like that. So Carolin it was. In November of that year I had to fly back to England for the annual conference of all Cavalry and RTR Commanding Officers, conducted by that great soldier, Jackie d'Avigdor-Goldsmid, and for this purpose Barry De Morgan, an expert cameraman, had made an excellent film depicting our Borneo operations. It lasted about twenty minutes with a commentary provided by myself – no better way of informing the RAC Conference of what we had been doing. It went down well. Wilfried then flew back to London from Germany, and then all four of us, Viola now two years old, Carolin a mere three months, flew to Singapore – met by Bill and Ann Currie – and on to Ipoh, where a house quite near our camp had been acquired for us.

We had also acquired two servants – Ah Lee who was Chinese and cooked, and Lim, a Malay girl, who looked after Viola and Carolin. Wilfried very nobly undertook to give a series of lunch parties for all the wives of the soldiers quartered in Ipoh. To start with gin and tonics were liberally handed out, but the resulting uninhibited behaviour of some wives brought about an abandonment of G & Ts in favour of a small glass of sherry before lunch. We also had a number of dinner parties for the officers and their wives or girl friends, and we were particularly delighted to entertain Colonel Richard Close-Smith, who had commanded the 4th Hussars in Malaya and who, together with his charming and elegant wife, Judith, was staying with friends in Ipoh. Richard also toured our camp with me to meet members of the Regiment, and was especially pleased to find that the traditional trumpet calls for various parade events were still sounded. Another most welcome visitor – although this time it was all done in Borneo – was Colonel George Kidston-Montgomerie, who was now Deputy Colonel of the Regiment, Winston Churchill still holding the position of Colonel. We took George round all the troop positions in Sarawak and he greatly enjoyed himself.

Back at Ipoh more formally, we staged a Trooping of the Guidon parade for yet another visitor, whom we were all delighted to welcome – Brigadier George Butler, first Commanding Officer of the amalgamated Regiment. For this parade we decided that Barry De Morgan, the Adjutant, and I would be mounted, so two of the less wilful polo ponies were recruited and practised. We decided to have the parade early in the morning before it got too hot and follow it by entertaining our guests with a kind of late breakfast in the Officers' Mess. One feature of the ceremony was a march past, and as every soldier knows, we have all been firmly instructed to 'look the inspecting officer in the eye' as we salute him with the 'Eyes Right!' This lesson must somehow or other have got home to my noble steed, Firefly, a useful mount on the polo field and one who did not take a Titan's strength to keep under control, for as the two of us reached the point opposite the dais where George Butler awaited our salute, indeed as I lowered my sword in that very act, Firefly came to a halt and turned his head in order to give George this very look. Only a smart application of my spurs averted a disastrous pile-up as the ranks of marching Irish Hussars closed up on Firefly and myself.

A few months before the Regiment was to be relieved by the 4th RTR, we heard that our next destination was to be Wolfenbüttel, a garrison town not far from Braunschweig. Wilfried and I decided that she and the children should return to Germany in advance of my own move back with the troops. They flew to England and on to Eisbergen to await my arrival later at Wolfenbüttel.

We duly handed everything over to the 4th RTR, flew to Stanstead and were allowed to have a few weeks' leave before reassembling at Wolfenbüttel where we took over from The Queen's Dragoon Guards, commanded by another old friend, Peter Body, a former fellow student at the Staff College and in 6th Armoured Division. To my great pleasure I found that my immediate superior officer was Brigadier Matt Abraham, a 12th Lancer, whom I had known in the war, a gallant, witty, cultured, loveable man, brimming over with good humour and intolerant of redundant regulation or military pomposity. We did quite a lot of training during the winter months of 1964 and 1965, as it was necessary to adapt to Cold War requirements, a somewhat different proposition from deterring Indonesian guerrillas. It was now known that in March 1965 I would be handing over command to my old comrade-in-arms, John Paley, and I was anxious that the Regiment should be in tip-top form when I did so.

There was, however, one event beforehand which dominated our thoughts and actions during the last days of January 1965 – the death of Sir Winston Churchill, Colonel, The Queen's Royal Irish Hussars. Operation HOPE NOT, a military document tucked away in the filing cabinets at HQ London District, had long been in existence and now at last was to be executed. Just as Churchill's life had been a pageant of achievement, so his funeral was a pageant of homage. As the Commanding Officer of his old Regiment, I was required to take part in the ceremony together with my regimental comrades. We formed a Vigil Party for the Lying-in-State in Westminster Hall; we carried his insignia and standards in the funeral procession; the Trumpet Major, Sergeant King, sounded reveille in St Paul's Cathedral; and a Bearer Party took the Colonel of the Regiment on his last journey from Waterloo Station to Bladon in Oxfordshire, and in the churchyard there laid him to rest.

Those of us who took part in that day, 30 January 1965, will never forget it. There is no other army in the world – and never has been – that could, under the splendid guidance and direction of the Household Division, have produced the dignity, solemnity, drilled perfection and sheer emotion of the procession from Parliament Square to St Paul's, the Dead March from *Saul* played by innumerable bands, the servicemen with reversed arms lining the streets, and behind them Churchill's people, silent, grave, some weeping, all filled with pride and awe. For those of us slow-marching in the procession who had been members of his Regiment and had been presented to him both during the war and at later regimental occasions, there was a very special participatory elation. Churchill had joined the 4th Hussars in 1895, had soldiered with them in India, played in the winning regimental polo team, charged at Omdurman – albeit with another regiment, the 21st Lancers to whom other regiments had assigned the motto 'Thou shalt not kill' because it was so long since they had been in action – become their Colonel, as we have seen, in the dark days of 1941 after serious losses in Greece, visited them no fewer than four times in war, attended their dinners and parades in peace, stayed on as Colonel after amalgamation with the 8th Hussars, and symbolized their twin mottoes, *Pristinae Virtutis Memores* and *Mente et Manu* as no other man ever had or could. He had been, as one former commanding officer, Lieutenant Colonel Sir George Kennard, had put it, the greatest Hussar of them all. Back in our barracks in Germany a few days later, we held our own simple and brief Drumhead Memorial Service, and during it I was able to remind the Regiment of the words with which Sir Isaiah Berlin had completed his infinitely rich miniature, *Mr Churchill in 1940*:

> A man larger than life, composed of bigger and simpler elements than ordinary men, a gigantic historical figure in his own lifetime, superhumanly bold, strong and imaginative, one of the two greatest men of action his nation has produced, an orator of prodigious powers, the saviour of his country, a mythical hero who belongs to legend as much as to reality, the largest human being of our time.

It was perhaps a fitting climax to my two or so years in command. I had often been told that command of one's regiment was the highlight of a life's soldiering and I found this to be true.

I was fortunate in that most of my time had been taken up with operations in Borneo with only the last few months in Germany, where many cavalry commanding officers had passed their entire tours. It had been an honour and a joy to have commanded The Queen's Royal Irish Hussars, and to the officers, warrant officers, sergeants, corporals and men of that great Regiment, I owe a debt of gratitude for their loyalty, their humour, their efficiency and their dedication. Jackie Goldsmid's great cry had been 'Wilkoness Wins'. I totally agreed with him and was happy indeed to find those under my command notoriously Wilko.

The time came to hand over to John Paley. On the afternoon before my departure he and I took a last hack together on two of the polo ponies [as 4th RTR did not play polo we had brought the best of our ponies back from Malaysia by sea and the Regiment continued to play both at Wolfenbüttel and elsewhere]. The animal I was riding stumbled badly as we crossed a ditch and I was ejected from the saddle, holding on to the reins. I remounted and we continued. My comment to John was that it would have been a fine thing indeed if on my last day in command of a cavalry regiment, I had been obliged to walk back to the stables in the wake of a loose horse.

Chapter 14

Soldiering On

> 'The profession, either navy or army, is its own justification. It has everything in its favour; heroism, danger, bustle, fashion. Soldiers and sailors are always acceptable to society. Nobody can wonder that men are soldiers and sailors.'
>
> Jane Austen

Towards the end of March 1965 we piled into our rather ancient Mercedes and set sail from Wolfenbüttel to drive to a small village in Buckinghamshire called Drayton Parslow. There were five of us – Wilfried, our two daughters, Trifine Kirby, Humphrey Weld's niece who had come to stay and help us with the children, and myself. I had been posted as Colonel GS, Military Operations 2 in the newly formed Ministry of Defence, and we had decided that rather than live in the hustle and bustle of London, we would stick to a rural life. I would find lodgings in London for weekdays and join the family for weekends. Drayton Parslow was a quiet, friendly village. We had agreeable neighbours and the local shop still observed that most helpful service of delivering ordered goods to the doorstep. The railway station at Bletchley was quite near and Viola, now four, was recruited to the local school, where she acquired a distinctly bumpkin-like accent which required severe correction. Trifine stayed on until we were well settled, then returned to her parents' home in Dorset. Our routine was established. I would catch an early train each Monday morning and return each Friday evening. During the week, thanks to the kindness of another old friend, David Walder, I was able to stay in London as he made available to me a room in his flat.

David Walder was a man of many parts. A lawyer, a Member of Parliament, a novelist, a witty, urbane and polished man, who had done his national service with the Royal Artillery and while serving in Malaya at the same time as we, the 4th Hussars, were there, had come across John Paley. Both were in hospital, David as a result of a stomach wound, John with a damaged back caused by falling into a pig-trap while on patrol in the jungle. They were in next door beds in the hospital ward, and David had been ordered not to laugh, as such contortions of the stomach muscles might prolong his recovery. But John Paley was a well-known raconteur of hilarious stories, and as a result it became necessary to move David into a different ward. Nonetheless he became so attached to our Regiment that after national service he applied to be on our books as a reservist. We were delighted to have him and his association with both the 4th Hussars and later The Queen's Royal Irish Hussars lasted until his untimely death from a heart attack while still in his forties. Married to Elspeth Morrison and with a large family, they had a spacious flat and were able to accommodate me. It was a very happy arrangement.

MO2 was the Army Department branch which dealt with operational matters in the Far East and advised the Chief of General Staff on policy and procedure for meetings of the Chiefs of Staff Committee. Having just come from Malaysia and having been engaged in operations there, I was fairly well up to date with the military problems facing the armed service there, and I was fortunate in finding my immediate assistants in MO2 of such high calibre. Henry Brooke, 16th/5th Lancers, I had known for many years. Later to command his regiment and to become their colonel, he had a sharp mind, a fluent pen and intimate knowledge of the new MOD organization and methods, and was thus infinitely well qualified to assist me in getting to know how things were done and whom to deal with. Much to my pleasure his half-section was an officer in my own Regiment, Gus Anson, who had commanded troops in Brunei and Singapore. Thoroughly able, a great sportsman, perhaps a little intolerant of the Army's occasional lapse into superfluous regulation, he had a nice sense of humour and a great zest for living. He later commanded a Yeomanry Regiment and also did sterling work in advising the Kuwaiti armed forces about the intricacies of British armoured vehicles. In short I had an admirable team of officers, backed up by a high class clerical team, loyal, hardworking and efficient, who were particularly adept at turning rapidly written briefs into wholly presentable documents. If I were notably fortunate in my subordinates, I was equally so in my masters, for the Director of Military Operations was none other than Victor Fitzgeorge-Balfour, with whom I had worked when in SD4. Worldly, urbane, cultured and steadfast, he was an ideal man to work for and deeply appreciative of the efforts we made. The one thing that Victor did not care for among his military duties was lecturing. As chairman of a meeting, he excelled but for what is known as public speaking, he had little taste. When therefore his programme forecast the requirement to give a lecture at the Staff College on Far Eastern operational matters, he declined the honour and passed it to me.

Knowing as I did that many of my former colleagues on the Directing Staff there, now promoted to higher positions, including such powerful beings as Dwin Bramall and Mark Bond, would be amongst the audience – and students at the Staff College are about as critical as any – I made a special effort, committed to memory some forty minutes of reviewing the situation in Malaysia, Vietnam, Thailand and other south-east Asian countries, and in full khaki fig, cross-belt and pouch gleaming, delivered my words of wisdom. It went down well. During my second year in MO2, Guy Alvingham, Coldstream Guards, replaced Henry Brooke, and Gus Anson's place was taken by Thomas Boyd-Carpenter, Scots Guards, two absolutely first-class men who made my job agreeably comfortable.

One of the perquisites of being Colonel GS MO2 was that a tour of the area for which we were responsible was one of the agreeable duties involved. The ideal opportunity then presented itself towards the end of my time in Whitehall – a conference of all the military attachés in south-east Asian countries to be held in Singapore and to which I was invited. Still in possession of all the hot-weather kit in which I had carried out my duties in Malaysia during the Confrontation campaign, I set forth. First port of call was Karachi, still at that time the seat of government, where I was greeted by Colonel Philip Panton, whose former service with the pre-partition Indian Army had enabled him to become fluent in Urdu. He and his wife gave some parties in their bungalow which allowed me to meet officers of Pakistan's army, and they were able to show me the somewhat limited delights of Karachi. Next stop was Delhi, this time to be met by a former MOD colleague, Colonel Vincent Budge, Grenadier Guards, who joined with his charming, accomplished wife in extending me their admirable hospitality, taking me about to savour the historic sights of Delhi, and to meet senior members of the Indian Army. It was all a most useful and enjoyable prelude to the Singapore conference.

My return to Singapore was marked by several events. First I was able to renew my friendship with Peter Kemmis Betty, whom I had known well during the Malayan Emergency days at Ipoh, and who was now Military Attaché, Kathmandu. We had many friends in common and were able to bring each other up to date with various darings and doings. I was to see much more of Peter, both while still soldiering and after we had both retired from the Army and found ourselves within striking distance for tennis parties and other jollifications. Secondly I found that another old friend from Staff College days, Brian Tayleur, 14th/20th Hussars, was on the staff of GHQ Far East. A very keen and competent polo player, he was also a brilliant teacher of the game and was a star of Singapore Polo Club. He thereupon arranged for me to take part in several matches and even fitted me out – we were roughly the same height and weight – with boots, breeches, polo helmet and sticks. I enjoyed a number of chukkas, and felt that even if nothing else came from my trip to Singapore, it would have been worth it for the polo alone. There was one regret. I was unable to accept an invitation to visit Afghanistan, so much in the news today, and always revealed as a savage and fascinating place. Familiarity with all our adventures there during the playing of the Great Game tempted me to go, but time's winged chariot was hurrying near, and I was obliged to decline. The conference itself was valuable in that each military attaché was able to give an account of military and political affairs in his particular country and we all went home wiser, or at least better informed, men.

Back in Whitehall – it was now the summer of 1966 – I had some excellent news. One morning Victor Fitzgeorge-Balfour came into my office and thrust a piece of paper at me and, with a smile, hoped I would like what was written on it. I did like it. It was my appointment to take over command of 39 Infantry Brigade in Northern Ireland from the end of that year. My own Irish connection was limited to having commanded The Queen's Royal Irish Hussars, but it was, of course, largely from Ulster and to a lesser extent from Eire, that my Regiment recruited its soldiers, so that, it could be said, I was going back to Regimental roots. In any event command of a brigade was something devoutly to be wished for. I remembered my former days as Brigade Major to Freddie Graham, and wondered what sort of Brigade Major I would be presented with. I need not have worried. My old friend, Mark Bond, at this time a Colonel GS at the Staff College, had been keeping his eyes and ears open and had already selected from his own bunch of students about to finish the course, the very man – Tony Jeapes, formerly of the Devon and Dorset Regiment, an SAS veteran, Military Cross for gallantry in Dhofar, who became a rock of sound support and a great, lasting friend.

In Drayton Parslow, where Wilfried had been kept fully occupied with two young children, gardening, being nice to neighbours and posting to and from the railway station for my picking up and dropping off, we made our plans for the move to Ireland. The cottage owners wanted it back at the end of the summer, so we decided that Wilfried, Viola and Carolin would go to Germany to stay first with her aunt in Essen, then with her father at Eisbergen while I should remain in London – David Walder was quite content that I should continue in his flat until I moved to Ireland. I was required to take over from Brigadier Chandos Blair in December to allow him time to find somewhere to live in England [his home was in Scotland] not too far from London where he would be attending a year's course at the Imperial Defence College. All went according to plan. I duly arrived in Belfast, drove to Lisburn, where HQ 39 Brigade's barracks were, lived for a few days in the Officers' Mess there, while taking over from Chan Blair the Brigade itself, but also the thoroughly satisfactory and comfortable married quarter. I inherited too Chan's staff car driver, who knew all the routes to visit the regiments and the Royal Ulster Constabulary stations, which I would shortly have to get on with, and also a treasure of a housekeeper/cook, Mrs Flanagan, who became a great ally of our two daughters, especially when they had merited our displeasure to the extent when a raised voice – or hand – had become necessary.

I was very fortunate to be in command of 39 Brigade during the two non-turbulent years 1967 and 1968. In the former and future years, the troubles caused much anguish among the people of Ulster and among the security forces positioned there to protect them. Apart from the last few months of my time there, when the Civil Rights movement got going and was subsequently exploited by the IRA, leading to bloody confrontations between the British Army and IRA gunmen, with the Royal Ulster Constabulary heavily and gallantly involved, we – that is my brigade staff and the regiments under my command – were able to pursue a programme of training and sporting activity which, whilst rigorous at times, was also hugely rewarding.

I was blessed with an excellent staff at Brigade HQ and also with a Squadron of Royal Signallers, which made it possible to conduct elaborate manoeuvres with reliable communications. Among my immediate assistants were Tony Jeapes, of whom I have already spoken, and who with my full support was keen to give our soldiers, who made up the HQ and the Signal Squadron, the opportunity of turning themselves into an SAS squadron; Jimmy Hellier, a dynamo of activity, efficiency and enthusiasm; Adrian Peck, 3rd Hussars, with whom I had played polo in Malaysia, and whose genial, Falstaffian exterior concealed a man of shrewd judgement and determined perseverance; John Morrogh-Bernard, Irish Guards, indefatigable in searching out new areas for us to train in, including the Island of Skye, the Orkney Islands, Otterburn ranges and others [alas, John was killed in a skiing accident by being over-bold while off piste]; Jasper Archer, 4th/7th Dragoon Guards, son of my former squadron leader, Porgy, but no more like his father than I to Hercules. These admirable officers were backed by a team of drivers, signallers, cooks, clerks, mechanics, and excellent NCOs, all of whom welcomed our ideas of making Brigade HQ as competent in the field as a fighting force, as the very battalions under our direction.

I was fortunate too in these battalions. One was The Kings, commanded by Geoffrey Errington; the other the 5th Queen's Regiment (Middlesex) with John Shipster DSO in command. Both welcomed my frequent visits to them and my idea of getting to know their officers and men by spending days with each company. During the winter months training was largely individual, but once the better spring weather had arrived, we were able to take to the field. One of the duties of a brigadier is to carry out what is somewhat inaccurately called an administrative inspection of each unit under his command, normally taking the form of a dull day in barracks for the Brigade staff to check the general running of the unit – discipline, equipment, turnout, drill, vehicle maintenance, accounts, the messing standards, recruiting, tradesman skills, state of barracks and so on. There might or might not be a ceremonial parade. We hit upon a better idea. Each battalion would be set an operational task, which would not only test command and tactical skills, but also exercise the administrative elements of the battalion. In the case of The Kings, they were required to prepare a fully operational battalion defensive position, with all that this involved in the way of siting companies, mutual support, depth, support weapons-deployment, concealment both from ground and air observation, ammunition supply, cooking and feeding arrangements, communications, reporting procedures and so on. It was a three-day affair and involved properly dug defences and strict umpiring. The battalion had never been required to take part in anything similar before, and they counted it a very fair test of their operational and administrative readiness.

For The Queen's, we thought of something different. A long march from Ballykinlar to Fort Magilligan with lots of hazards on the way, including embarking in boats at the southern shores of Loch Neagh, making their way north, disembarking under fire, and being subjected to numerous ambushes and counter-attacks en route. It was a severe test, made worse by appalling weather on the second day, but The Queen's did their stuff admirably and afterwards we received the gratitude of the Commanding Officer for having put his battalion through so imaginative and demanding a test.

The other principal regiment of the Brigade was the 4th/7th

Dragoon Guards, stationed at Omagh; a regiment I knew well from serving alongside them in Germany, and I knew many of their officers, including the CO – Robert Ford. For his administrative inspection, and at his own request, as he would shortly be handing over command, we conducted a more conventional day of tests, including a parade and march past [again the Ulster weather obliged by presenting us with a torrential downpour during my inspection of the parade and the march past, so we all got wet], but we also included a number of troop problems – rather as I had with our own regimental Sword and Lance competitions – which added some variety and spice to the day. Soon after this, Robert Ford – who was to return to Northern Ireland in later years and be implicated in the Bloody Sunday controversy – handed over command to Nigel Bagnall, of whom I have already spoken. For his day at the mercy of Brigade HQ, we reverted to an operational test in the field which, as the regiment was equipped with armoured cars, scout cars and helicopters, demanded a country wide deployment. But again it gained high marks as the regiment had never been subjected to so novel an examination before. It may be imagined that I found the helicopter squadron of the 4th/7th DG invaluable in touring the Province and getting about during Brigade manoeuvres, of which two in particular were memorable.

The first was an exercise set for us by HQ Northern Ireland, whose Commander, General Sir Tommy Harries, was a genial Ulster Rifleman. His principal interest was racing and his family ran a yard in Eire to which he ultimately retired. He was a great supporter of all that we did in 39 Brigade and never interfered. There was a great romance about his wartime affairs in that when in command of his battalion during the invasion of Normandy, he had established his HQ in the house of a substantial Norman landowner, and promptly fell in love with the daughter of the house, Anne-Marie, courted and married her while the war was still in progress. At the time of which I am speaking she was the chatelaine of Cloona House and from there dispensed good will and hospitality. Meanwhile Tommy's staff dispensed this exercise, which, in brief, required us to search a huge area for a band of 'guerrillas' supplied by the Queen's Regiment and to prevent their crossing a certain 'border' within a given time. To do the searching we were supported by a squadron of RAF Puma helicopters.

My Brigade Major, Tony Jeapes, conscious of his SAS experience, proposed that he should organize a troop of SAS to come over before the exercise started, establish themselves in the area of activity, win the cooperation of the locals, and so be in a strong position to inform us where the 'guerrillas' were hiding. Unwisely I declined to take what might be thought as an unfair advantage. This was not the only mistake I made. Forgetting altogether my memories of the Borneo campaign, when the presence of the helicopters *side-by-side* with the infantry they were supporting and so ready for instant action, I allowed the RAF Squadron Commander to keep his Pumas centrally concentrated. Sure enough, when the exercise got under way there were several incidents when helicopters arrived too late for the infantry they were to lift to get to the sighted 'guerrillas' on time. But the Brigade had an enjoyable and rewarding exercise. Of the thirty or so 'guerrillas' at large, we captured more than half, but failed to prevent some of them reaching the safe area on the other side of the 'border'. It was during this manoeuvre that I was wholly reliant on the 4th/7th Troop of Gazelle helicopters to get me quickly from place to place, to visit my battalion commanders, and to provide the aerial surveillance to assist me in determining deployment of my forces.

The second exercise was one in which 39 Brigade was essentially deployed as the 'enemy' for the benefit of testing the ability of one of the 3rd Division's brigades, commanded by my old Rifle Brigade friend from Minley and 7 Armoured Brigade, Hew Butler. His task was to 'invade' Ulster and establish a proper bridgehead, into which further reinforcements could later be dispatched. We, therefore, did our stuff, allowed ourselves to be pushed back, while attempting to make life difficult for the invading forces. It was judged a success, and we basked in the thanks and appreciation of the divisional commander.

The best manoeuvre of all, however, took place far from Ulster. The Commander of our Strategic Command was, in 1968, General Sir John Mogg, one of the best-loved, most versatile, able and all-round sportsmen that the Royal Green Jackets could field – and this is saying something. He had decided that an exercise in

Libya [at this time still available for British Army training] to test the battle worthiness and deployment skills of 16 Parachute Brigade would be timely, and thereupon called on us in 39 Brigade to lay something on. At this time 16 Para Brigade was commanded by an exceptionally distinguished soldier, Tony Farrar-Hockley, whom I had known for some years. Not only was he a man who had shown great courage in battle, endurance in a North Korean POW camp, and was overflowing with ideas, eloquence, enthusiasm and determination, but he was also a writer of great ability, so much so that he later was responsible for the *Official History of the Korean War*. We met again to discuss how best to frame the Libyan manoeuvre, and he was insistent that there must be at least two parachute landings during the week-long exercise. Tony Jeapes and I therefore put our heads together and devised what we thought would be sufficiently testing an affair, and duly presented it to John Mogg and his Chief of Staff, Michael Fitzalan-Howard, Scots Guards, of whom I was to see rather more after leaving the Army than during our service. Our plan was approved and, leaving the admirable Adrian Peck to look after things in Lisburn, Tony and I, with much of Brigade HQ, flew to El Adam to prepare everything for the exercise.

At El Adam, still an RAF station then, I found an officer of my own Regiment, Steve Daniell, in command of a troop of Gazelle helicopters, and Nick Vivian [who later in life did so much to champion and promote the interests of the armed forces from his position in the House of Lords] commanding a squadron of the 3rd Carabiniers. It was this squadron, together with a company of infantry mounted in APCs, which would provide the 'enemy' for 16 Parachute Brigade to deal with. The basic idea of the plan was for the parachutists to capture an airfield in the desert, secure it, patrol from it, and then be required to re-plane in order to carry out a further drop to secure another tactically important area. Before D-Day therefore, we deployed in the desert not far from the initial objective. One of my principal assistants was Nigel Bagnall, commanding 4th/7th DG. Also of this regiment was my GSO3 at Brigade HQ, Jasper Archer, who pre-D-Day gave us a most amusing sketch of how not to behave as an exercise umpire. This showed him concerned only with his own comfort and welfare and caring nothing for these conditions for those he was supposed to help. It was an admirably fitting prelude to what was to be a most rewarding week of action.

It was characteristic of Tony Farrar-Hockley that when the fleet of Hercules aircraft appeared as we watched from Exercise HQ, the leading parachutist from the leading Hercules was the Brigadier Commander, Tony himself. I rode in a jeep to the landing zone and had a word with him there to ensure that what we had in mind for the week's training ahead would suit him. He expressed himself well satisfied and we got on with it. There is something especially rewarding about military exercises in the desert – the sheer emptiness of it, the feeling that tanks and guns could do no damage to the countryside, glimpses of gazelles, the glorious weather and the complete freedom from the distractions of civilization. All these added up to an atmosphere of well being. And after a long day, swanning here and there by one of Steve Daniell's helicopters or motoring across the hard sand in a jeep, to return to the simple, but agreeable, pleasures of a whisky and soda before tucking in to supper, followed by a few hours' sleep under the stars made us all feel that the life of a soldier had much to recommend it. All went well with the planned mock battle, which culminated in an armoured counter-attack by Nick Vivian's mixed force of tanks, motor infantry and guns, and having conducted a post-exercise discussion, we all moved back to El Adam to await the VC10 which would take us back to Aldergrove airport near Belfast.

Back at Lisburn, Wilfried and I were able to entertain a number of visitors. George Kidson-Montgomerie, Colonel of the Regiment, came to stay, as did Kenneth Bidie, who was about to take over command of the Regiment from John Paley, and needed to visit our recruiters, our Home HQ – wonderfully well run by another regimental friend, Cliff Jones – and our affiliated Yeomanry Regiment, The North Irish Horse. Other visitors included my brother, Peter, and his wife, David Walder, Jack White, who had commanded C Squadron, 4th Hussars, during the Gothic Line battles. I had invented a game called Roof Tennis, which was played by two. The server struck his tennis ball on to the roof of our house; it would then bounce down to the other player – only allowed to bounce once on the ground – who would return it to the roof; thence to the server and so on until a point was won. All three of the visitors named took to the game enthusiastically and a good deal of rushing about and laughing took place. There was plenty of time and opportunity for other sporting activities. I regularly enjoyed morning hacks with Mike and Jill Oliver, members of the Regiment; we organized Brigade cricket and squash tournaments; tennis was very popular, and of course there were fiercely fought rugby matches between the battalions and other units of the Brigade. Another member of the Regiment, Richard Hoare, a most skilful angler, caught lots of salmon and then sold them to us for our lunch and dinner parties. And then there was the occasion when I was appointed Chieftain of the Day!

It all began in my office at Brigade HQ when a certain warrant officer of the Irish Guards, Mr Kenny, well known on both sides of the water, stood in front of my desk and eyed me. His look was a mixture of dutiful respect and quizzical assurance. Would he still have the power to surprise me? As soon as I heard his question, I knew that he had.

'How would you like to be a Chieftain of the Day, sir?'

I was determined not to be thrown off keel easily, nor would I start asking questions yet.

'Very much,' I replied.

Mr Kenny eyed me again.

'With respect, sir, do you know what it would involve?'

'No, but I'm relying on you to tell me. Sit down.'

Mr Kenny grinned and obeyed. He knew now that whatever it was he wanted, I would do my best to help. His request was straightforward. Would I allow this year's meeting of the All Ireland Pipe Band Championships to be held in the Brigade HQ compound for which I was responsible? It would mean that we would be invaded by hundreds of pipers and drummers; the skirl of the bagpipes would be heard for some four or five hours; we would organize car parking, feeding, drinking – a major, indeed except for the actual piping, perhaps *the* major consideration – putting up tents, preparing the field on which the playing would take place and so on. We would have to be prepared for a huge audience, all of whom would need facilities of every sort and who would, no doubt, distribute litter all over our militarily neat barrack area. Mr Kenny then played his trump card. I would be

Chieftain of the Day, a supreme honour, he emphasized. Moreover lots of money would be spent. What with NAAFI rebate and bar profits, we should do well in augmenting the fund for soldiers' welfare. The great day was several months away and after consulting my staff and the garrison Sergeant Major, we decided to accept the challenge and Mr Kenny was given the green light.

There followed lots of consultation and planning. Numerous agencies had legitimate fingers in the pie. The local Borough Council, the Chamber of Commerce, the two pipe band associations, Scottish and Irish, had their say. At Lisburn itself the garrison staff and the NAAFI managers made known their requirements. It was not easy to plan for an event for which the number of people who might turn up was not known. How many cars would there be? How many bottles of beer would be wanted? There had to be some guesswork. The military machine has often been accused of 'over-insuring'. But piping is thirsty work. Think of the uproar if we ran out of drink! We also wanted to ensure that there were plenty of ways of allowing spectators to part with their money – for the Army Benevolent Fund. One-armed bandits, strawberries and cream, a gift shop?

Yet we had to keep our eyes firmly on the main ball. The facilities for the pipe bands themselves, their assembly, their tuning-up areas, their marshalling and their actual playing had priority over all other considerations. We were lucky in having a large sports field, well sited and surrounded by tall, noble trees. Tents would be erected round the edges and a rectangular ring with posts and ropes would allow two bands to compete simultaneously, for drum majors to march and counter march, and for a final grand parade of all the bands. We were expecting sixty bands, at an average of fifteen per band, a total of nearly 1,000 men.

During the week before the great day, tents sprang up, the field was cut and rolled, flag poles erected – apart from the Union flag, there would be flags of the Brigade and my Regiment. After all the Chieftain must do things properly. There was intensive activity throughout the garrison. It was not every day that we were honoured by hosting pipe bands from all over Ireland. The garrison Sergeant Major produced a joker from his ample sleeve – a saluting base of great magnificence, with a door at the back, steps leading up to it, a roof, windows at the sides, and the whole thing painted a gleaming white. It had been constructed for a former visit by the Queen Mother. Flanked by flags, surrounded by flowers, with the Regimental plaque firmly in the centre of its gable and a so-called VIP bar immediately to its rear, it was indeed a fitting stage for the Chieftain of the Day to take the salute.

When I awoke on the morning of the Day, the sun was shining in a cloudless sky, but I had been in Ulster long enough to know that I could draw little comfort from this agreeable sight. By the time I joined my staff for a final look round the field, grey, rain-laden clouds were scudding low across the sky, the wind was strong and cold. Next stop the Assembly Rooms for a civic reception for the mayor, judges from Scotland and Ireland, officials of the two pipe band associations and their President. Mr Kenny, who loved to spring surprises, took me to one side.

'You'll have to make a speech in a minute, sir.'

'What?'

'Oh yes, just on behalf of the Army, you know, welcoming them as Chieftain and all that. Surely I briefed you on it sir?'

'No, you didn't, but I'll do what I can.'

Whenever we are required to put together 'a few words', we are, of course, assailed on all sides for our opinions on urgent matters. So it was on this occasion. Not until the mayor was making his speech of welcome did I have a moment to think. Through clenched teeth, I rehearsed a few phrases and when the mayor had finished, brushed through it tolerably well. After the President had droned on for a bit we dispersed to meet again at 2 o'clock when the curtain would go up. Shortly after two I arrived at the field. Our hopes, our expectations, could not have been better rewarded. Already there was a large crowd, eagerly looking at and listening to the competitors; already the NAAFI and Mess tents were doing a roaring trade; already the strawberries and cream were in serious demand. Everywhere was activity. In the ring itself two pipe bands, well separated, were performing. The judges were looking sage and serious. More bands were positioning themselves to be next on parade. Everywhere there was a general feeling of confraternity, all enjoying themselves, all relishing the sound of the pipes and drums. I strolled round having a word here with a soldier, there with a piper. The crowds were gathering. It was amusing to note that the VIP tent and bar was patronized by anyone who in his or her own eyes was up to the mark. This gave the tent far wider, more profitable and more entertaining a clientele than its designators had planned.

Bands entered the ring with that deliberate, rhythmic step, a variety of tartans on display – Maclean and Cameron, McKenzie and McGregor, an occasional Green or Saffron, a single Macbeth and, more numerous than any other, the Royal Stewart. They marched and formed their circles, played their strathspeys and reels with at least four parts, formed up and marched out again, only to be replaced by yet another band. On and on it went, until it was time for me to dash back to the house to change into uniform. Never had it seemed to me more fitting that I should belong to an Irish Regiment. When I returned properly accoutred, I ran into my administrative expert, looking worried. He was concerned that we were running out of strawberries. I asked if there were still plenty to drink.

'Oh, yes.' He brightened.

'Well, let's go and have one.'

As we entered the VIP tent, we were joined by Mr Kenny, himself resplendent in uniform. Freed momentarily from his judging of the bands' style and turn-out, he had come in search of me. Equipped with a glass each, he broached the point.

'You know you'll have to make another speech, sir?'

'You can't mean it.'

'Certainly. After the "Salute to the Chieftain" and "The Battle's O'er" you must address your bandsmen. It's the Address of the Chieftain. Very important. They'll carry your words back into every village in the South. I'm just organizing the microphone now. Thought you'd like plenty of warning.' He strode off, as purposeful and self-possessed as ever.

There was time enough during a parade of the drum majors for me to think what I was to say to *my* bandsmen. The weather, clearly aware of the climax approaching, took a sharp turn for the better. Indeed it turned on the charm. The sky became blue, a few straggling clouds sank, the wind dropped and the sun glinted down across the length of the field. The march past of all bands and their assembly prior to the prize giving was about to start. I took up my position on the saluting base and in marched three bands who would then play the others in. I took their salute. Then in they all came, band after band, swinging past, their tartans and kilts, drums and pipes as colourful and brave a sight as one could wish for. Sixty-one bands in all. At last all were assembled. Over the loudspeaker came the words that the 'Salute to the Chieftain' would now be played. When nearly 1,000 bagpipes play 'Highland Laddie' for you, you begin to appreciate the honour paid you. Then came 'The Battle's O'er' and the announcer's voice again: 'The Chieftain will now address his bandsmen.'

What did I say? What could I say? Brevity is the soul of wit; never more so than on an occasion like this. I thanked them for coming, some from so far south, to give us an unforgettable day. I thanked them for the singular honour they had awarded me and assured them that no future march past could ever equal this one. I recalled that my own Regiment had long lacked a pipe band, but was eager to reconstitute one [they did and it now flourishes as the Pipes and Drums of The Queen's Royal Hussars], and I suggested to them that if any of them felt the call of soldiering not to forget that apart from Mr Kenny's famous Regiment, there was also my own. And I told them to come back again to this garrison where they would always be welcome. It was enough. It served.

Prize giving followed. How splendid to hear the roar of delight which went up from a band as it heard of its own success. Bonnets were hurled in the air, drum majors carried high on the backs of their fellow bandsmen, clapping and handshaking came from their less fortunate rivals. When the National Anthem had been played, I asked the VIP barman to produce a large number of glasses filled with that beverage which only Scotland and Ireland know how to make. As we drank each others' health, the bands began to leave the field to march the mile or so down to the town. The great day was over.

After two years I handed over command of 39 Brigade to Peter Hudson, Rifle Brigade, who had a much more difficult time than I had had, for in 1969 the troubles began all over again. But memories of our time in Ulster are pleasant ones. One of the officers in my Regiment was Patrick O'Neill, son of Northern Ireland's Prime Minister, Terence O'Neill, and Wilfried and I were greatly honoured to dine with him and his wife at their Stormont house. The relatively non-confrontational conditions of the time also allowed us to travel to Eire and we much enjoyed holidays in County Donegal and County Cork. I had hoped to see my old 4th Hussar fellow troop leader, Claud Thompson, by this time again Joint Master of The Black and Tans, but his illness prevented it. We were also blessed by finding, as a companion for our daughters, Petronella, whose family lived in Lisburn. She was an absolute treasure – gentle, loving, patient and sensible, we owe her a lot for her care of Viola and Carolin, and we have kept in touch with her ever since .

I referred earlier to Colonel [later General] Bill Jackson, a highly decorated sapper, who had been in charge at Minley Manor and who was a distinguished military historian. While I was still in Ulster, he suggested that I should write an account of the battle for North Africa, as the publishers, Batsford, were doing a series of such battles. As a result I was put in touch with Peter Kemmis Betty [a cousin of my Gurkha friend] who was a director of Batsford. We rapidly agreed a contract, and during my final months in Lisburn I set to work on my first volume of military history. I shall always be immensely grateful to Bill Jackson for this introduction which led to many more historical and biographical ventures. What is more, immediately following my command of 39 Brigade, I was lucky enough to become a student at the Imperial Defence College in Belgrave Square. The course there, which lasted a year, was undemanding and gave me plenty of time for writing.

Chapter 15

Three Years' Sabbatical

> 'You ought to be getting command of a division, but unfortunately there isn't one for you.'
>
> The Military Secretary

The three years consisted of one at the Imperial Defence College and two at SHAPE in Belgium, where my job, with the aid of an international staff, was to ensure that access to Berlin from the west, by air, river, road and rail, was not interfered with or denied by the German Democratic Republic or the Soviet Union. In the early part of the 1970s this was not a demanding task. Preceded as it was by a year's holiday in Belgrave Square, the pattern of leisure for reading, writing, travel, sport, plays and opera, and dining well had been well established.

Sticking to our preference for living in the country, Wilfried and I rented a charming East Sussex farmhouse, from which I would take the train to London on a Monday morning, returning for the weekend, while once more most kindly accommodated in London by David Walder who now had a large flat in Queen's Gate for his wife, Elspeth and their four children, and was able to allow me one pleasant room. The IDC course with some sixty students, made up of brigadiers, naval captains, RAF group captains plus a mixed bag of Commonwealth and United States officers, civil servants and diplomats, was designed to give those attending a broader outlook on the political, economic, industrial and strategic aspects of world affairs in order to fit them for senior positions in their respective spheres of service. Most days – I should say mornings, for afternoons were invariably free – required our attendance at a lecture beginning at 11 o'clock, followed by questions and lunch. Those delivering these lectures were of a very high quality – cabinet ministers, university professors, eminent men of business, top ranking men of the Armed Services, ambassadors, politicians not in office, historians and so on. It was at once a pleasure and a privilege to be present at such a wealth of erudition, wit, experience and contrasting points of view.

For me, and I believe for others too, one of the most agreeable aspects of Belgrave Square was once more to be with old friends, particularly those from Minley Manor days, Mark Bond and Hew Butler. There was also a former holder of the same liaison duty as I had had at Fort Knox – Bob Britten, a sapper, with a great sense of humour and a notable skill with the camera, of which more later. Also on the course was one of my fellow troop leaders in C Squadron, 4th Hussars, Ronald Arculus, who made good use of our Italian campaign by perfecting his fluency in the vernacular [he eventually became our ambassador in Rome, and on one occasion grandly entertained Wilfried and me to lunch in the splendid ambassadorial palazzo]. The senior Army member of the IDC staff was Digby Raeburn, Scots Guards, with a fine war record, a sharp intellect and a most clubbable disposition. I was to have much more to do with Digby when I agreed to take over from him as Chairman of the Cavalry and Guards Club, and I will have something to say about this later on. The junior Army member of the staff – and this particular post was normally offered to an up and coming lieutenant colonel expected to reach great heights [the choice was unerring in this case] – was John Stanier, originally a 7th Hussar who later commanded The Scots Greys. He ended up as Chief of the General Staff and a field marshal.

At Beeches Farmhouse in Sussex we enjoyed family life. A good local school had been found for Viola and Carolin, now respectively eight and six; Wilfried found pleasant friends amongst the neighbours; a largish garden kept us busy; we had inherited two cats from the owners of the house, a ginger called Fudge and a one-eyed black called Nicholas. At night Fudge would climb onto the sloping roof and tap on the girls' bedroom window, demanding entrance, while Nicholas, and except for one other I had never come across this in a cat, would accompany us on quite long walks. The garden contained a tennis court, and one most welcome visitor was Richard Parsons, the potential diplomat who played the part of George Wickham in the amateur production of *Pride and Prejudice* at Salisbury Playhouse, and whose wife was a keen tennis player. At this time Richard was Private Secretary to a minister in the Foreign Office. Later he became our ambassador to Spain and to Sweden. There was also a small nine-hole golf course only a mile or so from the farmhouse, and when Mark Bond came to stay one weekend, we much relished opening our shoulders on one of the longer holes.

Perhaps the best part of the whole IDC course was the overseas tour. We had a broad choice between the United States, India and Pakistan, the Far East or – and this is the one I chose – Yugoslavia, Greece, Turkey, Iran and the Persian Gulf. There must have been a dozen or so of us on this particular tour, including Hew Butler, Bob Britten and John Stanier. I was looking forward to the opportunity of reading during the various flights for, following the reasonable reception of my Batsford book about North Africa, I had signed a further contract to write another one – *Hitler as Military Commander* – and had with me several biographies of Hitler, including, of course, Alan Bullock's great work. I was able to make useful notes for my own forthcoming book and there was plenty of room in the special RAF aircraft which took us first to Belgrade.

I will not compose a travelogue. I will say that Belgrade was dull and made considerably duller by briefings from grey, hard-faced civil servants of the Tito regime, who told us what a splendid country Yugoslavia was and how the economy was booming. Sarajevo, by contrast, was colourful, exciting and pulsating with activity, putting us in the way of appreciating the star of the show – Dubrovnik. As Hew Butler and I paced its, what seemed like, marble pavements in search of a superlative restaurant [we found one and dined excellently] I could not but recall that Marshal Marmont, Napoleon's great friend and fellow artilleryman, had been made Duke of Ragusa – the former name for Dubrovnik – by the Emperor after Marmont's Peninsular failure at Salamanca – and that when Marmont failed to respond to Napoleon's call on his return from Elba, the French language acquired a new word – *raguser*, to betray.

Next stop Athens, where the colonels were still in charge, and one morning we were treated to the sight of these same colonels arriving at a government building in a fleet of cars with military escort and not another vehicle anywhere in sight. Their grip on Greece, however, did not prevent our close inspection of the Acropolis and other antiquities, nor interfere with a trip to the border with Bulgaria to study the problems of defence. A lightning visit to Crete enabled us to follow the fortunes of Theseus as he grappled with the dreaded Minotaur. We were delightfully entertained by the British Ambassador at his house on the coast, but so fleeting and controlled a vision of Greece did little to further our understanding of its former glories. And so on to Turkey, where Ankara, like Belgrade, had nothing but dreary briefings to offer. Istanbul, by contrast, brought us face to face with the splendour, the mystery, the enchantment, the glamour of Byzantine art and the Eastern Empire. The Sea of Marmara, the harbour of the Golden Horn, the Great Mosque had us in thrall, a trip by boat to the Topkapi Palace and the inspection of its treasures there – such sights set us reflecting – while a visit to Ephesus reminded us of Diana's virtues.

We then hurried on to Tehran. At this time the Shah was still on the throne and the Iranian Army was very much in charge of what went on. They looked after us well and there were two unforgettable parts to our Iranian visit. One was Isfahan where the most beautiful mosques captured the eye and mind, situated as they were to the flank of a huge open space, a kind of padang, if you like, where it was said the game of polo was first played, no doubt with the heads of malefactors rather than the wooden balls of today. The other was Persepolis and, once again having admired the exquisite columns of Darius's masterpiece, I was able to offer my fellow students an echo of Tamburlaine:

> Is it not passing brave to be a king
> And ride in triumph through Persepolis?

Ever conscious of the requirement that on our return to Belgrave Square we would, like all the other parties whose tours had taken them elsewhere, be called upon to give an account of ourselves, Bob Britten had been filming everything of interest, so that our task would be lightened by simply showing the film with a suitable commentary which I could put together.

After the glories of ancient Persia, the final stop – Bahrain – where my old friend Roly Gibbs was the British general in charge – was clearly going to be somewhat thin, so I obtained permission to fly with a regular supply aeroplane to Abu Dhabi, where my 4th Hussar fellow troop leader, John Paley who had succeeded me in command of the Regiment, was now Commander, Abu Dhabi, Defence Force. Together we visited his various battalions and other units and I met a number of former colleagues who, like John, were fluent in Arabic. Little was I to know then that after leaving the Army some half dozen years later, I too would find myself working in an Arab country and struggling to master a smattering of that most difficult language. From Abu Dhabi I returned to Bahrain to join the rest of my party and was able to see a little of Roly Gibbs and his elegant, art-loving, versatile and wholly delightful wife, Davina.

During this five week tour, Wilfried and the children had been in Germany at Eisbergen, and we so arranged things that they flew back from there on the same day that our IDC tour ended. We were able to meet in London and return to Beeches Farmhouse, which had been looked after for us by David Walder and his family. Back at Belgrave Square Bob Britten and I showed our film which went down much better than some other presentations consisting of a mere talk. Mark Bond, who spoke about his look at America, could hardly restrain a yawn during his own offering. Soon after this we were to learn what our next jobs would be. It was then that the Military Secretary spoke to me the words that appear at the head of this chapter.

So, instead of a division to command, I was appointed to be Chief of Staff, *Live Oak*. This group of British, French, German and American officers, men and women, had been established during difficult times with the Soviet Union and the East German Government, who kept threatening to cut off all access to Berlin from the west. The Berlin Airlift had thwarted the most serious of actions taken by those attempting to force the Allies out of Germany's former capital, and since then the so-called *Live Oak* staff, positioned next door to SACEUR's headquarters at Casteau in Belgium [General de Gaulle's hostility to NATO had obliged both NATO and its military headquarters to move from Fontainebleau] had developed plans to overcome any further efforts by the East Germans or the Soviet Union to block any of the routes from West Germany to Berlin, whether the air corridors, the roads, the railways or rivers. It had been agreed from the outset that the Chief of Staff of this organization would be a British major general and so, early in 1970, I found myself taking over from James Lunt, whom we last met playing polo in Aden. He and his wife had found a charming, but small, house at Asquillies, a few miles from Mons, and thus near to SHAPE at Casteau. There had been so little activity on the part of those formerly trying to isolate Berlin that those appointed to join the *Live Oak* staff were by the time I came on the scene designated as being a component of Dead Wood. But, as James Lunt confided to me, the opportunity for improving one's golf handicap, for travelling in Europe, for skiing and for adding to one's bank balance – for the allowances were generous – more than made up for the somewhat unexciting nature of the job.

So we took over the Asquillies house, inheriting Jeannine as a general *femme de ménage* and her husband as an occasional tidier of the garden. Our neighbours M et Mme Cretur were agreeable and hospitable – to participate in a Sunday lunch party in Belgium requires an infinite capacity for food, wine and sheer endurance. M Cretur, whose profession was the manufacture of artificial limbs, had one great passion – *la chasse*, and his walls were all decorated with masks of foxes, heads of deer and wild boar, which made it clear that in spite of having only one eye, it was a deadly one. His great ally was the local *garde de chasse*, M Couvreur, a wizened peasant with whom I would occasionally exchange courtesies, although our comprehension of each other's French was sometimes questionable. Into this friendly environment we fitted, notwithstanding *l'odeur belge* which from time to time permeated the atmosphere as a consequence of faulty drainage. By this time Viola was at St Mary's Convent, Ascot, while Carolin went to the SHAPE school, picked up and redelivered each day by a huge school bus.

My duties were undemanding. There was only one serious incident during the two years that I was there. I reported direct to SACEUR, General Goodpaster of the US Army, an able, quiet, courteous and conscientious man, whom I would see more of on the golf course than in the office, for he was a keen golfer and greatly enjoyed his *Live Oak* games. My staff amounted to some forty or so service men and women from all three services of the four countries already referred to. One or two characters stood out from the rest. My deputy, General de Brigade Jacques Pol, had spent most of his service in France's north African colonies. He and his enchanting wife, Paule, gave the most enjoyable dinner parties, and had the unusual way of addressing each other with *vous*, rather than *tu*. Early on it became clear to me that he had never been able to reconcile himself to France's capitulation in 1940, and his sensitivity on this point was not eased by the demeanour and character of the senior German officer, Oberst Heino Graf Vitzthum, who had all the careless swagger of an aristocratic Prussian cavalryman. But the peace was kept. The American officers were competent but somewhat neutral. My British staff included some good fellows; the Chief Clerk an absolute treasure, and I was fortunate enough to have my faithful driver of 39 Brigade days, Corporal Edwardes.

We took full advantage of the opportunities for getting about. Twice we went to Grindelwald for the skiing, and one summer with the generous assistance of another French colleague, Roger de Courville, we spent two highly enjoyable weeks in Brittany. It seemed that his family, who lived in a Normandy château owned a holiday home on the Brittany coast, and we would be welcome to make use of it – gratis. We duly set off, finding our way first to the Normandy château, where we stayed one night with Madame de Courville, Roger's mother, and drank a lot of their cider, a pastime rendered more dangerous than I had imagined, for as Madame's son-in-law began to open one bottle the cork flew out with such violence that, narrowly missing his wife, daughter of the house, it shattered one of the windows.

Next morning we motored on to Brittany and having picked up the key found ourselves opening the door of what can only be described as a mini-château, complete with tower and winding staircase, only fifty yards from the sea. Roger had warned us that it was *un peu primitif* and indeed it was. But the sun shone, the sea sparkled and the local market yielded a superb variety of good things to eat and drink. The mini-château holiday was long remembered by all of us.

Already fairly fluent in German, *Live Oak* enabled me to polish my distinctly rusty French. Every now and again there would be a formal dinner for the *Live Oak* officers and their wives, often in order to bid farewell to those who were leaving, and on these occasions I would say the fitting things in three languages. But I must confess that my French was never more than passable, whereas Wilfried was admirably trilingual. In order to improve my French I attended, somewhat irregularly, the SHAPE language school for half an hour's chat with one of the competent and attractive Belgian instructresses. I had also at the very outset of my appointment interviewed all the staff and had, in each case, attempted to converse in their native tongue, as well as seeing how good their command of English was.

My duties demanded frequent visits both to Berlin itself, thus enabling me to use the three main means of access – road, rail and air – and also to Bonn to liaise with the British Embassy people with whom it would be necessary to confer in the event of a real crisis. Throughout my two years at Casteau there was only one real flap. It was relatively early on in my time there and was created by the Soviet declaration that on a certain evening their anti-aircraft missile units would be practising with live missiles in one of the three air corridors reserved for commercial aircraft to fly to and from Berlin. There was but one response to be made to such a threat. Our policy, well known to the Soviet Union and the DDR, was that these corridors must be permanently and without exception open to military and civil flights. After consultation with SACEUR, Bonn and the Ministry of Defence, we made it plain to both regimes – USSR and DDR – that two military flights would be using the southern and central air corridors at the time of these proposed missile practices. Normally my office and those of my assistants were fairly quiet during the evenings. On this occasion, however, it was necessary for me to give orders for dinner to be served to me in my office, as I was subjected to an endless flow of telephone calls from the Commanders-in-Chief, Rhine Army and RAF Germany; from the Embassy in Bonn; from the Foreign Office; from the Ministry of Defence; from the Paris Embassy, as one of the flights would be carried out by the French Air Force, the other by the RAF; and even from the Prime

Minister's office in London. Never before had I felt myself and my current position to be so important. The time for our flights came. The RAF mission in the central corridor was perfectly on time and carried out without incident. The French flight in the southern corridor was half an hour late, not because of any technical or political hitch, but simply because the two French pilots had lingered over their dinner. It too then went without a hitch and everyone heaved a sigh of relief and got back to their less exciting routines.

Those of you who know Brussels will know too that just round the corner from the Grande Place is an area housing the most superb restaurants. One of them in particular was a favourite of ours – Vincent – where the most exquisite sole was to be found. We did our best to do justice to those gourmet delights and sampled many other establishments' wares. We also gave dinner parties at our Asquillies house and it was particularly pleasing for Wilfried [amongst her many other virtues and accomplishments she is an exceptionally good cook] to receive the effusive appreciation of Jacques Pol. On one occasion we gave a drinks party for the officers and their wives, notable for two events. Our neighbour, Mme Cretur was one of our guests, and for the delectation of all those present I had mixed what was known as a Seventy-Five – the base being a White Lady [gin, Cointreau and lemon juice in equal parts] topped up with champagne. Having consumed one or two of these, Mme Cretur approached me for replenishment, but insisting that she would like *seulement le jus*, little realizing in her somewhat tipsy state that it was *le jus* which was doing the damage. The second point was the diplomatic skill with which my faithful driver, Corporal Edwardes, handled the rather tricky parking problem. He invited the local gendarme to supervise arrangements and then plied him with sufficient alcohol to ensure that the flagrant breach of parking regulations went unnoticed.

We were fortunate in being able to put up a number of visitors to SHAPE, including that great cavalryman, Charles Sloane of the 3rd Carabiniers, who when in charge of the musical arrangements for some important parade for the benefit of General de Gaulle, had chosen 'Charlie is my Darling' for one of the finale pieces. I remembered, in particular, his careful and meticulous schooling of polo ponies when he came to stay with us – the 4th Hussars – at Bredebeck for some nearby polo tournament. His wholly charming wife, Patricia, was a keen tennis player, whom I had partnered in a Rhine Army match, and who had persuaded Charles to play in a game partnering her father during their engagement. Charles recounted the story of his serving with his potential father-in-law at the net and succeeding in hitting the neck of this august figure not once, but *twice* with consecutive balls. I also recall now that later on in our lives Charles, who like myself had become Colonel of the Regiment, gave wise and shrewd advice at Cavalry Colonels' conferences. For his visit to SHAPE on this occasion, he stayed with us and presented us with a huge Melton Mowbray pie, which sustained us for some weeks. It was always a great pleasure for me to see Charles at the Cavalry Colonels' dinners held each year at the Cavalry and Guards Club – of which more later.

Other visitors gave us much pleasure with their company. My former Minley Manor colleague, Bill Cooper, and his wife came to stay for a few days, bringing with them a framed reproduction of a George Stubbs *Mares and Foals* painting, which has adorned every drawing room in which we have found ourselves since then and, as every soldier will confirm, there have been many of them. Bill Cooper, who spoke excellent French, was also a great trencherman and was deeply appreciative of Vincent's offerings. We worked up appropriate appetites in order to do justice to these culinary delights by striking golf balls about with careless confidence on the local course and by similar treatment of tennis balls on our somewhat dilapidated Asquillies court. Next to arrive was an old friend from 4th Hussar days in Italy after the war, Tony Morrison who, having worked for some years in Rhodesia, where he found and married his talented and charming wife, Diana, was now Chief Executive of the Hereford Herd Book Society, or what I preferred to call it – Commander-in-Chief, Hereford Bulls. He had telephoned from our Embassy in Paris to see whether it would be convenient to look in on his way back to England. I thereupon dispatched the faithful Corporal Edwardes, accompanied by Jacques Pol's elegant secretary to ensure that no linguistic problems arose, to the Paris Embassy to pick him up – a gesture which greatly impressed the Embassy officials with whom he was dealing. He too much enjoyed his few days at Asquillies and we shall hear much more of him and Diana later, for in the mid-1970s we acquired a house in Herefordshire, although we did not stay there long. Another of Corporal Edwardes' adventures involved his meeting yet another visitor at Brussels airport, this time Tom Tilbrook, one of my troop leaders during the Malayan Emergency and now on the Berlin staff. On the way to the airport and not far from it, the staff car suffered what Edwardes described as a 'complete mechanical breakdown'. On hearing this from his telephone message, I ordered him to run to the airport and bring Colonel Tilbrook to Asquillies by taxi, leaving the staff car to look after itself. The order was duly obeyed and Tom arrived just in time to have a bath and don a black tie for the dinner party we had arranged for him. Corporal Edwardes' final picking-up requirement was one he disapproved of. We had heard from Peter Kemmis Betty that his second son, Charlie, was back-packing through Europe and would be in Brussels at such and such a time. We offered accommodation and victualling. A rendezvous in the Grande Place was therefore given to Charlie when he telephoned and a disgruntled Edwardes, who clearly disapproved of such privileged treatment of someone so young, so scruffy and – not to put too fine a point on it – so unwashed, duly found him and delivered him to us, where the comforts of baths, laundry, kitchen and bed were more than welcome.

The Deputy SACEUR, a post held always by a British general, was at this time Sir Desmond Fitzpatrick, formerly of The Royal Dragoons, and whose previous appointment had been C.-in-C. Rhine Army. He was a man of keen intelligence, a gallant and successful commander in war, a competent field sportsman, whose sometimes intimidating manner concealed an agreeable sense of humour, and whose standards of integrity, loyalty and duty were very high. His wife, Mary, was refreshingly frank and quite unimpressed by either the position her husband occupied or by the dignitaries whom she was obliged to meet and often entertain. I well recall overhearing her response to Desmond's plea:

'Will you come and be nice to the Mayor of Mons?'

'No!'

My own dealings with him had little to do with either his

military position or mine. They were more of a social or private nature. On one occasion he asked me if we would like to give a dinner party for the then Chief of General Staff, Sir Michael Carver and his wife, Edith, who were staying with the Fitzpatricks for some NATO conference. We duly did and I remember the CGS's first comment to me: 'I've just been reading your book' [he was referring to *Hitler as Military Commander*, which had received a favourable review from Michael Howard, who had been persuaded by James Lunt to do a piece about the book]. He did not, however, say what he thought about it. He was himself a most distinguished and prolific military historian and his opinion would have been worth having. But, like his great ancestor, Wellington, he was never lavish with praise.

Apart from Grindelwald, the mini-château, sole at Vincent, receiving visitors and other distractions, I had plenty of time for writing. It was made known to me by that delightful 12th Lancer, Matt Abraham, that Lady McCreery, widow of the renowned General Sir Richard McCreery, who had commanded the Eighth Army, was a brilliant horseman and perhaps the greatest cavalryman of his generation, wanted a short portrait of her husband to be written for the sake of the grandchildren and other descendants. It was thought that someone, not himself a 12th Lancer, might produce something more objective than one too close to Dick McCreery's life and career. Matt, who was familiar with my own writings, therefore asked me to undertake the task. After talking it over with Lettice McCreery herself, I agreed to do so, but I insisted that there would be no question of remuneration. I would look upon it as an honour to be trusted with such an undertaking. I consulted widely and received the most gratifying response from many of those who had known and admired Dick. One of these was Desmond Fitzpatrick, and in his office at SHAPE we had a long talk about Dick McCreery's life as a soldier, a horseman, a family man, a countryman, and all that he had done for the world of racing. Happily the little book was well received and was exactly what Lettice McCreery had hoped for. She presented me with a lovely reproduction of Roy Beddington's painting of the 4th Hussar Mounted Escort to Sir Winston Churchill at the Queen's Coronation in 1953.

There was also the opportunity to write pieces for *Blackwood's*

Magazine, to which I had contributed for some years. My first success there had been with a portrait of Bella, that beautiful mare who carried me so willingly and boldly in my mastership of the Staff College Drag, and while at Asquillies I was able to complement this original piece with one called *Memoirs of a Drag-Hunting Man* [shades of Siegfried Sassoon]. Many years later I had the good fortune to produce a book – for that great equestrian publisher, J.A. Allen – called *On Drag-Hunting* and incorporated into it some of the stories which had appeared in the *Blackwood*'s articles.

It was in the latter part of 1971 that I heard of my next appointment. I was to take over from Bill Scotter as Chief of Staff, United Kingdom Land Forces at Wilton, near Salisbury. There then followed a round of farewell visits to Berlin, to Bonn, to my SHAPE contacts and to General Goodpaster himself. Desmond Fitzpatrick and his wife came to have drinks with us one morning, bringing with them Major General Alan Cathcart, Scots Guards, and his decorative half-section, Rosie. Alan asked me if I knew his brother-in-law, General Sir Basil Eugster, Irish Guards, Commander-in-Chief, UK Land Forces – that is my future boss. I didn't and said so, but I soon would and on assuming the position of his Chief of Staff, I came to like and admire him greatly. But my three year sabbatical would soon be over.

Chapter 16

From Brigmerston to Boyton

> 'I hope you won't bear a grudge against me that I was unable to find you a 3 star job.'
>
> The Military Secretary

There were several pleasing aspects about becoming the Chief of Staff at Wilton. The first and perhaps the greatest of these was the house that went with the job. Brigmerston Farmhouse, near Bulford, and on the River Avon, was Georgian, spacious, elegant, with a very pretty garden, an even larger vegetable garden, a lovely view across the river and a staff to go with it. Sergeant Smyth from my own Regiment was in charge, Corporal Scott was the excellent cook, Corporal Sturman, also from the Regiment, was my soldier servant. Mr Dark was the gardener, who spent much of his time studying *The Sporting Life*; nonetheless he kept the lawns immaculate, the flowers blooming and the fruit and vegetables flowing. There were also two very good loose boxes, a forage storeroom and a tack room. We had taken over the house from Colonel Jasper Browell, who was commanding an artillery regiment at Devizes, had formerly run The King's Troop, and was about as clubbable a man as you could find anywhere. Tall, well built, rubicund and kindly, he was a model of all that is best and most attractive about a British Army officer. An excellent horseman himself, he was a great supporter of the Royal Artillery Hunt, the race course at Larkhill, where many local hunts held their annual point-to-points, an organizer of Army Hunter Trials, an enthusiastic member of the Larkhill shoot and apart from all this a fine soldier. While at Brigmerston, he had allowed a nice 9th/12th Lancer, Richard Mackaness, to stable his two horses there [Jasper's own animals were at the Larkhill stables] and on taking over we were, of course, delighted to continue the arrangement. I should perhaps add that our Brigmerston staff also included a cleaner, a somewhat disgruntled female, whose ill temper totally failed to cast a damper on our enjoyment of being there.

The second agreeable feature of the job sprang from the people with whom I had to work. The staff officers, HQ personnel, clerks and typists were a lively and competent bunch, and my closest colleague in charge of administration was Major General Ronnie Buckland, Coldstream Guards, whom I had known previously and who was a model of efficiency, industry, loyalty and good humour. His speech impediment somehow rendered his gift for witty, pithy comment more attractive. And then there was the man we both worked for, the C.-in-C. UK Land Forces, General Sir Basil Eugster, Irish Guards. Gigantic in stature, brave in battle, distinguished in appearance, kindly in manner, he would spend much of his time touring round the country visiting regiments, headquarters and other military establishments in order to get a general feel for how things were going, what, if anything, needed change or improvement and making officers and soldiers alike aware that there was such a thing as HQ UKLF concerned with their wellbeing and their ability to carry out willingly, effectively and enthusiastically their respective duties. Basil and his diminutive, enchanting wife, Marcia, would give the most splendid dinner parties in their official residence, Bulford Manor. Their thoughtfulness for guests would be illustrated by Basil's announcing that as he had been lunching at White's that day and had seen a surplus of plovers' eggs, he had bought the lot for our delectation; or Marcia's insistence – I was on this occasion seated on her right – on demonstrating to me with faultless dexterity the best way to peel a peach. Basil was, at this time, Colonel of the Irish Guards, and it may be imagined how imposing a figure he cut when mounted on a huge grey of some 17 hh or more, with bearskin towering above and accompanying HM The Queen for her inspection at the Birthday Parade. On one of these days when Ronnie Buckland and I, accompanied by our wives, were spectators of this most impressive of all military spectacles and when Philip Ward, Welsh Guards, was the Major General, we all went to lunch at Philip's house in London, where his wife Pam, whose diction – she had studied at RADA – was the most perfect I ever encountered in an Army wife, gave us the most sumptuous repast, before we motored back to Salisbury Plain. I was fortunate enough still to have Corporal Edwardes as my driver, and I am happy to report that during his service at Wilton he found and married an intelligent, comely and good-natured member of the Women's Royal Army Corps.

A third advantage of my new appointment was that it allowed plenty of time for sporting activities. My old friend, Guy Wheeler, fellow troop leader in wartime C Squadron, 4th Hussars, was about to leave UKLF, where as a brigadier he had been overseeing the activities of all the RAC regiments, and asked me if I would like to take over the half-gun he had in the Netheravon Shoot which was run by none other than Robert Ferguson, whom I had succeeded some dozen years earlier as Master of the Staff College Drag. Robert's gamekeeping skills, enhanced by careful organization and preparation, resulted in some very good sport. It was principally a partridge shoot and at this time, 1972, there were plenty of English grey partridge on Salisbury Plain. The Netheravon Shoot did not take itself too seriously and was uncritical of those, like myself, whose marksmanship was not of a high order. As many as twenty guns, accompanied by wives, would assemble at The Officers' Mess, Netheravon, each Saturday during the season and be briefed by Robert Ferguson or one of his deputies. We would take it in turns to walk up the birds with other beaters and then stand in line of guns. For lunch we would return to the Mess for a particularly excellent stew, followed by a somewhat heavy treacle pudding. There were normally five drives before lunch and three afterwards. The bags were modest, but there was usually enough game – apart from partridge there were numerous hares and some pheasants – for most participants to take something home for the pot. It was great fun for members of the shoot were all very good natured and sporting, and there was the great advantage of feeling well exercised after a day of walking and standing.

In coming to grips with my actual job as Chief of Staff, the first priority, apart from getting to know the staff and the HQ element of drivers, clerks, cooks and mechanics led by John Elliot, an admirable artilleryman, both parachutist and pilot, and RSM Ayres, Welsh Guards, another soldier of high quality who ran a superb Sergeants' Mess, was to visit all the districts in the United Kingdom, some ten or so stretching from the south-west to the north-east and including the Midlands, to say nothing of Wales, Scotland and Northern Ireland. Ulster, of course, was in a class by itself as the troubles were still dominating affairs there and directions as to policy and its execution came directly from Whitehall. But for all the other districts I set off usually by helicopter, accompanied by Colonel Lionel Harrod, Grenadier Guards [he subsequently became a general and Colonel of the Royal Regiment of Wales] to the various headquarters at Taunton, Aldershot, Preston, Shrewsbury, Brecon, Edinburgh and Colchester, not forgetting the Horse Guards. My purpose? To see the people there, hear about their problems and plans, put over my own intentions and generally get a feel for what I and my assistants at Wilton could do to help. There were some fine men among these District Commanders – Hugh Cunningham, a genial and sporting sapper, who later was a most valued friend in Wiltshire; Corran Purdon, a keep fit fanatic, who, it was said, once took the wind out of the Physical Training Inspector's sails by parading his entire battalion in PT kit and running on the spot for this dignitary's approval; Chandos Blair, whom we last met in Ulster, now commanding in Scotland and able to indulge to the full his exceptional skills with gun, rod and mounted on one of his fast galloping hunters; Bob Britten in West Midland District who persuaded me to give a talk on leadership to a large group of Birmingham-based industrialists. Surprisingly it went down rather well. Bob lived in Wrockradine Hall, a lovely old Georgian house, with an enormous dove-cote and excellent stabling. We recalled with pleasure our joint film presentation of the IDC tour. London District was commanded by Philip Ward, whom we have already met at the Trooping of the Colour. Philip was a man of keen intellect, exquisite taste and with a natural charm which won him golden opinions from all those who came in contact with him. If you came across him by chance, he instantly made you feel that you were the one person in the world whom he had been anxious to see. Many years later he took over from me as Chairman of the Cavalry and Guards Club. But that, as Kipling would have observed, is another story – which will duly be told. With such men as these – and all the others were equally able and competent – there was little, if anything, to find fault with in the handling of their commands, and it soon became clear to me that we at Wilton would do well to make sure they had the resources and support they needed and to fight their battles for them in Whitehall.

There was also at UKLF a Deputy C.-in-C. and again the two occupiers of this post, with whom I worked, were stars. The first, Frank King, had won his spurs at Arnhem, had subsequently commanded formations and was shortly to become respectively C.-in-C. Northern Ireland and Rhine Army. A fine-looking, steady and utterly straightforward man, gentle of speech, strong in character whose integrity was absolute and whose honesty was transparent, he was a very keen golfer, and I recall his saying once, when reporting on the situation in Ulster, that his principal concern had been the sinking of four-foot putts. His main task in UKLF was the supervision of training, both that conducted in the various arms schools and of major exercises both at home and overseas. These were the tasks he handed over to his successor, my former fellow Brigade Major in 6th Armoured Division, Allan Taylor, as it happened another very keen and hugely skilled golfer [I had one game with him at Tidworth Golf Club, of which we were both members, and he gave me a stroke at every hole which enabled me at least to make the final outcome uncertain]. Allan undertook a major review of Army training, which took him many months and distant travelling and resulted in a most comprehensive and valuable report. Here was another senior soldier, totally unspoiled by success, courteous to all who did their duty well, but sharp enough when required to correct some failure of thoroughness.

At Brigmerston we received, one day out of the blue, a most welcome visit from Douglas Macrae-Brown, my former fellow student at the equitation course in Palmanova in 1946. He had left the Army in 1958 and with his Italian wife, Letizia and their four children had set up a school in Eastbourne for teaching English as a foreign language. He seemed to be doing rather well as he arrived in a Rolls Royce, and insisted, over the years to come, on taking us to Royal Ascot for two days [for which

Wilfried would provide the most splendid picnic consumed in No. 1 Car Park] and also to Glyndebourne, which, of course, was not far from his home in Eastbourne. I suppose he was the most generous man I ever came across. He derived great satisfaction from giving pleasure to his old friends and was, besides this, brimming over with good humour, having too an excellent taste in wine – when he came to stay he would always bring bottles of good champagne and claret – plus profound appreciation of the delights of the table. He also possessed, to the dismay but reluctant toleration of his wife, an eye for the girls. Being good looking and charming his success in this field was perhaps not surprising, although going right back to our days at Palmanova, I once had reason to question his selection of a somewhat severe looking redhead, who was a sister at the local military hospital. His justification? 'I never look a gift mare in the mouth.' We had some fine times with Douglas. Friends like him were few and far between.

But another old friend to appear on the scene was Clodagh, who had so efficiently typed my Napoleonic essay at the Staff College, now married to John Grotrian, formerly Grenadier Guards, and living in the Woodford Valley. Clodagh was bright, intelligent, a great party girl, seeming to know everyone who mattered, full of fun and laughter. She had captivated the devotion of Nigel Bailey, a former naval captain, a bachelor, who lived at Lake in a beautiful house [now owned by Sting] with a superlative shoot and excellent fishing on the Avon. Both Nigel's nephews, Peter and Robin, served in my Regiment, and he made us most welcome, particularly as we were old friends of Clodagh.

Nigel would give us the most enjoyable parties at Lake, and there we would meet a number of good friends – Tom Inglis and his wife, Diana, the Curries, who had looked after Wilfried so well for the Balaklava Ball almost twenty years earlier, Alan Cathcart and his Countess No 2, Ronnie Hay, an intrepid naval airman with whom I had been at Latimer and many others. There never seemed to be any shortage of champagne or caviar, salmon or partridge, and the Lake cellar was all that a discriminating toper could desire. In the shooting season we were frequently asked to take part, and in order to do justice to the high pheasants which Nigel would arrange, I tried hard to better my performance by taking instruction from that excellent teacher of shooting, David Olive, who ran the Apsley Shooting School. On these occasions the lunch was such that the post-prandial drives were dealt with in a somewhat cavalier fashion, apt to enhance accuracy.

There were plenty of other opportunities for indulging in sporting activity. Brigmerston Farmhouse was ideal for a meet of the Royal Artillery Foxhounds, at this time the Master being another old friend, Peter Heaton-Ellis who, like Jasper Browell, had commanded The King's Troop, and who later settled in the charming village of Chitterne [where after some comings and goings we too found our 'everlasting mansion']. Peter came to reconnoitre Brigmerston, and we agreed a corner where the hounds could be positioned, where horse boxes and trailers would unload and later reload their hunters, the arrangement of the field. I asked about likely numbers so that we would not run out of stirrup cup material, and all seemed set. It was half-term in February so that apart from the staff and ourselves, Viola and Carolin were on hand to dole out glasses of port and fruit cake. We had about thirty members of the hunt mounted and a dozen or more on foot, so that the stirrup cup suppliers were kept busy. I was pleased to note that Jasper Browell, mounted on a large and powerful looking bay gelding was among the field, heartily approving of keeping up the tradition of Brigmerston meets. This encouraging start was then enhanced by hounds' finding almost at once after moving off. In short a great day.

Once a year Basil Eugster would invite all the District Commanders to attend a conference at Wilton to discuss current matters and to plan future activities. The Eugsters, Bucklands and ourselves would put up the various generals, some of whom brought their wives, and the great aim was to keep them amused when not actually conferring. Tidworth Golf Club assisted us here, and I recall one classic battle in which Chandos Blair and I took on Peter Leuchars and Pat Howard-Dobson and won on the last hole. Dinner parties and bridge provided further entertainment. The most valuable contribution to our deliberations came from those District Commanders who had been wrestling with vicissitudes of Northern Ireland 'Troubles', a strike by dustmen in Scotland, security at Aldershot.

About half way through my three year appointment as Chief of Staff, Basil Eugster retired from the Army, and his place as C.-in-C. was taken by my former Latimer fellow student, who had also been commander, Persian Gulf, during our IDC tour, then Corps Commander in Germany – Roly Gibbs, whose beautiful and talented wife, the divine Davina, wrote poetry, painted and gave entertaining dinner parties at Bulford Manor. She had no interest whatever in military or political affairs. Roly Gibbs himself was one of the finest soldiers I served with. Outstandingly brave in battle, quiet in manner, an all-round field sportsman, a shrewd judge of character, endowed with natural authority, he had climbed to the heights of his profession [and was to climb still higher as a field marshal and Chief of General Staff] in what seemed to be an effortless way. His lightness of touch and ready humour were infectious. He was universally liked, admired and respected. I found that, like Basil Eugster, he left the detailed matters to Ronnie Buckland and me, spent much of his time touring to visit regiments and other units to get the feel of how his command was getting on, and where needed, inviting us to correct any failings of administration or support that he had identified. These, I am happy to say, were few and far between, a tribute to the calibre and diligence of the District Commanders.

Once in a while we were able to persuade Roly and Davina to dine with us at Brigmerston, and I recall one particularly successful and enjoyable dinner party when Matt Abraham and his wife, Iona, were staying with us. Apart from the Gibbs, there were present another great 12th Lancer friend, Robin Brockbank and his enchanting wife, Gillian, Ronnie and Judith Buckland, John and Christina Paley [John, it will be remembered, had succeeded me in command of the Regiment, later was in charge of the Abu Dhabi Defence Force and was now running Salisbury Plain Area]. Corporal Scott excelled himself in the kitchen, Sergeant Smyth smoothly oversaw the service, Berry Bros. & Rudd were responsible for the Montrachet and the Lafitte-Rothschild, the Memsahibs were not too displeased by our lingering over the port, and it was all pronounced, as Davina put it, 'a fun party'. No compliment could have been more appreciated. Roly was sensible enough to take part in as many sporting activities as he could. He hunted regularly, he shot – indeed we found that we were occasionally fellow guests and neighbouring guns on one of Nigel Bailey's shooting days. And I believe I saw as much of my Commander-in-Chief on the golf course at Tidworth as I did in the office. Every now and again I would receive a note from his office while working in mine suggesting a round of golf that afternoon. I would duly accept, arrive at the clubhouse and be joined there by Roly, who had taken the opportunity to practise his helicopter-piloting skills and land on a nearby sports field.

There was one quite serious matter which arose during my time at Wilton – the reorganization of the Field Army, a Whitehall exercise being overseen by perhaps the most acutely powerful intellect and fountain of erudition amongst the Army's serving officers [I exclude Shan Hackett who had retired] – David Fraser – the Razor – who at this time was Vice Chief of the General Staff. His biographies of Alanbrooke, Rommel and Frederick the Great are models of industry, perception, judgement and fine writing.

He had that priceless gift of handling words, whether written or spoken, in such a way that he was able to make the dullest matter of organization or procedure sound interesting. Distinguished service with the Grenadier Guards battalion which had formed part of the Guards Armoured Division, he had later commanded a brigade in Borneo during the Indonesian Confrontation campaign, and then a Division in Germany. I could comprehend his *not* having been appointed Chief of the General Staff only by putting it down to some prejudice or hostility from on high. Instead he became our senior military man at NATO. On leaving the Army he was able to devote more time to writing, much to the benefit of those discriminating enough to read his books. I was much gratified when – at a chance meeting in Hatchards – he told me that he had derived both pleasure and knowledge from one of my own books. As for the exercise dealing with the Field Army, although he did not agree with the suggestions I made, he was at least willing to discuss them in a responsible way. I was further gratified when he invited me to read his excellent biography of Erwin Rommel before its publication and to comment on it.

At Wilton life went on. Ronnie Buckland retired and was appropriately dined out, when he spoke most eloquently without a trace of his stammer. He had been a pillar of strength in his administrative management of UK Land Forces, and happily remained a friend. His successor, Len Garrett, filled his gap with easy going distinction. I still found both the time and inclination to write articles for *Blackwood's Magazine*, touching such themes as leadership and the Army's future. In the summer of 1975, we staged a cricket match between the officers and sergeants of UKLF, and Roly Gibbs was pleased to observe that the officers' victory was, in large measure, the result of accurate bowling by his Military Assistant, Garry Johnson, and – I say it in all modesty – his Chief of Staff.

Also in 1975 I was awarded the great honour of being appointed Colonel of The Queen's Royal Irish Hussars, a position I held for ten years. As Colonel of a Regiment you are the guardian and champion of that Regiment's interests. Your voice in selecting Commanding Officers is a powerful one. Duties include arranging for a steady supply of good officers by interviews at school, at home, the Cavalry and Guards Club, getting likely ones to visit the Regiment, and attending their Sandhurst passing out parade. It is important for the Colonel to visit the Regiment regularly – to suit them and, of course, to keep the Colonel-in-Chief, in our case Prince Philip, advised of the Regiment's condition and future deployment. You also arrange for HRH to make periodic visits, once a year if possible, and certainly at least once every two years. All the customary making of speeches at Old Comrades' and Officers' dinners, keeping in touch with Home HQ, the Regimental Association, the Museum and attending sporting functions fall to your lot. Above all you must keep a strong eye on what the Regiment is required to do, where it is posted and whether it is receiving all the support from senior officers under whose command it is. One later, but most important, task is to ensure that your successor as Colonel is the right man and in deciding this it is essential to consult widely. I found my time as Colonel infinitely rewarding and it reinforced my conviction a thousand fold that the British Army's great strength lies in its regimental system, and woe betide those attempting – as some misguided generals are now doing – to interfere with it. I found Prince Philip the most agreeable Colonel-in-Chief, and I will say more about this later.

It was also in 1975 that I heard from the Military Secretary, as indicated at the head of this chapter, that my military career was coming to an end, so that two urgent questions arose. Where were we to live? [We had no house of our own] and what was I to do? We then made a mistake, by acquiring a house *before* deciding what I was going to do after leaving the Army. Our friendship with Tony and Diana Morrison, who lived in Herefordshire – with the bulls – had resulted in our staying with them there, and our liking that beautiful, unspoiled county. After some false starts we liked the look of The Vicarage at Yazor, a hamlet, north-west of Hereford. It needed quite a lot doing to it, but we went ahead and bid for it successfully at auction. One of the great advantages of buying houses from the Church is that these things are always done at auction and there is no question of gazumping – as we were to discover on a subsequent occasion. While still living at Brigmerston we set about putting the Yazor Vicarage in order and by the time we had completed the work, one or two offers of future employment had come my way. One possibility was to run the Royal United Services Institute, another to join the staff of the Institute for Strategic Studies, a third to take over from Sheriff Thompson as Defence Correspondent of the *Daily Telegraph*. All these were in a sense a kind of extension of military commitment, without being part of the inner circle. So instead – far more challenging, innovatory and adventurous – I took up the offer from Westland Aircraft of becoming their senior representative in Cairo with a specific mission – to persuade the Arab Organization for Industrialization to manufacture the Lynx helicopter.

We will come to my adventures in Egypt later, but the requirement to live in Cairo, yet make frequent visits to Yeovil –Westland's headquarters – meant that I would have to move from Yazor to somewhere more or less equidistant from Heathrow and Yeovil. We therefore moved to Wiltshire. Initially the Army demonstrated their helpfulness by allowing us to occupy a pleasant married quarter in Tidworth, which was not in use, and here I must award full marks to Len Garrett for his instant readiness to assist, thus enabling us to find a suitable house to buy after disposing of the Old Vicarage at Yazor. But before we leave Herefordshire I must record how greatly we enjoyed our time there. The Morrisons were unfailingly kind, and introduced us to other Herefordshire people, notably Ernle Gilbert and his sweet Austrian wife, Hely. Ernle, whose family had long been prominent there with a particular reputation for knowing more about fishing on the Wye and bringing down high pheasants than most other landowners, was a man larger than life. Tall and well built with an almost always benevolent expression on his face, minutely knowledgeable about country life and field sports, bubbling over with enthusiasm for life and activity, generous to a fault, it was impossible to be in his company without a feeling of well-being. He radiated magnanimity mixed with genial eccentricity. His first question to Wilfried on meeting her was: 'Do you like moths?', leaving her in no doubt that he did and knew all about them. At dinner parties he would pour gin or whisky into glasses, while looking away from what he was doing, involuntarily half filling the glass with spirit before leavening it with tonic or soda water. I shall long remember walking with him, both of us suitably armed, to see whether the duck would oblige by quitting their pond within range. On another occasion when he took me fishing for salmon on the Wye, there was great excitement when my line became encouragingly tight, only to find when we landed the fish that it was a huge pike. Undismayed he at once promised to describe to Wilfried how to prepare pike pâté. This was duly done, but was not a success.

We also were most kindly welcomed by our Yazor neighbours – the Davenports and the Cotterills, both extensive landowners. Tim Pierson, from whom I had taken over command of the Regiment, and whose family had long been based in Herefordshire, took us to a Hunt Ball which, being given in a country house long unoccupied, was distinguished by fires lit in cold fireplaces which resulted in so much smoke that, as Piers Bengough commented to me: 'I'm afraid we're all blubbing.' Another good Herefordshire friend was Arthur Denaro of my own Regiment, who commanded in the first Gulf War and subsequently was most fittingly appointed as Colonel.

Leaving the Army was a wrench, but mitigated by the circumstances of having had a most satisfying time as a soldier – the wartime adventures, the internal security campaigns, the comradeship, the sporting activity, the people I had served with, commanded and been commanded by, the great and enduring friendships made, above all the pride and honour of having been part of a truly magnificent Regiment, the 4th Hussars, and helping to make as illustrious the succeeding Queen's Royal Irish Hussars. Besides, as Colonel of the Regiment I would still be closely involved with military matters and would continue to be with my friends and colleagues. There was also the point that I was going to be so busy adjusting to my new position with Westland, to say nothing of helping Wilfried find, buy and organize a house in Wiltshire, that I would have little time to nurse regrets about doffing my military uniform.

Having taken our farewells at Wilton and Brigmerston, with Wilfried at Yazor and both girls at St Mary's Convent, Ascot, I set about two tasks – first to learn some simple Arabic before taking up my job in Cairo; second finding a house. Again the Church obliged. The Rectory at Boyton, a tiny hamlet in the Wylye valley was for sale. We looked at and liked it – a Victorian stone house, spacious and elegant, with a two acre garden, including lawns for croquet and tennis, and an excellent wine cellar. There came the day of the auction, expectation to the fore, and after a few anxious moments precipitated by a rival bidder, we silenced opposition. Boyton Rectory was ours and we will return there shortly. But first I will offer a taste of what life in Cairo was like for me in 1976 and 1977. The best way to do so, I believe, will be to describe a typical week of activity.

Chapter 17

Cairo Diary

> 'Dealing with Arabs is like trying to hold water in your hand.'
>
> Magdi Wahba

5th October

It is eight o'clock in the evening. For the eighteenth time in eighteen months, I land at Cairo. I know the airport well, having spent far too long in it, fighting my way to the exit or waiting for aircraft to leave. I've learned by now to have only hand baggage with me – no waiting for the stuff to be unloaded. The bus takes us to the reception building and I swoop through it to the immigration desk as if the Security Police are after me. My visa is in order, my cholera inoculation up to date – not that it is ever asked for. I am through all the barriers and past the customs before some of the passengers have reached the airport buildings. My light suit, just right for the journey from Wiltshire to Heathrow this morning, is just tolerable for the relative cool of an early October Cairo evening. At the end of the long barrier of railings flanked by a crowd of friends and families meeting travellers, I sight Mustafa Kemal, my driver. He relieves me of my attaché case.

'*Ah'lan wa sah'lan, liwa-t-ee*' – Welcome, my general.'

'*Izay-ak, Mustafa? Ana mabsoot ashuf-ak*' – How are you, Mustafa. Glad to see you.'

We exchange more courtesies on the way to the villa, only a few kilometres from the airport and in the centre of Heliopolis. Mustafa's English is far better than my Arabic, for he spent the best part of ten years working with the Royal Army Service Corps before and during the war. Nonetheless he encourages me to converse in the vernacular.

'*Wa, ela-t-ak, Mustafa, kull haga Kewayesa?* – Your family all right?'

'*Ham'du lil lah* – God be praised'.

We arrive at the villa, which is a combined office, visitors' Mess, conference facility, and for me home from home. The staff greet me. Lots of welcome, handshakes, beaming smiles, rushing about to get glasses, soda water, whisky, ice for a suitable sundowner to be mixed. Abdel Tawaab Soleiman, the cook, is a tall, grave, elderly man who pads around the villa in a purposeful fashion and produces consistently appetizing food – food, moreover, which does not have that dreaded effect which the veteran's flesh, as much as the novice's, is heir to: gyppy tummy. His English too is good as he has worked for British families over the years. He listens solemnly to my instructions for next morning and takes himself off. Tawfiq, the *bauwab-sofragi*, short, plump, always good-humoured, without a word of English, obliges me to address him in Arabic – he is too courteous to indicate that he hasn't the faintest idea of what I'm talking about – while I make efforts to comprehend him. *Ensal'lah*. God willing.

Some of my colleagues arrive. We exchange news and I hand over letters from home and the day's newspapers. By this time it's getting late. They depart and I go to my room, cool enough now to dispense with air-conditioning. Sleep knits up the ravell'd sleave of care.

6th October

Armed Forces Day and a holiday. Anniversary of the 1973 war, and as usual huge military display at the parade site of the War Memorial and Tomb of the Unknown Soldier. Egypt's President, the Vice-President, commanders of the armed forces, political leaders, the Diplomatic Corps – everyone is here, even Mr Yasser Arafat, leader of the PLO. He is awarded a warm embrace by the Egyptian Head of State and a cool handshake by the Commander-in-Chief. Addresses of welcome and speeches to recall military achievements precede what everyone has come for – a march past by the Army and Navy, a fly past by the Air Force. Tanks, guns, trucks, soldiers, sailors, missiles. With rather less emphasis on

Russian equipment than in previous years, no doubt to demonstrate Egypt's growing independence of Soviet support. It is an impressive show. The soldiers are smart, with proud bearing and excellent drill, the weapons of war gleaming and menacing. The military attachés and journalists look hard at some unfamiliar items and at each other, and begin to form in their minds the phrases with which they will later on make their reports and indulge their speculations.

The biggest spectacle is the Air Force's fly past with a timing, precision and symmetry that the Royal Air Force would consider first-class. First come the helicopters [British, I'm glad to say] – the majestic and shiny blue Sea Kings, the yellow desert-painted Commandos, droning past in well-kept formations. Some of the Commandos have rope ladders hanging from them with soldiers spread-eagled at the ladders' ends and national flags streaming behind them. Then, after an interval, the fighters, screaming past in close order and suddenly shooting up into the sky and dispensing coloured smoke. Mirages, Russian Migs and Badgers are followed by transport aircraft, including the American Hercules. All in all it is a splendid display of air power and skilled flying.

It has, of course, been impossible to motor anywhere for hours, from well before the parade had started until everyone has gone home again, but by early afternoon the roads are back to normal. 'Normal' in Cairo means a remorseless stream of every sort of vehicle – trams, buses, taxis, cars, military trucks, donkey carts, horse-drawn wagons, camel trains – jamming the three or four lane roads. Horns hooting, people shouting at one another, ignoring traffic lights and policemen, avoiding pedestrians by inches, arranging for frequent crashes, above all showing a single-minded aggressive determination never to be put off the great aim of demonstrating that no matter who else might think differently, it's your road, for your exclusive use, and it is for you to forge ahead of whatever mass of vehicles may be in front of you. Fortunately Mustafa has learned my ways – not to use the horn except to save life, not to weave in and out more often than every five minutes, not to kill any pedestrians, not to 'Trouble the engine' by exceeding seventy kilometres an hour in second gear.

Three o'clock in the afternoon and it is time to go to the airport to meet a colleague, with whom this evening, holiday or not, I must attend a meeting to discuss an Arab-UK industrialization programme. After it's over we repair to the villa for dinner by courtesy of Abdel: soup, lamb, cheese, fruit and glasses of Omar Khayyam, the locally produced red wine, the vintage of which is measured in months – of the current year.

7th October

Friday, *yawm el goma*, a day of prayer, the equivalent of a Sunday at home and in theory the one day of the week off. I say in theory, for Friday is a favourite for visitors from England to arrive, knowing as they do that they can get two days' intensive work done and be back home by Monday. Very good, except for those meeting them and looking after them. Today the pattern is normal and two more colleagues are arriving. For me it makes little difference, as Friday is my morning at the British Embassy to compare notes with the Defence Attaché and his staff. It's a good day from their point of view, as there are no Egyptians in their offices and they can catch up and also send signals to the FCO and the Ministry of Defence, rounding up the week's events before *their* weekend starts. It's also a good day for driving from Heliopolis to Garden City with minimum traffic. I drive myself so that Mustafa Kemal, a devout Muslim, can have his day of prayer.

Off I set at about nine forty-five, into the Saleh Salem, the main thoroughfare between el Masr el gedeeda, new Cairo, and el Qaahira, the Victory; Cairo itself. Past Abassia and the barracks where I did that Sherman gunnery course some thirty-five years earlier, past the City of the Dead, that fantastic collection of tombs and mosques, biggest graveyard of any city I have ever seen, past Saladin's Citadel, with the great ramp opposite built by Napoleon Bonaparte for his artillery to gain the necessary height and reduce the fortress in 1798, past the beautiful Mohamed Ali mosque, replica of Istanbul's Blue Mosque, down the hill to the Roman aqueduct, round to the Corniche and along the Nile to Garden City and the Sifaara el Britaaneeya, the Embassy. I spend half an hour with each of the three attachés, exchanging news and views.

I also take the opportunity to check arrangements for the ceremonies at the el Alamein war cemeteries in just over two weeks' time, then motor back to the villa where Abdel gives me a glass of *limoon*, that delicious mixture of fresh lime, sugar and water. I sit at the typewriter and begin to compose the weekly Sitrep. I had thought that on leaving the Army, I had done with writing Situation Reports. Not so. If you don't play golf or tennis or ride in Egypt, you're missing something. The facilities are excellent and the weather – reliable. But we don't go to the club immediately after lunch. There are four of us in the villa. One quite unashamedly goes off to his room for an hour or so of what used to be known as Egyptian PT or 'Studying for the Staff College'; two others busy themselves on the dining room table with lists of spare parts and prices in preparation for the next day's conference with Egyptian Air Force officers; I go to my office, which has one very comfortable chair – known as the thinking chair. I read over my Sitrep notes and amend them, then pick up today's copy of *The Times*, kindly brought by our visitors, and gently scan it until an unseen figure wielding a cudgel creeps up behind me and deals me a telling blow which ensures that I am not awake until about 3.30. A quick cup of tea, and three of us make our way to Heliopolis Sporting Club, enlist one of the professionals, who makes up the four and raises the game's standard for three sets of tennis. It is Abdel's night off, so later that evening we dine at the Swissair restaurant by the Nile. Shrimps and sole, with some *nebeed abyad*, a slightly sweet white wine, go down well.

8th October

For my colleagues, contract negotiations; for me a day of administration. First, villa victualling and the accounts. I suppose during the many years I lived in Mess when serving with the Regiment, I had been President of the Mess Committee as often as anyone. I had never expected to become the Mess Sergeant. But here I was, living in the villa [although Wilfried and our daughters came to Egypt for the summer holidays I was once more living a bachelor life] from which to promote Westland's bid for its helicopters to be manufactured by the Arab Organization for Industrialization, and inevitably saddled with the task of running the villa as well. I found that what with soothing the staff, maintenance, putting up endless visitors, accounts, the garden and patiently dealing with electricity failures or hot water problems, it was like being manager of a small, exclusive hotel.

We need more cash for paying the rent, so Mustafa drives me to the Banque du Caire. I recall the day I turned up there with a cheque for £250,000 burning a hole in my pocket. It was in respect of some completed contract with the Egyptian Air Force. When I handed over the cheque to a small plump female, she took one look at it and said she couldn't accept it without a copy of the contract. Banking bureaucracy gone mad. Back in my pocket goes the cheque and I then cash a more modest one for our villa expenses. On I go to Swissair office to confirm my tickets for the next trip home. Impossible to park so Mustafa drives round and round the block until I reappear. Then trying to outdo a shiny Mercedes, he manages to jam our car between two donkey carts. All three vehicles are immobilized. We're surrounded by the turbulent bustle, colour and variety of a Cairo street. All kinds of people, some in European clothes, many more in *gallebeyas* or the traditional black *milaaya laff* which the women wear; horse-drawn carts with twenty locals sitting on top; bicycles, shops teeming with goods and food; street vendors of vegetables and fruit, noise, smells and good humour abound. Yet the donkey drivers are menacing Mustafa. It is clearly time for me to exercise my authority, but before I get out of the car, Mustafa must have somehow mustered a team of eight passers-by and between them they bodily lift the car with me still in it and move it backwards clear of the carts; 'a few words' are exchanged with the donkey drivers, and we are once more showing Cairo that Mustafa was not in the RASC for nothing. I re-enter the villa. Enough excitement for one day. Tomorrow I shall be driving some 200 kilometres – but without Mustafa.

9th October

Five a.m. Tawfiq switches on the light in the upstairs hall. I'm downstairs twenty minutes later and Tawfiq produces scrambled egg, toast and coffee. Somewhat early for breakfast, but there'll be no more food for seven or eight hours. One of my colleagues, a logistic expert, pulls up at the villa just before six. We're off to Alexandria to visit Air Force units to see that all is going well with our helicopters. We speed along the Saleh Salem, cross the Nile to Giza, down to the Pyramids – no matter how many times you see them, they always fill you with awe – and take the desert road to

Alex, which so many British soldiers had taken on their way 'up the blue' half a lifetime ago.

It's about 212 kilometres from the Pyramids to Alex. We do it in two and half hours and arrive at our first port of call, west of the docks, just as life is getting going there. After seeing what I want and arranging a later rendezvous, I set off in the car along the coast, through the western part of the town, on to the Corniche, past the Cecil Hotel, off the Corniche again to circumvent a one-way stretch, through the crowded streets once more, back to the sea front, grey rollers breaking over the sea wall, past King Farouk's great Montazar Palace, now open for all to see, and on to the scene of one of Nelson's greatest triumphs, Aboukir. More business, more talk, more plans. Then back to the flat we have opposite the Alexandria Sporting Club, where racing thrives and even polo is still played. Payment of rents, discussion about future lease, some sustenance, and then – golf. The caddies at the Sporting Club speak French. I cannot persuade them that my Arabic is worth acknowledging. But following refreshment after the game, I set off leaving my fellow players there, a *sofragi* has come rushing after me waving a piece of paper. I look at it, return it to him with a phrase indispensable to the traveller in Arab lands: '*SaaHib-ee yedfah el Hisaab.*' My friend will pay the bill.

There is no difficulty about falling asleep this evening, despite the frightful traffic noise outside. The journey, the wonderfully fresh sea breeze you always get in Alex, the game, the plain but plentiful food at the Cecil have done their stuff. Tomorrow back to Cairo.

10th October

When we come downstairs, the *bauwab* – all houses and apartment blocks have a door-keeper – is polishing the car. Off we set, this time by the Delta road, the *route agricole*, a dual carriageway, each one double laned, with a dividing island of straggling bushes. It's just about the most dangerous road I know. Huge lorries with trailers hurtle towards Cairo from the Alexandria docks, loaded with every sort of cargo, extremely unwilling to keep to the right-hand lane or suddenly pulling out to avoid a donkey cart or a train of camels. Taxis, some of them the large station-wagon types, packed with people, trying to prove that they are the fastest vehicles in Egypt, bully their way past you. Little boys leading camels or riding donkeys rush across the road as soon as a momentary gap in the traffic gives them a chance. You need to concentrate hard. But what sights there are to be taken in: the Delta, rich in crops, every inch under cultivation, rice, alfalfa, oranges, corn, dates, potatoes and, of course, cotton. It's all green as far as you can see, the *fellahin* working as hard as any farmers anywhere, all the family involved: a boy attending the buffalo, which is either ploughing or treading blindfold round the irrigation well; girls with pots or loads on their heads; women tilling the fields or taking in the crops; camels treading disdainfully along with unbelievable volumes of alfalfa or corn. What industry!

All forms of transport seem to run in parallel. The railway flanks the road, and passenger trains, overflowing, the carriage roofs alive with people, clank past. On the other side, across an expanse of green, are the canals on which the *feluccas* glide, their great masts and sails towering upward, apparently floating gently over the fields. On and on we drive. It takes us three hours to reach the outskirts of Cairo, then slowly through the mass of people and vehicles to Heliopolis and the villa.

'*Abdel, fingaanayn awah, min fadlak.*' Two cups of coffee, please. My companion leaves. I turn my attention to the villa. Have we enough soda and tonic water? Abdel and Mustafa have been at odds over some petty matter. *Malesh*. Never mind. Three more visitors are expected this evening. Is there plenty of food? Why the devil hasn't that light bulb on the stairs been replaced? *Bukra, ensal'lah*. Tomorrow, God willing.

11th October

Today is different. Our visitors want to see Memphis and the Sakhara Pyramid. In the cool of the tombs and outside, with those superb views across the desert, patience – a commodity badly needed in Egypt – will return. The imagination will be sweetened. Another week will have gone by. Soon I'll be dashing home to report to Yeovil, as Colonel to deal with Regimental matters, and, most important of all, to see the family. As the soldiers awaiting demobilization used to say, roll on. *Ensal'lah*.

After two years of negotiation, presentation and consultation, the

Arab Organization for Industrialization agreed to manufacture the Lynx helicopter in Egypt and contracts were signed. My task was done, but I stayed on in Cairo until the proper Westland people had been deployed there to manage and supervise the actual work. It all went smoothly until that day in 1979 when President Sadat of Egypt signed a peace agreement with Mr Begin of Israel. So appalled were members of the Arab League that financial backing for the entire Lynx operation was withdrawn by those providing it – Saudi Arabia, Qatar and the United Arab Emirates. Then began a wearisome process involving not only Westland [together with Rolls-Royce whose engines powered the Lynx], the AOI officials, the British Embassy in Cairo, but the Egyptian military hierarchy and our own Ministry of Defence, plus countless lawyers and an international tribunal which arbitrated in such disputes with regard to the key question – what compensation was to be paid to Westland for the resultant loss of multi-million pounds' worth of business?

During the years that followed – seven in my case – I was required to make frequent visits to Cairo, Jeddah [at that time all the Embassies to Saudi Arabia were there, later moving to Riyadh], Qatar and Riyadh itself to discuss these matters with our Embassy people, AOI officials and Arab armed forces commanders. Westland's Secretary, a most able and likeable lawyer, John Bayley, drawing on his capacity for infinite patience and titanic labour, was the mainspring which kept the process alive, and he was eventually rewarded by the arbitration of the tribunal which sat in Geneva and awarded Westland several hundred million dollars in compensation. My own principal contribution to the hundreds of meetings and discussions which took place was to negotiate with Dr Mulhem, a Saudi Arabian Secretary of State responsible for AOI matters. We would meet at his office in Riyadh and while he deplored the resort to arbitration which we had initiated, I would point out how easily he could bring it all to an end by conceding that compensation was justified and by leaving it to the Tribunal to determine what amount of money would constitute a fair settlement. But while our discussions were amicable enough, I once again came to acknowledge the prescience of Magdi Wahba's comment that dealing with Arabs was like trying to hold water in your hand. Meanwhile I continued to act as a general military adviser to Westland. My ready access to our own Armed Forces dignitaries assisted me here, and I was able to offer guidance to the main board of Westland Aircraft.

In doing so I had two able colleagues, both retired colonels and old friends. John Waddy, Somerset Light Infantry and Parachute Regiment [he had also been Commander SAS Regiment and gave me indispensable help with my *History of the SAS*]. A veteran of Arnhem he had been with Shan Hackett there and had, like Shan, been badly wounded. Then there was John Moss, Royal Artillery and Army Air Corps, a skilled pilot and incidentally an excellent shot – we both had guns in a Salisbury Plain shoot. The three of us did a lot of work together preparing submissions to the various arbiters of Westland development policy. It was a happy, fruitful collaboration. It was during our work together that the question of writing the SAS book came up. One evening when we were in Herefordshire, home of 22 SAS Regiment, Wilfried and I were dining with Ernle Gilbert, whom you have already met. Other guests included Michael Rose, at that time commanding 22 SAS, and his accomplished and decorative wife, Angela. Michael was familiar with some of my other military works, and asked me if I would be willing to write a history of the Regiment. I replied that if the Regiment would give me their full support and cooperation – Yes. One of Michael's cousins was Barley Alison, that well-known and much admired SOE member, colleague of Duff Cooper and at this time a pillar of Secker and Warburg. One of her colleagues, Tom Hartman, was of enormous help to me in copy-editing several of my books. So it came about and after talks with Barley and Tom Rosenthal, plus the invaluable assistance of Bruce Hunter [Director of David Higham Associates], a contract was agreed. John Waddy and I then got to work. The book was published in 1984 and was well received.

During my years with Westland I was fortunate in working for two most able and remarkable men. One was Lord Aldington, the Chairman. He had been a gallant and distinguished member of the 60th Rifles, a prominent lawyer, Member of Parliament, Minister and head of the Sun Life Insurance Company. He was also Warden of Winchester College. I admired his acute mind, his readiness to listen, his humour, magnanimity and affability. He was ready to undertake tedious and sometimes fruitless discussions with AOI officials without losing either patience or perseverance. He also enjoyed the delights of the table. His experience was formidable, his acquaintance with sources of power substantial and his capacity for hard work admirable. I got on well with him, but I shall never understand why he allowed himself to become involved in a legal action brought against Count Nikolai Tolstoy who, in one of his books, had implied that Aldington – then Brigadier Toby Lowe, on the staff of General Keightley's 5th Corps – bore responsibility for the repatriation of Russian soldiers who had fought for the Third Reich, repatriation which would lead to their merciless extinction.

For a lawyer to become involved in so questionable a duel was a puzzle. Everyone of consequence knew that so relatively low-level a player in the game could not possibly be held responsible for such an act. The finger pointed much more accurately at those in positions of political power, such men as Macmillan and Eden. No one without governmental authority could have made so grave a decision. Besides, all those who mattered knew Aldington's character and record far too well to countenance so damning an accusation.

Equally difficult to comprehend was the vendetta conducted by Tolstoy. His outrage at the fate of his fellow countrymen is wholly understandable. His apportioning blame to Aldington is not. I had met Tolstoy on several occasions at Balaklava memorial parties arranged by that most eccentric and *simpatico* Welsh Guardsman, Robert Pomeroy, and I had found him charming, tolerant, knowledgeable and gentlemanlike. For him to involve himself as an accuser of Aldington, smacked of serious misjudgement. If any military man were to be held even remotely indictable for the return of those Russian soldiers, it would be necessary to look higher up the military hierarchy than a mere brigadier – the Corps Commander [Keightley], Army Commander [McCreery], Supreme Allied Commander [Alexander]. But the idea of its having been a military decision, as opposed to a political one, does not hold water.

In his leadership of Westland, Aldington was both a rock and an inspiration. So too was his right-hand man, the Chief Executive Basil Blackwell, to whom I was directly responsible. If a keen intellect, a robust constitution, an imaginative turn of mind, a strong character and an all-round understanding of industrial, financial, technical and engineering matters, combined with sympathetic man-management and an open, friendly demeanour sum up the attributes required by someone to run an aircraft manufacturing business, then Basil Blackwell was made for the job. His directions to me were clear, his demands for results were fair, his appreciation of good work done was sincere, and his day-to-day manner and conduct, appealing and generous. He was very much on top of his job, and would never hesitate to go and see for himself. He was accessible, had a care for those under his command, valued the particular contribution I was able to make, and in the frequent half social, half business get-togethers, which are all part of the industrial game, was a charming and considerate host. He was also a dedicated and skilful gardener. I greatly admired and liked him.

After some nine years with Westland, I decided I had had enough, and thus brought to a close what might be called my wage-earning career. But there were other spheres of activity which made demands on my time. I was sixty-four when I left Westland, but I was still Colonel of The Queen's Royal Irish Hussars, had become Chairman of the Cavalry and Guards Club, and still was committed to writing some more books of military history. It is at this point that my memoirs cease to be a kind of chronological account of events and turn to some reflections and memories of pastimes pursued and people with whom both duty and inclination had brought me into contact.

Chapter 18

Field Marshals and other Brass Hats

> 'We may pick up a marshal or two, perhaps; but not worth a damn.'
>
> Wellington

On the other hand most of the field marshals whom I met *were* worth a damn. I suppose the nicest of them all was John Harding, who commanded 7th Armoured Division in the desert, was Chief of Staff to Alexander when Alex commanded 15th Army Group, later commanded a Corps and ended up as Chief of the General Staff. I did not meet him during the war, but afterwards, when we, the 4th Hussars, were stationed near Trieste and Loopy Kennard was Master of our pack of foxhounds, John Harding and his wife, Mary, were often to be seen, well mounted, Mary riding side-saddle, and thoroughly enjoying the bustle and excitement of drag hunting. It was then that I first had the good fortune to be introduced to General Sir John Harding as he then was. Together with other members of the Regiment, I later chatted to him in his Mess at Duino Castle [shades of Rainer Maria Rilke's *Elegies*] and at a parade in the Piazza del'Unita in Trieste when the US Bronze Star was pinned on my chest. Many years later after I had written the short biography of Dick McCreery, Wilfried and I were frequent guests of Lettice McCreery at lunch, and John Harding, now a widower, was often there too. The two families had been close friends. John Harding wore his fame and his achievements very lightly. He was charming, modest, ever ready to recall old times and friends in common, with a most delightful smile and a rich store of memory and anecdote. Diminutive, kindly, with a shock of grey hair and a twinkling eye, he was the absolute antithesis of the blimpish, pompous, self-important figure caricatured by some writers who know little of soldiers or soldiering. While working for Westland I was again invited to lunch with him, as Lord Aldington had been a member of his staff during the Italian campaign. John Harding left a name, at which the world did not grow pale, but rather glowed with its readiness to point a moral, or adorn a tale.

The field marshal with whom I had the most business to conduct was HRH Prince Philip, Colonel-in-Chief of the Regiment. As Colonel it was my duty to arrange with his staff and the Regiment itself the programmes for his frequent visits to see how we were getting on. The first occasion in which I was involved was earlier, when I was still in command. We had not long since returned from the jungles of Borneo and Malaya and were stationed at Wolfenbüttel, near Brunswick. George Kidston-Montgomerie was then Deputy Colonel – it was winter 1964 – and he accompanied Prince Philip.

They arrived at the barracks in time for tea, and we then showed Prince Philip the film that Barry De Morgan had made of our operations in Borneo, paid a visit to the Sergeants' Mess for drinks, and then returned to the Officers' Mess for dinner. The Colonel-in-Chief was and is, particularly good at talking to soldiers and listening to them. He would move from group to group, that is squadron to squadron, much to the delight of the senior warrant officers and NCOs. At this time, of course, the majority of senior ranks were from Northern Ireland or the South, and such men are in no way overawed when talking to members of the royal family. On the contrary, they tend to make the running. It was all very informal and friendly.

Back in our own Mess, I ensured that all the officers were able to have a word with Prince Philip, before we trooped into the dining room. One of our number, Randle Cooke, was especially pleased to see him, having been HRH's equerry for two years and was all too familiar with the ins and outs of such royal visits. We dined well and Prince Philip went off to his bedroom in the Mess. Next day it was fine but cold, and the programme was so arranged that our royal visitor could meet and talk to as many of the soldiers as possible while we demonstrated our operational role of forming a reconnaissance screen along the border with the German Democratic Republic, together with the busy patrol activity which, apart from keeping an eye open for any unusual border deployment by GDR forces, enabled our own squadrons to get to know their operational area in detail. Back in barracks after a busy morning, Prince Philip visited the Corporals' Mess, the dining hall and the Wives' Club, where Wilfried presented a selected number of wives to HRH, and we then retired to our own Mess for lunch. Prince Philip was to fly an RAF Wessex helicopter to his next port of call, but before doing so he presented me with a signed photograph of himself, dressed as Colonel-in-Chief. It had been a brief, but enjoyable visit, and next time I was present at such an occasion, I would myself be Colonel of the Regiment.

Before I handed over command to John Paley in March 1965, there was, of course, that great, solemn and unforgettable day when the Regiment played its part in the funeral of our Colonel, Sir Winston Churchill, which I have described earlier. This led to a further piece of regimental business. Who was to succeed the great man as Colonel? I was myself in no doubt that it should be George Kidston-Montgomerie, who had so admirably carried out the duties of Deputy Colonel and was dearly respected by all of us. The soundings I took confirmed my views, particularly strongly supported by General Shan Hackett, and George's appointment was formally confirmed. Ten years later, and for a further ten years, I was myself Colonel of the Regiment, having taken over from General Shan Hackett, and so it fell to me to be present at and help to arrange the Colonel-in-Chief's visits. There was one nearly every year for Prince Philip seemed greatly to enjoy these occasions. They varied both in nature and location. The first one for me was at Paderborn, when Dick Webster was commanding. Following a formal parade at which the Guidon was trooped, Dick, who wore the responsibilities of command with a light, imaginative and good natured air, had devised something original – a luncheon for the Colonel-in-Chief, which would be partaken of by all ranks in the main dining hall. To be sure that all went smoothly on the day, Dick had arranged a kind of dress rehearsal, during which he explained to the Regiment what would be the procedure, including two short speeches by himself and myself, together with fitting toasts. All went well on the day, and the Regiment's enjoyment of it all was admirably summed up by one corporal who, when I asked him what he had thought of it all and Prince Philip's part in it, replied: 'Sheer magic, Sir!'

Subsequent visits by Prince Philip occurred at Tidworth and Münster. The Tidworth affair, Robin Rhoderick-Jones commanding at the time, was noteworthy in that *two* Lord Lieutenants were required to be on parade, as our first port of call was at Warminster, where one squadron was based, so that Lord Margadale, renowned sportsman, political wizard, owner of Fonthill and about as clubbable a man as you find anywhere, lent his convivial presence to proceedings. Then we helicoptered to Tidworth, where the bulk of the Regiment was stationed. There was the Earl of Malmsbury to greet us, for we were now in Hampshire. After our round of inspections and chats to the soldiers, the Sergeants' Mess entertained us before we moved to the Officers' Mess for Prince Philip to meet wives and have lunch. I could not but observe that as our royal guest was the first to be served with food, and he wisely got on with it, by the time his two neighbours at table, the senior wives, had been themselves supplied, Prince Philip had more or less consumed his portion and engaged his table companions in conversation while they struggled to talk and eat at the same time.

The Münster affair was special, as the Colonel-in-Chief was to present the Regiment with a new Guidon, so that an elaborate parade was organized. Steve Daniell, now commanding, ably assisted by Charlie Lowther [son of that great 8th Hussar, Guy Lowther, who had so distinguished himself in Korea] and the Regimental Sergeant Major, had devised a splendid sequence of events, including a mounted cavalry escort for Prince Philip, consecration of the Guidon, a march past by the Regiment's Challenger tanks, with trumpet calls to herald various manoeuvres and – happily the weather was fine – a general air of ceremony and dedication. An open air lunch for all ranks and their wives followed, and that evening a ball to bring to an end our celebrations of the tricentenary of the raising of the Regiment, for it was in 1685 that James II realized one of his ambitions – to augment his standing army by the formation of nine more regiments of infantry and six of cavalry, including 4th Dragoons. This triumphant acknowledgement of the Regiment's 300th anniversary was my last performance as Colonel. Prince Philip clearly enjoyed himself, particularly at the ball when he danced with all the prettiest wives. Throughout my time as Colonel, I had found him a wonderful support, always ready to attend a dinner for the Old Comrades and to make a short, appreciative speech, most generous in his offers for me to fly with him for an overseas visit, and above all so enthusiastic and sympathetic in his contact with all ranks of the Regiment. We were – and are – fortunate indeed to have him as our honoured Colonel-in-Chief.

Other field marshals must receive *shorter notice*, although there are some giants among them. They fall into two categories – those who were of another, earlier generation, and those who were contemporaries of mine.

My first meeting with Gerald Templer was not auspicious. It was in 1951, when I was Freddie Graham's Brigade Major and we were taking part in some manoeuvre for the benefit of another brigade in the Stamford Battle Area near Thetford in Norfolk. The exercise was about to get under way, and I had asked one of my liaison officers to check something and report back, undertaking to have a drink ready for him when he did. I was studying the map with my back turned to the entrance to the command vehicle, when footsteps on the short ladder leading into the vehicle told me that Ricky Vallance, the LO was back. Without turning I called:

'Is that you, Ricky? I have your whisky and soda here.'

A stern bark replied:

'It is not Ricky. It is General Templer. What is the situation?'

I recovered and attempted to explain how we had deployed the brigade and what information we had about the 'enemy'. He was far from satisfied with our reconnaissance activity and was not mollified by my offer of the whisky and soda to himself. All this, of course, was before he went to Malaya, where he made so profound an impression, so much so that he was later appointed Chief of the Imperial General Staff, sure route to becoming a field marshal. Templer was honest, honourable, straight and forthright. He is said strongly to have opposed the Suez operation, saying that of course we would take Cairo, but what would we do then? Years later, when Templer was Chairman of the Ogilby Museum Trust, and I was a trustee, the more human side of his nature emerged. He was incapable of subterfuge; his own man – strong and decisive to the end.

Another man of his calibre was Frankie Festing. Large, jovial and uncompromising, dressed more like a gamekeeper than a field marshal, he exuded good nature, a refusal to put up with any damned nonsense, and furiously outspoken in committee, when the circumstances demanded it. It was said that when at No. 10 in discussion with senior members of the government, he would strike terror into ministers by the sheer violence with which he would thump the table before exposing their proposals to the ridicule and rejection that they warranted. He was a powerful, much respected figure, and would have been appalled at the mess current members of the Army Board are making of the Army's greatest and most precious feature – the regimental system. He had four sons, all of whom soldiered at one time or another. Two of them, Michael and Andrew, whipped-in for me when I was Master of the Staff College Drag Hounds. I fear that men like Festing are in short supply nowadays.

Although my meeting with him was brief enough, I must not fail to include that most elegant, gentlemanly, gallant and urbane soldier – Alexander. He may not have had the battlefield management skills of Montgomery, but Alex had the charm, the tact, the persuasiveness and the good manners to get on well with our American and other allies at times when smooth relations and effective cooperation were of supreme importance in the conduct of Middle East and Mediterranean operations. My first meeting with him I have already described when his distaste at having to plunge down into the anti-tank ditch in the wake of Churchill during the Prime Minster's visit to us in Italy was all too obvious. He enjoyed Churchill's absolute confidence, and in the summer of 1944 showed his strategic grasp in the plans he made for the break-out from Cassino and the capture of Rome. It was ten years later, in 1954, when I was again presented to him. He was at this time Minister of Defence in Churchill's second administration – a role not suited to his temperament or talents – and the occasion was a huge manoeuvre in Rhine Army, called *Battle Royal*. I was commanding C Squadron, 4th Hussars, and at one point in the exercise Alexander, accompanied by General Windy Gale, required an explanation as to what was happening. At this point I had just led the squadron through the cleared passage of a mythical minefield and was about to launch forward to support a further brigade advance. But a halt was called, I was ordered forward and asked to 'paint the picture'. I seemed to do this adequately enough and Alexander with his customary charm thanked me and recalled previous occasions when he had had the good fortune to encounter members of the 4th Hussars.

I will just touch on a few more field marshals, before extolling the virtues of some other admirable brass hats who did not reach that highest of military ranks. Dick Hull, whom I had first met when he was a major in the War Office, commanded 1st Armoured Division in the Gothic Line battles, which I have mentioned earlier. He did not, in my view, deploy or manage his division to the best advantage, yet when it was disbanded some months later, he was immediately given command of another division. Such are the fortunes of war. Later in his career he wholly redeemed any former deficiency by his wise handling of Far Eastern affairs and his performance as Chief of the Imperial General Staff. He was also an effective Chief of Defence Staff. He was friendly, approachable, listened to advice, faced ill-health with courage and cheerfulness. He was a fine representative of his famous regiment, the 17th/21st Lancers.

Field Marshal Michael Carver, with whom I had both military and literary dealings, had a brilliant mind, a somewhat severe manner, an understandable confidence in his own judgement, and an equally understandable dislike of criticism. When, in one of my books, I was bold enough to criticize one of his pronouncements in a book of his, he was extremely cross. I had done no more than suggest that there was no final version of history and that new evidence might throw new light on the conduct of former commanders in crucial battles, little enough one might think and certainly not warranting so sharp a rejoinder. But Carver was a great man, with a profound sense of duty, a dedicated head of the Army, although not as devoted a believer in the regimental system as he should have been, a prolific historian, with lots of humanity under a veil of austerity, a man of absolute integrity, a brave and brilliant commander in action, honourable, loyal and true.

I move now to some of those who were more or less my contemporaries and whom Michael Carver had probably marked down as worthy to succeed him. Dwin Bramall, whom we have already met at the Staff College, was tailor-made to be Chief of the General Staff and Chief of Defence Staff. Extremely able, with a profound knowledge of Whitehall's workings, fully conscious of the Army's unique and precious regimental system, affable in discussion, quick in decision, liked and respected by his fellow men, he gave distinguished service both to the armed forces and the country. On one occasion he gave me the very support I needed when, as Chairman of the Cavalry Colonels, I fought against the removal of regimental bands, and with his aid succeeded in preserving them, albeit at reduced strength. The honours rightly showered upon him – a peerage, Lord Lieutenant of London, the Garter – have, in no way, altered him; kindly, amiable, direct, a proper soldier and a true, loyal friend.

What shall I say about Roly Gibbs, so gallant a leader in action, so casual a commander in peacetime, so shrewd in judgement, while concealing his perspicacity, so ready to see the comical aspect of any circumstance, who rose effortlessly from one position of command to another and seemed to be a reluctant Chief of the General Staff? His good nature and easy-going attitude were genuine, yet underneath it all lay a dedication to the task in hand and a fierce loyalty to the people and principles he valued. I was fortunate indeed to serve with him and to call him my friend.

Very different from Roly Gibbs were two cavalry associates of mine – Nigel Bagnall and John Stanier. Nigel, red-haired, quick in judgement, intolerant of woolliness, impetuous in manner, but cool and valiant in battle, he cared nothing for the opinions of those in authority if he found them faulty, and expressed his own views with clarity, conviction and force. I saw much of him when he commanded his regiment, the 4th/7th Dragoon Guards, and subsequently when he was a Divisional Commander. He was a powerful and effective Chief of General Staff and I suspect was only not made Chief of Defence Staff because the political leaders of the day were unwilling to be subjected to the scathing criticism and unanswerable argument that Nigel would have deployed to their discomfort. John Stanier was a much smoother proposition. Highly intelligent, an exceptionally fine public speaker, equipped with a charm of manner and a persuasive eloquence which won many a contest, he had supreme confidence in himself and had reason to do so. He was essentially practical and had an easy way with the great men with whom he had to deal. He was on one occasion of great assistance to me when as Chairman of the Cavalry and Guards Club, I had to wrestle with the problem of purchasing the freehold of 127 Piccadilly, which had been acquired by a hardened property company. John Stanier's support in this – happily successful – battle was wholehearted and effective.

'Fate doesn't always make the right men kings,' says the young aide de camp, Fritz von Tarlenheim, to Rudolph Rassendyll in *The Prisoner of Zenda*. Has fate always made the right men field marshals? It is a moot point. I have already suggested that had it not been for certain influences, David Fraser would have been awarded a baton. Another obvious candidate was the greatest soldier-scholar of his generation – Shan Hackett. A gallant, highly decorated commander in the field at many levels, an academic of prodigious powers, a master of numerous languages, with a great love for and knowledge of history and literature, himself a formidable writer and lecturer, he stood up peerless among his contemporaries. Yet there were also times when he displayed remarkable cleverness to the discomfort of others, and it may have been the fear that he would quote Greek to uneducated ministers that robbed him of the top Army job [which went to Carver instead]. Shan became Principal of King's College, London to the benefit of all concerned, including myself, as he called upon me and others to help write a book, which became a world best seller. It was called *The Third World War* and I will have something to say about its composition later on. Back to the generals who won golden opinions from all those who served with them.

Bill Jackson was a much decorated sapper, who had commanded squadrons in the ill-fated campaign in Norway [he was very eloquent on the problems of maintaining morale and discipline during a withdrawal when the enemy enjoyed air supremacy] and in the slow, bloody slog in Italy; and later instructed at the Staff College, did great things in the Ministry of Defence, ending his time there as Quarter Master General, before a final appointment as Governor of Gibraltar. It was he who helped me in my début as a military historian, having himself written numerous military books, including volumes of the *Official History* of the Mediterranean campaigns and a joint effort – with Dwin Bramall – about the Chiefs of Staff Committee. He showed his generosity of spirit in bullying the then literary editor of *The Times*, Philip Howard, to print his reviews of some of my own books, reviews which were invariably favourable. His own historical works are first class and his management of Whitehall affairs judicious and fruitful. He and his wife, Joan, were wonderful hosts. Bill himself was full of the milk of human kindness, incapable of envy, but always ready to lend a helping hand. He was wholly *simpatico*.

I have already had something to say about General Dick McCreery, who was too straight, too honest and too nice ever to be considered for the post of Chief of General Staff. How he would have hated Whitehall! Another cavalryman of his calibre, who, however much he may have disliked Whitehall, nonetheless was an outstanding Adjutant General, was Monkey Blacker. He possessed all the qualities of a first class commander – he was brave, imaginative, charming, persuasive, tactically adept, tough, intelligent, a fluent speaker and writer, full of pluck and perseverance. He was also one of the best horsemen of his generation, equally at home in the hunting field [he took over Mastership of the Staff College Drag from me], on the race course – he rode the Grand National course several times and his accounts of doing it were enthralling – in the show ring or on television indicating how to ride, school, jump and look after horses. His work with the Jockey Club and the British Equestrian Association was legendary. His horses Workboy and Pointsman were national heroes. His leadership in war was renowned. He was, in short, a star turn, and would have been a most effective head of the Army. His memoirs are a model of what such a treatise should be. To cap it all he was, like Dwin Bramall, a fine painter. Infinite talent in a single human being.

I could go on with praise for many more senior officers of the British Army with whom it had been such a pleasure and privilege to serve. Jackie d'Avigdor-Goldsmid was another fine cavalry-man, who set a great example to his fellow generals with his selfless devotion to all that the cavalry hold dear. A great goer in the hunting field, an ardent supporter of amateur racing, Director of the Royal Armoured Corps [his lectures to assembled commanding officers invariably ended with the exhortation 'Wilco-ness Wins', meaning that you had to deploy a positive willingness to get things done], a long standing Chairman of the Cavalry Club and a prime mover in its successful amalgamation with the Guards Club, a Conservative Member of Parliament, an essentially regimental soldier of prodigious achievement, a man held in respect and affection by all those fortunate enough to have known him well. One of his great friends from the same regiment, 4th/7th Dragoon Guards, was Ian Gill, whose gallantry in the field had brought him two Military Crosses, and who commanded his Regiment and a brigade with just the light, but firm touch to get the best out of his subordinates. Charming, a brilliant teacher, elegant, amusing and staunch, a keen horseman, married relatively late in life to his great love, who alas succumbed to cancer far too soon, I was lucky indeed to count him as a true and loyal friend.

Other names and other faces crowd my memory – that wonderful Irish Guardsman, Basil Eugster; Walter Walker who handled operations in Borneo so calmly and effectively; Tony Farrar-Hockley for his sheer zeal, courage, perseverance and versatility and for the excellent books he turned out so effortlessly; Philip Ward, Welsh Guards, the Major General at London District, who succeeded me as Chairman of the Cavalry and Guards Club, and who always made one feel that you were the one person on earth whom he was most pleased to see. Nor can I leave this particular subject without recalling those who were my colleagues at Minley Manor or the Imperial Defence College – Mark Bond, Hew Butler, Bill Cooper, Stuart Watson, Tim Creasey, Bob Britten, Geoffrey Collins, Neil Fletcher, *Que de souvenirs*!

We remember, too, Lady Bracknell's contention that whereas to lose one parent might be thought of as a misfortune, to mislay two smacked distinctly of carelessness. So we might say that whereas to have endured one regimental amalgamation could be classified as a misfortune – no matter how successful – to be obliged to undergo a second such upheaval was bound to raise the question as to whether sufficient care had been taken by those most nearly concerned. Yet some thirty years after the 4th and 8th Hussars had combined to form The Queen's Royal Irish Hussars – a Regiment which won golden opinions from all who knew it – the Ministry of Defence decreed that this same Regiment should itself be amalgamated with The Queen's Own Hussars which was the outcome of the 3rd and 7th Hussars being amalgamated at the same time as the 4th and 8th – in 1958. No amount of pleading or lobbying by regimental colonels and others prevailed upon hard-hearted ministers to change their minds. It was during the discussions as to what cap badges and collar badges the new Regiment, The Queen's Royal Hussars, should have that the opinions of former Colonels of the two Regiments concerned [General Sir Robin Carnegie and myself] were made known.

When The Queen's Own Hussars was formed, those in charge very wisely chose to keep the main feature of the 3rd Hussars' cap badge, a Hanoverian horse, intact, and simply substitute the new Regiment's name – The Queen's Own Hussars – for the former 3rd King's Own Hussars. At this point it must be made clear that the only cavalry regiment in the British Army to have a horse as its main insignia at this time was The Queen's Own Hussars. Yet far from hanging on to it, those planning the future of the new Regiment, The Queen's Royal Hussars, designed a curious and quite undistinguished badge, comprising a twiddly sort of scroll, with the Irish harp in the middle, the crown supporting a lion on top and the Regiment's name beneath. As a matter of courtesy, Robin Carnegie and I were invited to say what we thought of it. We both most emphatically made it plain that we favoured retention of the Hanoverian horse. It was a great disappointment to us, although perhaps not a surprise, that our views carried no weight whatever, and the newly designed, still wholly undistinguished badge came into service. The horse, however, was retained as a collar badge.

Robin Carnegie is a man I have long admired and am gratified to call an old, valued friend. Like Roly Gibbs he seemed to rise effortlessly from one position of command to another, ending his military career as a lieutenant general in charge of Army training.

Tall, calm, highly intelligent and articulate, with a nice sense of humour and a charming manner, we would often meet out shooting – he was, indeed is, extremely skilled with gun dogs, and apart from shooting, is much in demand for organizing picking up at various shoots in Wiltshire. His wholly delightful wife, Iona, has many talents, she paints, writes books and together with Robin converted an old barn on the Fonthill estate into an elegant, spacious and most inviting house. Moreover she has created a splendid garden from what was a ploughed field. In short, a great couple.

I have not in this treatise so far mentioned what Churchill once described as the greatest corps in the world – The Royal Marines – but I must do so because of being fortunate enough to have served with some notable members of that corps. One of my fellow teachers at the Staff College was Neil Maude, another excellent fellow, a keen shot, a competent horseman and married to an equally enthusiastic horsewoman – Dor [maiden name Pilkington-Ernle-Erle-Drax]. They would frequently come out with the Drag when I was Master, but having only one horse between them, it was customary for Neil to ride the first and third legs, allowing Dor to enjoy the second leg. All this demanded some careful briefing and map reading so that whichever one of them was not riding could reach the proper rendezvous – a check – in order, as it were, to change horses. Neil went on to command a brigade, but then suddenly decided to retire. His reason? I cannot think of a better one. To have more time for field sports, for sailing, for travel and for leisure.

During my time as Commander West Sarawak, which I have spoken of earlier, I was fortunate enough to have under command a company of Royal Marines from, I think, 42 Commando, led by Major Jeremy Moore, who later achieved great fame as overall commander in the Falklands. Jeremy was a highly competent, much decorated, commander, and I gave to him the task of defending Kuching airfield, the one absolutely vital piece of ground in the three divisions of Sarawak for which I was responsible. His appreciation of what needed to be done and his execution of the task were faultless. I met him several times later on, after we had both left the service, and he was the same as ever

– cheerful, positive, overflowing with good spirits and enthusiasm, a splendid example of Churchill's greatest corps in the world.

There were others who did much to reinforce the point. Ian Gourlay, who commanded, again I think, 41 Commando, was one of those responsible for a sector of Sarawak, and I remember sharing a tent with him at our camp near Kuching during an operation involving both our regiments. Steady, firm, assured, brimming over with good nature, clearly regarded by his subordinates with affection, respect, confidence and loyalty. It was no surprise to any of us who knew him well that he became Commandant General of the Royal Marines.

Another character with whom I shared the supervision of some major military exercises in Malaysia in 1964, was Leslie Marsh, who had taken over from Billy Barton as the head man of 3 Commando Brigade. We had established our control headquarters in the hutted buildings of a rubber plantation in Johore and had set up an agreeable Officers' Mess for our hours off duty. We would frequently have a stengah together and at one point I learned from him that he had long been enamoured, entirely innocently, of a brother officer's wife, and as a result was still a bachelor. There was a happy ending to the story for after leaving the service, the fellow Royal Marine had abandoned this world for the next, and Leslie at last was joined to the being whom he had for so long cherished. But the moment most bright in my memory of him occurred on the nine-hole golf course which this well-chosen plantation boasted, when he and I were relaxing from our, by no means arduous, duties and had reached the sixth hole. There suddenly appeared from behind a clump of bushes a corporal of Marines moving swiftly, despite his ample proportion, and clearly pregnant with some urgent tidings for his Brigadier.

'By heavens,' declared Leslie, 'it's my steward, Perkins. There must be some frightful flap. No doubt HMS *Bulwark* is getting up steam now and I'm wanted aboard.'

An almost breathless Perkins slid to a halt, saluted and announced: 'Sir, the Director of Infantry has arrived at Control HQ and wants to know how the exercise is going.'

Leslie regarded him with a tolerant smile. 'Is that all?' he asked. 'Tell him to wait'; and turning to me: 'I've always admired Francis Drake,' he said. 'We will finish the round.'

I am most conscious of having omitted from my narrative mention of many friends and colleagues who played a large part in my life. I will name a few but there will still be many players not listed in the cast.

Regimental comrades inevitably figure largely in my memory. General Sir Brian Kenny, my successor as Colonel of the Regiment and the only 4th Hussar since the days of Winston Churchill's contemporaries to reach four star rank, is about as fine a soldier as you would find anywhere. From winning the Sword of Honour at Sandhurst he graduated as a pilot and commanded our Air Squadron in Malaysia and went on to command the Regiment, a brigade, division, corps, Rhine Army and was a most distinguished Governor of the Royal Hospital. An easy going charm, great sporting enthusiasm and competence, and an astonishingly youthful appearance even into relative maturity concealed a natural leader of sound judgement and steady determination.

Nor can I forget the two Regimental Sergeant Majors who served The Queen's Royal Irish Hussars so loyally and well during my command – Hugh Burroughs, who radiated good nature, infectious confidence and morale-building spirit, and his successor, Mr Holberton, stalwart, upright, conscientious and authoritative; both of whom exercised calm control of the Sergeants' Mess, so indispensable a part of the Regiment's well-being and competence. I have said little of our Home Headquarters, whose activities in relation to the Old Comrades and their various get-togethers, to say nothing of production of every sort of help to those former members in need, constitute an absolutely vital part of the whole Regimental structure. Those who ran the Home HQ – Cliff Jones, Jock Ferrier, Bob Smith, and now David Innes-Lumsden and Timmy Timmons – deserve our wholehearted and eternal gratitude. I will mention two other members of the 4th Hussars, who made a profound impression on me – Clem, as Major Clements was always known, tall, lean, a man of few words but a brilliant horseman, who was said to have kicked Loopy Kennard down the platform of a Greek railway station for insubordination and who on leaving the Army generously presented me with his sword, which is still in my possession; and Kenneth Bidie, who came to us from Hodson's Horse in 1948 and later commanded the Regiment. He set so high a standard of personal integrity, devotion to duty, immaculate dress and faultlessness of conduct that he was indeed a model of what a British cavalry officer should be.

I shall always remember with gratitude and affection our next-door village friends, Nick and Carol Gow, when we first arrived at Brigmerston Farmhouse. She had lost a leg as a girl in a serious riding accident, but from her cheerfulness, activity, resolution and sheer good spirits, you would never have known it. He, a former Colonel, Royal Horse Artillery who had become an Air OP pilot, had a slightly blimpish manner which concealed a powerful sense of fun, much common sense and a most kindly disposition. He was a keen golfer and bridge player and a most dutiful church warden. They made us most welcome in their charming house. I still treasure his wide-eyed expression of approving astonishment when, at lunch with us, he exclaimed:

'By Jove! Starched napkins! Not since I left the Service have I been so indulged. I trust the memsahib will take note!'

He would, from time to time, assume the manner of an Imperial master. But it was all part of the fun.

I will close by paying tribute to two general officers whom I greatly admired. General Sir Frank Kitson was one of the first to understand the nature of what became known as counter-insurgency operations, such campaigns as the British Army was required to conduct in Malaya, Cyprus, Kenya and Aden, to name but a few. He himself had shown outstanding courage and daring during the Mau-Mau campaign and subsequently commanded a Rifle Brigade company in Malaya. He quickly came to understand that the recipe for defeating such insurgencies was fourfold: good intelligence, a proper triumvirate of government, police and military to direct operations, winning hearts and minds, and, most important, isolating the guerrillas from their sources of food, information, money and support. As a result of a year's defence fellowship at Oxford, Kitson produced an excellent book on the subject, *Low Intensity Operations*. He went on to become a four star general, and to indulge his love of field sports, with the able support of his wife, Elizabeth, an excellent horsewoman and painter, and to write several more books of biography and military history. Like Monkey Blacker, he is an impressive all-rounder.

Another such is Maurice Johnston, who was a star pupil of mine at Minley Manor, transferred from the RHA to The Queen's Dragoon Guards, commanded the Regiment and a brigade, rising to the rank of lieutenant general and, on retirement, succeeding Roly Gibbs as a most dedicated and effective Lord Lieutenant of Wiltshire. Maurice excelled at all field sports, as a gardener, a glass engraver, as a most valued friend. He and his musically talented wife, Belinda, were greatly admired examples of what it is to be wholly *simpatico*.

Enough of those who brandished the sword. Let us turn now to those who preferred to wield the pen.

Chapter 19

Words, Words, Words

> 'I would rather be a beggar in a garret full of books than a king who did not love reading.'
>
> Macaulay

Well, yes, but the king might acquire a taste for reading and the beggar might be unable to buy any more when he had gone through those in the garret. But like Macaulay I have always loved reading. The encouragement of my father and mother and their taste for the classics, was of greatly beneficial influence. So apart from the early devouring of Lewis Carroll and A.A. Milne, I soon graduated to John Buchan, A.E.W. Mason and Anthony Hope. The Father Brown stories of G.K. Chesterton followed, before embarking on a serious course of Dickens, the Brontës and Jane Austen. In my latter teens I read D.H. Lawrence and was especially fond of his poetry. Keats, Shelley and Coleridge were great favourites, Byron later, but above all Shakespeare. The study of Shakespeare's plays at school was never a necessary labour, always an enrapturing joy. To see the plays at the Old Vic in the late 1930s, when John Gielgud headed a cast which included Kathleen Nesbit, Joyce Redmond, Peggy Ashcroft, Alec Guinness, Jack Hawkins, Harry Andrews and Andrew Cruikshank – the two pieces in question were *King Lear* and *The Tempest* and tickets were to be had for shillings rather than pounds – was surely a theatrical experience only to be compared with those two giants of the stage, Laurence Olivier and Ralph Richardson, in *King Henry IV*, Parts 1 and 2, Olivier playing respectively Hotspur and Justice Shallow; Richardson, of course,

Falstaff. The number of times I have been reminded of Shakespeare's use of words in putting over some particular point, and then making use of them to reinforce a piece of my own writing is countless. In a similar way I have found the rhetorical antitheses of Macaulay prompting me to emulate his captivating style. His *Essay on Milton* was the first of his works that I read, before graduating to the *History of England*, which never fails to astonish with its scholarship, insight into human nature and sheer dazzling eloquence. Milton himself, despite *Paradise Lost*'s nobility of theme, depth of erudition and felicity of verse, I found somewhat overwhelming. Coming right down to earth I have found the novels of Anthony Trollope so readable, enjoyable and true that I return to them again and again. I must, in all honesty, also confess to a liking for some of Georgette Heyer's Regency romances. And, of course, the Flashman books were just up my street. So are those by Raymond Chandler, P.G Wodehouse and James/Jan Morris. I almost forgot Kipling's poems.

'Read no history,' declared Disraeli, 'nothing but biography, for that is life without theory.' He didn't mean it, of course. It was just another *bon mot*. Not he, nor anyone, would neglect the wonder of Gibbon or the magic of Macaulay. And moving to more modern times, the *Oxford History of England* is not to be missed. Arthur Bryant, for all the faults pointed out by Andrew Roberts, is eminently readable. For those so inclined, the Marquess of Anglesey's *History of the British Cavalry* is a gem of scholarship and a source of pride. On the other hand how pleased Disraeli would have been with Buckle and Monypenny's massive tribute, how gratified by Robert Blake's great work, how diverted by André Maurois's light-hearted portrait.

Many of us, who have relished reading, have found ourselves wanting to write. It was certainly so with me. Schoolboy jottings in imitation of Lawrence, blank verse in praise of a fellow creature, essays on current affairs in preparation for examinations were unproductive beginnings. But when it came to the composition of squadron notes for the 4th Hussar Journal, publication was assured. What is more, following Dr Johnson's advice, the lure of prize money for winning essays promoted by *The Army Quarterly* lent fluency to my pen. *The British Army Journal* welcomed articles and reviews of military books, but it was not until I broke into the covers of that delightfully old-fashioned magazine called *Blackwood's* that I went beyond the somewhat limited readership of military circles. I wrote lots of stories for *Blackwood's Magazine* and was sad when, in 1980, the last monthly number was published.

Well before this, however, by virtue of Bill Jackson's kind intervention, I began to write my first volume of military history, *The Battle for North Africa*. It was 1969 and at that time Batsford had embarked on a series of military books depicting both the history of battles and the performance of military commanders. It was then that I first met and immediately liked one of Batsford's directors, Peter Kemmis Betty, cousin of my Gurkha friend. One thing led to another and during the next three years, I did three more books for Batsford, one about Hitler's command of the *Wehrmacht*, the others describing the Ardennes counter-offensive, and the Battle for Berlin. All this activity was only possible because I was enjoying the three-year sabbatical referred to earlier. It was when this period of relative leave from military duties came to an end that there was a pause in literary output, and I concentrated on my duties as Chief of Staff, UKLF. No sooner had I retired from the Army and taken up my task in Cairo for Westland, however, when perhaps the most interesting of my writing ventures came about.

General Shan Hackett, from whom I had, a year earlier, taken over as Colonel of the Regiment, had been persuaded by William Armstrong, a man of great charm and discrimination, the Managing Director of Sidgwick & Jackson – persuaded, I should add, by three glasses of Armagnac to round off an excellent lunch at the Garrick – to embark on what was designated as 'A Future History' – *The Third World War, August 1985*. In order to do so Shan had enlisted a team of co-authors. They were a retired Air Chief Marshal, Sir John Barraclough, a retired Vice-Admiral, Sir Ian McGeoch, Norman Macrae, deputy editor of *The Economist*, Sir Bernard Burrows, former British Permanent Representative at NATO, Brigadier Kenneth Hunt, International Institute for Strategic Studies, and myself. A series of meetings had produced a broad scenario for the book's structure; we were all allotted parts of the narrative to be written and submitted to Shan and William Armstrong with a view to checking progress at another meeting to be held later. My part in it was to write two chapters, each of some 10,000 words on the conflicts in the Middle East and Africa. In gathering together facts and figures I was greatly assisted by Hugo Meynell [a former 12th Lancer, son-in-law of Lettice McCreery, now a pillar of *The Economist* – he had arranged for the printing of my short biography of Dick McCreery]. Hugo kindly supplied me with many of those short reviews of affairs in various countries covering political, military and economic matters at which *The Economist* so excelled.

I was able to compose my two pieces in my Cairo office and duly dispatched them to Shan Hackett, who expressed satisfaction and warned me of a further meeting of all co-authors to be held at the offices of Sidgwick & Jackson. I was able to fly back to England for this meeting, combining it with Westland work and a family reunion. I shall always remember William Armstrong's opening comments as he reviewed the contributions we had all submitted. General praise for style, content and compatibility, together with broad sanctioning of all the contributions. He then interjected the word 'however' and went on to say that there was a lack of sparkle, drama, excitement, urgency and expectation about the opening pages of the book.

It was therefore agreed that several of us would produce something to remedy this fault, and I was charged with writing a passage which would depict a young officer of the *Bundeswehr* finding that his Leopard tank was no match for the Soviet superiority of armour and fire power. Happily my chapters on Africa and the Middle East were accepted. Further amendments and additions to other parts of the book were discussed and agreed. There would be a further meeting, this time with lunch at the Cavalry and Guards Club shortly. Gradually *The Third World War* was getting under way.

As the time of publication approached we all met again for lunch at the Carlton Club, this time with our wives in attendance. William Armstrong had pronounced himself satisfied with the latest revision, illustrations had been assembled and a race for being first in the market had developed with a rival team of writers who were putting together a comparable story about what they called *World War Three*.

We won the race with some months to spare and the reception

of the book was most gratifying. An instant bestseller in Britain and the United States, it was translated into almost every European language and some Oriental ones. Shan dryly recommended the Japanese version as a good read, and we all received large cheques in royalties, much of which was promptly removed by the Inland Revenue. It had all been great fun and so successful had the venture been that a sequel was written, again by the same team. This did not sell so well.

I had by this time acquired an agent – David Higham Associates, and in particular was looked after by Bruce Hunter, a most intelligent, agreeable and enterprising man. We would often meet for lunch in each others' clubs to discuss a further project. Bruce had seen to the production of the SAS book, published by Secker & Warburg, and this was followed by an account of *The Italian Campaign* and *Gentlemen in Khaki*, also published by Secker. Barley Alison had become a great friend. Next I was approached by Richard Cohen, then with Hutchinson, and we agreed on a further book about the British Army, *Beggars in Red*. Bruce Hunter then put me in touch with Constable, and after a most rewarding talk with Robin Baird-Smith, we agreed that a short joint biography of Wellington and Napoleon might do well. The resultant *The Duke and the Emperor* was well received and graced by a favourable review from Elizabeth Longford. The Robertshaws who own Warminster bookshop generously gave a launch for this book and subsequent ones. I could not have asked for more.

There then followed a meeting with Benjamin Glazebrook, whom I found, as all who know him will agree, a most charming, stimulating and clubbable man. We agreed that a joint study of Churchill and Hitler, as war leaders, might appeal, and so in 1997 this volume appeared, and despite a somewhat sour review from John Charmley, whose ideas about making peace with Hitler in 1941, ideas preposterously endorsed by Alan Clark, I had comprehensively demolished, did quite well both here and in the United States.

In 1999 came something very different. I had long wanted to record some of my equestrian adventures, and the Government's attack on fox-hunting presented me with the opportunity to write a book about drag hunting in order to show that, fun as it was, it could not be a substitute for the real thing.

Thanks to the enthusiastic and highly effective help of Caroline Burt, Publishing Director of J.A. Allen, Pat Sutton, long time Master of the Staff College Drag Hounds, Jane Westcott and many other advisers and contributors, the book, *On Drag-Hunting*, was published in 1999. It was lavishly illustrated with paintings of various drag hounds by such experts as Lionel Edwards, Gilbert Holiday, Snaffles and John King, together with some of the woodcuts in books by 'BB' and Siegfried Sassoon [*Memoirs of a Fox-Hunting Man*] and photographs. My son-in-law, Tim Barker, did splendid work in making transparencies of all these pictures and they did much to enhance the text. It had been one of the easier books to write, as it required relatively little research, and it is agreeable to observe that today many packs of foxhounds have remained active by resorting to drag hunting, at least to start the day. Indeed it seems that the major effect of the anti-hunting legislation has been to increase the support country-wide for the chase.

A little while after this venture Bruce Hunter put me in touch again with William Armstrong, now semi-retired, but still active on behalf of Pan Macmillan, who had had some success with some 'What If' books, and William thought that another one might be worth doing. After some false starts we hit upon a number of campaigns in which the element of chance had been significant. What I had to do therefore was to explain the strategic circumstances of a particular battle, show what effect chance had in determining its outcome, and then speculate as to what might have happened if things had fallen out differently, so leading to the resultant longer term consequences. Among the commanders and battles I chose to examine were Nelson at St Vincent, Napoleon at Marengo and Waterloo, Hitler during the Dunkirk affair and Rommel at the gates of Egypt. *If By Chance* was published in 2003 and had a fair reception.

This is a catalogue of my contributions to military history. I must emphasize one major factor in my churning out all these historical efforts. The support and assistance given to me by Wilfried in proof-reading, index checking, typewriter maintenance, general advice and sheer patience was incalculable. And, apart from this, from the moment we acquired The Old Rectory at Boyton in the

Wylye valley, at a time when I was heavily committed to my Westland duties in Cairo and elsewhere, Wilfried set about making our new home, both house and extensive garden, all that it should have been to give us and our daughters twenty most happy and fulfilling years. It is to the Wylye valley, therefore, that we will now go.

Chapter 20

Boyton Rectory and the Wylye Valley

'The Very-Own House.'

Rudyard Kipling

Just as Kipling and his wife took an instant liking to 'Bateman's' – 'We entered and felt her Spirit – her Feng Shui – to be good. We went through every room and found no shadow of ancient regrets, stifled miseries, nor any menace' – so we were at once captured by the feel of the former rectory in the tiny hamlet of Boyton in the Wylye valley. As with all church properties it was to be sold by auction, and when the day came, there were some anxious moments as the bidding in the Red Lion Inn, Salisbury reached and passed the amount of money we had realized by the sale of the Yazor Vicarage. But we emerged the winners and our mortgage people were happy to oblige.

At the beginning of 1976, just before I set off for Cairo, we took possession. It was, indeed is, a Victorian [1873] house, stone built, with a half a dozen bedrooms, drawing and dining rooms, a study, where no doubt countless inspiring sermons had been composed by the former Rector, Dr Richardson, and would now be given over to the production of military history – when I was at home and had the time – kitchen, scullery and so on, plus, to my delight, a spacious wine cellar. High ceilings, shuttered windows, an imposing hall with a most impressive bookcase and a gracious stairway. The two and a half acres of garden included a grass tennis court and a croquet lawn, some lovely trees, beech, willow, apple and cherry, with a paddock and a kind of rising stretch of meadow which went from the croquet lawn to a gate opening on to woods of the principal Boyton landowner. There was also a patch for vegetables and at the far end of the tennis court a box hedgerow and a beautiful laburnum tree. The short drive from the village road up to the house was flanked by bushes on one side, by the paddock fence on the other and there was plenty of space for Wilfried to create a herbaceous border. There was much to do in putting the interior in order, including the building of a proper fireplace in the drawing room. Viola and Carolin, both still boarders at St Mary's, Ascot had chosen their own rooms, and I was allotted both a dressing room and a walk-in wardrobe. At the far end of the house were two rooms for friends to stay and a second bathroom. The whole thing was just about perfect, and while I was obliged to dash off to Egypt, Wilfried got on with the business of putting house and garden in order. Advice as to whom to employ came from a near neighbour, Sheila Morris, who became a very dear friend. On my first return from Cairo to report progress to Westland HQ, I found Wilfried had done wonders, and all I had to do was to ensure that the wine cellar was properly stocked. Berry Bros & Rudd duly accommodated us.

In the Wylye valley we encountered nothing but kindness, hospitality and generosity. My old 12th Lancer friend, Robin Brockbank, whose Manor House at Steeple Langford was nearby, arranged a drinks party for us to meet many of the locals, including our own neighbours, Raymond and Anne Wheatley-Hubbard, who farmed several thousand acres, stretching from Boyton to Corton and beyond, and who also had a wonderful pheasant shoot. The Wheatley-Hubbards were exceptionally thoughtful in offering every sort of help to Wilfried particularly when heavy snow had to be cleared from the Old Rectory's roof and when a gale blew down trees which blocked the road. But their friendship far exceeded simple assistance of this sort. We were frequently guests at their dinner parties, and I was invited to shoot even though Raymond was well aware of my erratic marksmanship. Some of the other subscribers to the Boyton shoot also became close friends. Colin Thompson, a first class shot, would be accompanied by his enchanting wife, Bridget, who was also an excellent tennis player. Another regular was Teddy Kenney-Herbert, a delightfully old-fashioned former 60th Rifleman, who had his own rather more modest shoot, to which we were also invited. Teddy would assemble eight guns, all close friends, and five or six drives would be fitted in before lunch, prepared by his charming and keen hunting wife, Dawn. Teddy was always quite happy if there were enough game for everyone to take home a brace of pheasants, and at the end of a splendid lunch of stew and other delights, he would compare the number of birds shot with that of tonic bottles used to smarten up the copiously poured gin. It was just the sort of shoot which Max Hastings would have approved of and enjoyed taking part in. Another really fine shot, who graced both these shoots, was John Jardine Paterson, who rarely missed and whose elegant and accomplished wife, Priscilla, was a wizard at training and supervising her gun dogs. Two other friends with whom we would join these shooting parties were Leslie Addington [descendant of Pitt's friend and successor as Prime Minster] a man of great charm, with a keen interest in history and a pillar of the Roman Catholic Church and Hugh Cunningham, whom I had also worked with in my soldiering days and who, like Teddy, had his own smallish shoot, to which again we were regularly invited. I did my best to live up to all this liberality, and regularly attempted to improve my performance by taking lessons from David Olive. Yet, although I found myself knocking down the clays quite efficiently, I still missed too many pheasants. Now and again I would get my eye in and do creditably enough, but these memorable days were far too rare.

I have said that Boyton was a small hamlet. Apart from the Rectory and the Wheatley-Hubbard's newly built Broadleaze, the only house of consequence was Boyton Manor, originally residence of the Giffard family – the first Giffard said to have accompanied the Conqueror in his descent upon England – but for many years owned by the Fanes. The occupant when we arrived was Barbara Fane, widow of Edmund who had, by all accounts, been a man of admirable qualities, and it was alleged had been able to buy back his family home, Boyton Manor, which had fallen into other hands, by virtue of Barbara's extreme wealth. Barbara had re-married, a Frenchman, Comte de Brye, who was, to say the least of it, a fish out of water among the country pursuits-loving inhabitants of the Wylye valley, but was friendly enough and loved playing tennis. I was, therefore, often required to play against him. While giving him a good runabout, I never allowed him to win.

Another great advantage from my point of view which Boyton provided was that in the next door village, Corton, lived Diana, Duchess of Newcastle, a legendary steeplechase rider, breeder of thoroughbreds, and a great girl all round. Attached to her house were stables for about fifteen horses, the yard being run by Richard and Zara Caldecott. I was thus able to resume my riding, often accompanied by my old 4th Hussar fellow-soldier, John Paley and sometimes by Robin Brockbank too. My reputation as a competent horseman was severely tested when Diana, who was going away for a week, asked me to exercise her thoroughbred gelding, a grey called Cletus. As I mounted the animal I asked his girl groom if there were any quirks of conduct that I should look out for. She simply replied with a shrug that he was a thoroughbred. Nothing further was said. Neither she nor Diana mentioned the fact that Cletus, like many horses, hated pigs. One of the good circular hacks over the Boyton farm led straight up Pig Lane and when we were half way up this lane, with fields either side, Cletus suddenly reared up, turned a sharp 180 degrees round and broke into a furious gallop. It took all my skill to stay on board, but I succeeded in calming Cletus and we turned again and trotted up the gradually rising lane. It would have been a complete loss of name on my part had Cletus galloped riderless back to the stables, while I ignominiously trailed behind on foot. Much more frequently I rode one of the Caldecotts' mares, a delightful skewbald called Harlequin, whose only vice was a dislike of lorries approaching from behind – she had once been hit by one – when she would break into a canter and need making much of before settling down again. I had a lot of pleasure riding the Corton horses and was able to take Viola and Carolin for hacks as well. Later Mouse Berry, who was a fine teacher of horsemanship, took over the Corton stables.

We were most fortunate in having two splendid helpers at the Old Rectory. Mrs Dobson, wife of one of the Wheatley-Hubbards's farm workers, would come in once or twice weekly to clean. She was totally reliable, efficient and good natured, and we continue to keep in touch with her now, some dozen years after leaving Boyton. Then there was Mr Guerri who not only did sterling work in the garden, coming twice a week in the summer, but could turn his hand to practically any task in the house, painting, mending electric devices, wood chopping and storing, gravel laying on the paths, growing hedgerows, putting up fences and gates. These two made a huge contribution to our enjoyment of Boyton. It was an ideal time for entertaining both our own friends and those of our daughters. Anna Addington, Leslie's wife, had been wonderfully good in making sure our daughters were included in teenage parties, as were Derek and Octavia O'Reilly, who lived in a grand house at Stockton. He had been in the Royal Navy and his nephew, Mark, was in my Regiment. We were able to return all this hospitality and during holidays from school, Viola and Carolin had their friends to stay. What with a tennis court, croquet lawn, horses to ride and parties to go to, no dull moments were allowed.

Inevitably local duties arrived. I was persuaded to become Chairman of the Friends of Boyton Church, which involved the endless requirement of raising money for the maintenance of the very old and beautiful church. I was ably assisted by Robert Laird of Corton and John Rigby, both former soldiers. Eventually our financial problems were solved by the generosity of Barbara de Brye, whose death occurred during my chairmanship. She had bequeathed £100,000 to the church and the interest on this invested money covered our expenditure. Later I handed over as Chairman to John Rigby and accepted the position of President. Another less onerous task was to be Vice-President of the local Royal British Legion branch, Derek O'Reilly being Chairman, and later I was to succeed him. The principal events were the annual dinner and parade for Armistice Day service.

A much more difficult duty was thrust upon me when I was induced to take over from Digby Raeburn as Chairman of the Cavalry and Guards Club. Up until about 1983 the Club had paid a peppercorn rent to the Sutton Estate, but in that year the freehold of 127 Piccadilly passed into the hands of a property company, headed by Elliott Bernerd. Before I became Chairman, the Club Committee had decided that, as we could not possibly afford the rent of so desirably placed a building, we should seek to purchase the freehold. Now, if there was one thing that all my life in the Army had not prepared me for it was negotiating property deals with experts in that particular field. Help, however, was on the way. One of the Club's members, Peter Jones, was himself in the estate business and gave excellent advice. We, therefore, formed a small action group, which I headed and which included Peter Jones himself, Tom Hall, my Vice-Chairman, Ian Frazer, Jonny Hok, Philip Ward, John Stanier and the Club's legal advisers. Tom Hall's devotion to, and work for, the Club's welfare has been and is incalculable. The Club Secretary, David de Pinna, was a pillar of strength at this difficult time and the Club staff as a whole were solidly behind our efforts; loyal as always. There were four phases in our campaign. Another staunch supporter throughout the campaign was Dick Worsley who later became the Club's Vice-President.

First, we had to discover the situation, that is whether the new owners would be willing to sell the freehold and if so under what sort of conditions. Early reconnoitring established that they would be open to offers and had no other immediate plans for the disposal of the building. The second phase was to establish that 127 Piccadilly could not be used for purposes other than its existing one. This was done by upgrading its status as a listed building, and reinforced by a kind of PR offensive designed to make it clear to the new owners that certain powers in the land – banking, social, conservation, city, even Royal interests – would be displeased if 127 Piccadilly were to cease housing the Cavalry and Guards Club, but gratified if a way could be found to satisfy both parties in the resolution of the problem. This phase in the campaign seemed, intangibly perhaps, but detectably, to have the desired effect. Next came the third phase – negotiations to determine a price. It was clearly essential that a figure had to be arrived at which would both hold water in the property world and at the same time be within the bounds of realization by the Club itself. Eventually a figure which seemed to conform to these two requirements was agreed upon. Now came the last phase of all – raising the money. At this point we sought advice from various banking sources, including the then Governor of the Bank of England, Robin Leigh-Pemberton, our own bankers and David Barclay. Ian Frazer did wonderful work at this stage of the game. Certain debenture ideas were discussed and agreed, appeals to members were launched, responses began to be made; slowly, surely the amount of money being collected mounted, a further appeal was made after an Emergency General Meeting of the Club members which had its effect, and eventually the sum donated was sufficient to persuade bankers to make up the deficit. It had been a long haul, but the freehold had been purchased thanks to the members' generosity and at the next AGM I was able to hand over as Chairman to Philip Ward. The Cavalry and Guards Club is still going strong, although there are still financial problems, including paying back certain sums to members who came forward with reimbursable debentures. The problem is being vigorously tackled by the present Chairman and Committee.

Apart from the distraction of negotiations in Middle Eastern countries, wrestling with property dealers over the future of the Cavalry and Guards Club, writing books of military history and enjoying our family life at Boyton, the sporting world still loomed large. The Netheravon shoot, which I mentioned earlier, admirably run by John Oldfield and others, continued to provide coveys of partridges, superb stews in the Officers' Mess and good company. One of my fellow guns was George Morant, a splendidly old fashioned Major, long since retired, who was ready to have a go at anything which left the ground or indeed at the numerous hares who regarded Salisbury Plain as their own property. In the summer months George would take me trout fishing on the Anton, a tributary of the Test. I am not a skilful angler, but the sheer beauty of the river, the tranquillity, the thrill of tightening line, the subsequent enjoyment of a grilled trout were pleasures fondly remembered.

As for the shooting, quite apart from Netheravon and the other shoots to which we were so generously invited, my old friend Humphrey Weld, with whom I had hunted, had restarted his own former shoot at Chideock, and once a year we would set sail for Dorset and stay the weekend with Humphrey and Fanny, while their son, Charles, with the aid of his most accomplished keeper, organized a day at the pheasants and duck. It was an excellent shoot with some very high birds, most testing for an indifferent shot like myself, but I just about scraped through. Although in a totally different class, we managed to persuade the Welds to come for a day's shooting at Netheravon, and succeeded in getting two of Humphrey's former regimental comrades of The Queen's Bays, Jackie Harman and Douglas MacCallan, to lunch with us at Boyton on the Sunday.

Another couple, whom we first met out shooting with the Kenney-Herberts and Wheatley-Hubbards, were George and Anita Davenport, who farmed at Codford but subsequently moved to a most enchanting mill house at Sherrington. They were both keen and very competent tennis players, and many were the matches we played on their hard court or our own grass court, together with the Thompsons and others. George and Anita were, indeed are, about as nice as anyone could be, incredibly hospitable with their drink and lunch parties, always good natured, brimming over with friendliness and highly intelligent.

There are so many other friends and Wiltshire people who figured in our lives at Boyton. Harold Cassells who, as a young officer in The King's Dragoon Guards had won two Military Crosses, farmed extensively, asked me and others to shoot his partridges, and of whom a fellow officer, George Powell, once observed that it cost you sixpence to say 'Good Morning' to him. John Talbot of Wardour and his enchanting wife, Patricia, known always as Podge; Michael Fitzalan-Howard, with whom I had had dealings as a soldier and who was a model of graceful conduct, service to the community and devotion to his Regiment; Michael Stratton, a sporting landowner, whose generosity of spirit, goodness of heart and readiness to share his good fortune with others were legendary [I came terribly close to losing my name with him for quite misunderstanding his instructions at one particular pheasant drive]; his neighbouring farmer Nicholas Yeatman-Biggs, another life-loving and most likeable man, who was not altogether pleased when I declined to attempt a run while at the other end of the wicket in a local cricket match, resulting in his being run out. Robin Oatts, like so many of our Wiltshire friends, a keen and competent field sporting man, who helped Teddy Kenney-Herbert run his shoot, was excellent at training gun dogs and organizing picking-up, and whose wife, Mary, was an ardent follower of foxhounds [I had first encountered them in Malaya during the Emergency there and again during the Borneo campaign]. Gris Davies-Scourfield, 60th Rifles and renowned escaper from Colditz and his wife, Diana, both of whom would frequently turn out to help dispose of Teddy's pheasants. Gris paid me the most generous compliment by describing my book, *Gentlemen in Khaki*, as the best he had ever read about the British Army. Another old friend who each year would invite me to Lord's to watch whichever Test Match was in progress was Desmond Scarr of 6th Armoured Division days and visits to Salisbury Playhouse to see how well amateurs could present *Pride and Prejudice*. I must also record that Stuart Green and his wife, Nancy, became valued friends, as did Charlie and Phyllida Humphreys.

I have mentioned the opera in Italy and at Glyndebourne. We were fortunate enough also to have almost on our doorstep an opera enthusiast, Donald Birts who, with the aid of his delightful and accomplished wife, Trish, would, year in, year out, arrange for the Pavilion Opera to stage one of the great operas in their magnificent tithe barn at Hill Deverill. We always went, sometimes accompanied by our daughters and their friends, and we even persuaded Humphrey and Fanny Weld from the wilds of Dorset to join us for *Lucia* and *Bohème*. It was thus that we renewed our acquaintance with Puccini, Verdi, Donizetti and the others. But we also went to the source of all those wonders and would often take our holidays in Italy.

One of the advantages of working for Westland was that from time to time duty and pleasure could be amalgamated. A requirement that I should liaise with our representatives in Rome [for the Italian helicopter company, Agusta, was an important collaborator] enabled me to take Wilfried with me to Rome, where one day's work was followed by a week of renewing our acquaintance with all the wonders of that beautiful city. We walked everywhere. It is the only way to see Rome properly. And the choice of restaurants is infinite. We also had the good fortune to see something of my old friend, Filippo Senni, who had been our liaison officer in the last nine months or so of the Italian campaign, and who had made so pleasant my attachment to the Italian cavalry in the heady *La Dolce Vita* days of 1946. He took us to the Circolo della Caccia, that splendid club which he had made me an honorary member of all those years ago. We dined on the terrace there and recalled old times and old wartime comrades.

It was, we thought, also necessary to introduce our daughters to the delights of Italy, and we took them for two holidays in Tuscany, renting little villas, the first near Lucca [home of my favourite opera composer, Puccini, whose comment that he had spent his life chasing three things – beautiful women, wild duck and librettists – I had long regarded as one of the better summing-ups]. From Lucca we toured round in our hired Fiat to look at Pisa, Florence and Siena. While taking a reasonable interest in the beautiful cathedrals, churches, paintings, sculpture and so on, we found that Viola and Carolin would grow weary of so much edification after a while and demand to know where and when we were going to have lunch. I always made a point of discovering beforehand where there was to be found a good, reliable *ristorante*, far from the madding crowd. In Florence I knew of one such, north of the Ponte Vecchio, and we made our way there. That delicious combination of Parma ham and melon, followed by some luscious plate of pasta, with a *fiasco* or two of *vino rosso* did the trick. During a second holiday in Tuscany – this time we stayed in a garden cottage in the grounds of a landowning nobleman – we had been advised by the travel company on no account to ignore the culinary fame of an establishment called *La Toppa*, but to be sure to get there early as all the local Italians piled into it soon after midday. Thus after inspecting the towers of San Gimignano, we reported to *La Toppa* at precisely *mezzogiorno*. We were the first there and although we had not reserved a table were warmly welcomed by the *padrone* who then proceeded to sit down at the table with us and help us choose food we would long remember. The highlight was a dish of *balli di pollo*, chicken balls, which consisted of the tenderest portions of meat encased in a light covering of what must have been some sort of pasta. *Delizioso*!

Later Wilfried and I made many more visits to Italy. Two were organized by that most enterprising and *simpatico* of travel agents, Ultimate Travel. The first of these was an excursion by boat along the River Po, calling at all the medieval cities – Venice from where we started, Padova, Ferrara, Mantua, Verona, looking at all the beautiful churches, paintings, piazzas, eating sumptuously on board, and as we passed close to Lodi – scene one of Napoleon's triumphs – I was required by the tour leader to give a short talk about it, the leader having read my book about Wellington and Napoleon. We ended up at Bergamo and inspected the ancient part of that city, before flying home from Milan. On another occasion, still in the hands of Ultimate Travel, we indulged in a week crammed with the magic of Venice. It was organized by two youngish Italian brothers, totally bilingual of course, who had access to gardens, palazzi and individual Venetian notables who showed us their treasures and discoursed upon the history of their families. The final dinner at a palazzo, adjoining the one where Byron lived, was most gracefully conducted, and I was nominated to say a word of appreciation. Mustering the best of my Italian, I spoke the appropriate words, adding that as we were so close to the shades of Byron, it would be fitting to recall a few lines of his, recording surely his abandonment of wanton play by virtue of his love for Teresa Guiccioli:

> So, we'll go no more a roving
> So late into the night,
> Though the heart be still as loving,
> And the moon be still as bright.

And on that note we will leave Venice, although Wilfried and I returned there a year or two later and enjoyed a week of unbroken sunshine, endless walks through that most enchanting of cities and a most judicious choice of restaurants. We followed this by a week at Lake Maggiore, where the island gardens with their exotic plants and white peacocks never fail to please. But now we must return to more prosaic matters.

Chapter 21

Family Affairs

'There are secrets in all families.'

George Farquhar

Are there? I cannot instantly call to mind any such things. The idea that my father or mother had secrets from each other or anyone else is quite foreign. My father was headmaster of what was then called a secondary school. He could be a stern parent, but at the same time was anxious that my brothers and I, later my sister too, should be aware of the pleasure to be derived from literature and music, from cricket and tennis, from the beauty of nature, from mastering foreign languages. He taught us to play bridge while we were still quite young, he introduced us to opera with the aid of a wind-up gramophone and 78 rpm records, he took us for walks in the country to admire trees and flowers, he travelled with us to France. But he was not with us for very long. Four years' service in France during the Great War had undermined his health and his premature death robbed us of the opportunity for a more mature relationship with him. At this time my elder brother, Peter, had won a bursary to St John's College, Oxford. Financial difficulties made it necessary for me to leave school early and enter the Civil Service, from which I later escaped by joining the Army after the outbreak of the Second World War. My sister, Margaret, went to stay with my father's sister, Agatha, at Canterbury and finished her education there. She later taught classics at Downhouse.

I suppose my mother was just about the most unselfish human being I have ever encountered. Like my father she had a great love of English literature, played the piano, and after his death took up teaching herself. She was all that was kindly, loving, thinking only of the welfare of her children and prepared to make any sacrifice for them. Fortunately she enjoyed robust health and lived well into her eighties, much gratified to see the advancement of her sons in the academic and military fields, taking great pleasure too in the growing number of grandchildren she was presented with and continuing to enjoy re-reading the English classics together with occasional visits to the theatre [I remember in particular escorting her to see Paul Robeson play *Othello* at Stratford and Laurence Olivier as *Lear* in London].

If I were fortunate in having such parents, I was equally so with my brothers and sister. Galen, the eldest, was a man of very even temperament, a great lover of literature, music, gardens, the Lake District, France and good company. He was always good tempered, devoted to his family and friends, and would take endless trouble to help others. Next came Peter, who was head and shoulders above the rest of us in sheer intellect and learning. As an Oxford philosopher he was world famous, yet maintained an easy friendliness with all those whom he did not regard as either pretentious, pompous or stupid. He was a wonderful host with a numerous family, all of whom were musically talented, a charming, intelligent and loving wife, Ann. It was impossible to be dull in his company because of his wide interests, profound knowledge and willingness to adapt himself to whichever company he found himself in. Many were the occasions when he would take me to dine with him at High Table in Univ or Magdalen. Many were the plays we saw together in Oxford college gardens performed either by OUDS or the Amateur Dramatic Society. He was very distinguished, but wore this distinction with ease and assuming that the word – bounty – can be equated with generosity of spirit and conduct, I would say this of him:

> For his bounty,
> There was no winter in't; an autumn 'twas
> That grew the more by reaping. His delights
> Were dolphin-like; they show'd his back above
> The elements they liv'd in.

Such was my brother, Peter, knighted for his services to philosophy, liked and admired by all. My sister, Margaret, eight years my junior, shared with us a love of literature, music, sporting activities and learning. She became a highly competent bridge player, reared a family, but alas died far too young of heart failure. Although perhaps we four did not always see as much of one another as we should, we shared so many interests that we were always at ease together.

My greatest good fortune was, of course, in finding Wilfried as my wife, Viola and Carolin as my daughters and, as this memoir is written primarily for them to know something of myself and they know all that has happened to us as a family, I will say no more except to reiterate my profound love and gratitude. We had enjoyed happy times together at Boyton, but the time came when we had to say farewell to 'The Very Own House', and move to something smaller. Fortune favoured us once more when we found a small, easily run house in Chitterne, the heart of Salisbury Plain.

Chapter 22

Chitterne

'...loveliest village of the plain.'

Oliver Goldsmith

This treatise is approaching its end. Yet before bringing it to its conclusion, I must say a word about Chitterne which, unlike Boyton, is a substantial village. Before coming to live there, we were familiar with it. Indeed in my soldiering days I had frequently either motored through it, outflanked it with my squadron or earmarked it as a suitable leaguer area. And there were several of its long established inhabitants whom we knew well. No names, no pack drill, as they say, but all these friends were of the right ingredients. Mostly former soldiers, they and their families devoted much time and effort to Chitterne's well-being. It was because of this and of the whole-hearted cooperation of most of the villagers that it quickly became clear to us how enterprising a place Chitterne was and is. No sooner had we arrived in the village than we were invited to take part in one of their much-prized annual events – the so-called Grand National Lunch in the village hall, at which tickets were sold with a view to drawing a horse for the race. Food and drink were to be consumed and the great steeplechase was to be watched on television. Lots of money was thus raised for the Conservative Party.

Apart from this event, there were many others which had the dual merit of providing much enjoyment and raising money, either for charity or the church or the village hall. Until a few years ago there was a gymkhana – a fairly rare thing in villages nowadays – primarily for the Pony Club level of equestrianism, but hugely popular and well patronized. But like so many comparable initiatives, the hard work involved was undertaken, year in, year out, by the same volunteers who, at length, found it too much for them, so that with no younger people skilled in running such an event coming forward, this particular enterprise came to an end. But others went on. The immensely popular flower festival still brought in crowds of well wishers, the annual fête seemed always to be blessed with fine weather, the plant sale was still a draw, exhibitions of paintings and other fine arts graced the village hall, the Christmas lunch or supper went on, the Royal Artillery foxhounds met several times each season, and a few years ago the Chitterne Cricket Club was revived holding up to ten matches with neighbouring villages, the RA Hunt, Warminster Beagles and the Wet Bobs. Indeed the cricket enthusiasts also organized highly successful dinner-dances with a superb supper supplied by villagers and a traditional jazz band to persuade those present to keep their feet warm.

What was so pleasing to see was the willingness, enthusiasm, commitment and sheer effectiveness with which so many of Chitterne's people gave their time and took infinite trouble to make all these events successful. A special word should be said in praise of those innumerable, lovely ladies who tirelessly worked away in the village hall, laying tables, cooking food, serving Cricket Club teas, clearing up afterwards – all with a cheerfulness and spirit that did the heart good to observe. Even though I have mentioned no names, those who most deserve recognition and profound gratitude know full well that it is to them the village's appreciation and gratitude is directed.

And so we soldier on. It was, of course, by having been a soldier that my life took the shape it did. I have twice said that, second to my marriage, becoming a 4th Hussar was the best thing that happened to me. The Regiment gave me much and I trust that I gave something in return. Since 1994 officers of the 4th Hussars have dined together at the Cavalry and Guards Club thanks to the dedication of Captain Dick Wallington who served in the Regiment during the war. We are all profoundly grateful to him.

'Never forget,' declared Wavell, 'the Regiment is the foundation of everything.' Alas, the present Army Board have forgotten it. Their plan of disrupting the regimental system is so ill-conceived, impracticable and incompatible with the most precious quality of the British Army – the unique excellence of the Regiment – that I was obliged to write a letter to the Editor of *The Times* [which I am happy to say was published] pointing out how profoundly mistaken the Army Board's proposal is. My letter concluded thus:

> Does General Jackson really believe that he knows better than such men as Wellington, Wolseley, Templer and Festing? If so, he will, as Wellington informed a comparably misguided individual, believe anything.

It is not too late to modify this damaging policy. But heaven send us men of character, conviction and courage to head the British Army.

Soldiering is more than just service, adventure, command, action, the wonder of horses, seeing the world, meeting every sort of human being, the sense of belonging to something unique, priceless and yours. There is also a kind of nobility about it, as that great scholar, G. Wilson Knight maintained: 'the Shakespearian hero is usually a soldier...a symbol of faith in human values of love, of war, of romance in a wide and sweeping sense.' Quite a reputation to live up to. In this memoir romance has not been altogether absent without leave. And it has at least been an honest tale.

Index